POLITICAL

LANDMARKS;

OR

HISTORY OF PARTIES,

FROM THE ORGANIZATION OF THE GENERAL GOVERNMENT TO THE PRESENT TIME,

COMPILED FROM THE MOST RELIABLE AUTHORS, BY

DANIEL MUNGER.

DETROIT:
PRINTED BY FOX & EASTMAN.
....
1851.

PREFACE.

In presenting to the public this volume, entitled the "Political Landmarks: or History of Parties," we feel that we have undertaken a severe task; yet we hope that the facts we have endeavored to collect, from the most intelligent and reliable authors, and arrange together, will be satisfactory to the reader as being a faithful delineation of the political history of the country. It is of much importance that these "landmarks" should be kept constantly in view by those coming upon the political stage, as they must soon be called upon to guide the ship of state. Our great men are now arriving at an age which must ere long deprive us of their invaluable services. Among the number, we must mention Messrs. Cass, Clay, Buchanan, Benton, Webster, Woodbury, Dallas, &c. These men have occupied conspicuous places in the political history of our government, but the measure of time allotted to man for his sojourn upon this earth, has with them been nearly filled. The senate of the United States now embraces the most brilliant galaxy of talent and statesmanship that was ever assembled in a legislative body upon the face of the globe, unless perhaps a period antecedent, in the same body, would have found added to the glorious list of talented men, the late Hon. John C. Calhoun and Silas Wright, but the sand has nearly run, and new men must fill the places of the living. It is important, therefore, that our young men should make the effort to qualify themselves for public stations. None should think for a moment that even the highest distinctions are beyond their reach. Among the men here mentioned there is hardly one who does not owe his enviable position in the political world, to his own perseverance. We must say that we have fears as to the industry and application of those coming upon the stage as the successors of the great men of the nation alluded to. When they were young, times and circumstances were vastly different from what they are at the present time. Their fortunes and fame depended upon their own industry and perseverance, while at the present day a competency to carry one through life is more easily obtained, and frequently falls from estates, without the least effort on the part of the recipient. The great danger is, that such a state of things will have a tendency to paralize the efforts and energies of those who must fill up the scene of life upon the political stage.

Gen. Cass came upon the political stage poor, and with an ordinary education, in the practice of the law. Being possessed of an ambitious spirit, and an unusual degree of industry, he made himself what he is, probably one of the most accomplished scholars in the Union. Had he been brought up in luxury in younger days, it is quite doubtful whether he would have been prompted to attempt the Herculean task. He will live to enjoy his luxury in his older age, as the competency of this world's goods allotted to him probably far outstrips that of the others named.

Col. Benton is said to be the most studious man of the age. He is remarkable for his statistical information. Whatever subject arises in the senate he can put his hands upon the necessary papers or information relative to the same, or something analogous, either in his table drawer or in the library. His whole time, aside from his senatorial duties, are devoted to researches in his library.

The same can be said to a great extent of Henry Clay, and of John C. Calhoun, and Silas Wright while living. Mr. Webster is said not to be so studious, but never forgets any thing he has read or heard during his life. His early education was of the most complete order.

It has been our effort, in this undertaking, to place before the public, the prominent facts connected with political history from the organization of the national government to the present time. The low price fixed upon the work will render it accessible to all; and should our efforts prove satisfactory to the public, our object will have been accomplished.

TABLE OF CONTENTS.

POLITICAL LANDMARKS,

COMPRISING

A HISTORY OF PARTIES,

From the organization of the Government to the present time.

CONTINENTAL CONGRESS.

The sessions of the Continental Congress were commenced as follows: September 5, 1774; also May 10, 1775, at Philadelphia; December 20, 1776, at Baltimore; March 4, 1777, at Philadelphia; September 27, 1777, at Lancaster, Pa.; September 30, 1777, at York, Pa.; July 2, 1778, at Philadelphia; June 30, 1783, at Princeton, New-Jersey; November 26, 1783, at Annapolis, Maryland; November 1, 1784, at Trenton, New-Jersey; January 11, 1785, at New-York, which from that time continued to be the place of meeting, until the adoption of the Constitution of the United States

CONVENTION TO FRAME CONSTITUTION.—FIRST PRESIDENTIAL ELECTION.

In May, 1787, a convention was assembled at Philadelphia to frame a new constitution. General George Washington was sent as a delegate from Virginia, and was unanimously chosen President of that body In 1789, he was unanimously chosen the first President of the United States, by electoral votes given by States, as follows:

New-Hampshire,	5
Massachusetts,	10
Connecticut,	7
New-Jersey,	6
Pennsylvania,	10
Delaware,	3
Maryland,	6
Virginia,	10
South-Carolina,	7
Georgia,	5
	69

The legislature of New-York having omitted to pass a law directing the mode of choosing electors, owing to a disagreement between the two branches of the legislature, no vote was cast from that state. The ten states gave sixty-nine votes, all for General Washington; and thirty-four votes were given for John Adams, and thirty-five votes were scattering. By the constitution, as it then stood, the President and Vice President were voted for by the electors upon an equal footing—the one receiving the largest number of votes being elected President, and the one receiving the next largest number, being elected Vice President: John Adams was, therefore, elected Vice President.

The intelligence of the election of General Washington was first communicated to him at his residence at Mount Vernon, by Mr. Charles Thompson, secretary of the then late Continental Congress. The urgency of the public business required the immediate attention of the President elect at the seat of government; he consequently left for New-York immediately, in company with Mr. Thompson and Colonel Humphreys. On his way thither he was greeted by the people of the different places through which he passed, with the most enthusiastic and decisive evidences of attachment and respect.

Soon after the adjournment of Congress, General Washington selected his cabinet. Thomas Jefferson was appointed Secretary of State; Alexander Hamilton, Secretary of the Treasury; Henry Knox, Secretary of War; and Edmund Randolph, Attorney General. Mr. Jefferson returned from a mission to France and assumed the duties of Secretary of State in March, 1790.

John Jay, of New-York, was appointed Chief Justice of the supreme court; and John Rutledge, of South-Carolina, James Wilson, of Pennsylvania, William Cushing of Massachusetts, Robert H. Harrison, of Maryland, and John Blair, of Virginia, Associate Justices.

The second session of the first Congress was also held at New-York, in January, 1790, when Alexander Hamilton put forth various able reports, as Secretary of the Treasury, which shadowed forth the policy of the then existing administration. He recommended the funding of the public debt incurred by the war of the revolution; the assumption of state debts by the general government; the providing of a system of revenue from duties on imports, and an internal excise, which measures were adopted by Congress.

An act was passed for the permanent location of the seat of government in the District of Columbia, and the temporary seat of government at Philadelphia. The third session was held at Philadelphia, commencing on the first Monday of December, 1790. To complete the national financial system recommended by Alexander Hamilton, Secretary of the Treasury, a national bank was incorporated. The cabinet and members of Congress were divided upon this subject, but the bill passed, and General Washington gave it his signature.

The second Congress met at Philadelphia, in October, 1791. There was a majority in each branch favorable to the administration. The excise act, imposing a duty on domestic distilled liquors, similar to one passed in 1790, was one of the measures, and became very unpopular. Upon this subject the *Whiskey Insurrection* broke out in western Pennsylvania, and an army of 15,000 men was raised to quell the rebellion.

During the second session of the second Congress, from November, 1792, to March, 1793, much time was occupied in discussing the domestic and foreign relations of the country, without the adoption of any measure of particular importance. Party spirit ran high. The cabinet was divided, Hamilton and Knox advising federal measures, while Jefferson and Randolph acted in unison with the opposition in Congress, whom Mr. Jefferson denominated republicans. The difference of opinion existing between the members of his cabinet was a source of extreme mortification to the President. Entertaining the highest respect for both Jefferson and Hamilton, he was unwilling to part with either, and exerted all his influence to effect a reconciliation between them, without success.

The French revolution had an important influence upon the politics of the country at this time. Jefferson and his republican friends sympathized with the French nation in their struggles for liberty, and their contests with other nations, while Hamilton and his friends of the federal party, with whom Washington coincided in this particular, considered it important to the interests of the United States to maintain friendly relations with Great Britain, which power was then at war with France.

Under this state of public opinion, the presidential election took place. General Washington desired not to be re-elected, but finally yielded to the earnest wishes of his friends to serve a second term. General Washington, in 1793, again received the unanimous electoral vote, as follows:

New-Hampshire,	6
Vermont,	4
Massachusetts,	16
Rhode-Island,	4
Connecticut,	9
New-York,	12

New-Jersey, - - - - - - - -	7
Pennsylvania, - - - - - - -	15
Delaware, - - - - - - -	3
Maryland, - - - - - - - -	8
Virginia, - - - - - - -	21
North-Carolina, - - - - - -	12
South-Carolina, - - - - - -	7
Georgia, - - - - - - -	4
Kentucky, - - - - - -	4
	132

John Adams received 77 votes, and George Clinton of New-York received 50 votes, (New-York, Virginia, North Carolina, Georgia ;) consequently Mr. Adams was declared elected Vice-President.

December 31, 1793, Thomas Jefferson resigned his seat in the cabinet, as Secretary of State, in pursuance of notice given some months previous. The President appointed Edmund Randolph to succeed Mr. Jefferson, and Wm. Bradford, of Pa., to succeed Mr. Randolph, as Att'y General.

In April, 1794, the President selected John Jay, then Chief Justice, as a special Envoy to England. Mr. Jay arrived in England in June, 1794, and in November following a treaty with Great Britain was signed. It arrived in the United States on the 7th of March, 1794, and was ratified by the Senate on the 24th of June, by precisely the constitutional majority, (two-thirds,) after much opposition.

In 1794 the French government requested the recall of Gouverneur Morris, the Minister to that country. The request was complied with, and James Monroe was appointed his successor. In 1796 the President recalled Mr. Monroe, and appointed Charles C. Pinckney to succeed him.

At the close of the year 1794, General Knox resigned the place of Secretary of War, and Timothy Pickering was apppointed. Alexander Hamilton resigned the post of Secretary of the Treasury, in January, 1795, and Oliver Wolcott, of Connecticut, was appointed his successor.

We have thus far been very particular to give a minute history of all events which have transpired, it being the starting point in the political events of the country. We shall proceed to put forth the most reliable authorities for the purposes of our history of parties, and shall for the present quote from Niles' Register, a "History of Parties," prepared by him in 1823. It will be noticed that Mr. Niles was a violent opponent of the congressional caucus system:

Presuming that I know something of what *were* the landmarks of the old political parties in the United States, a brief notice of them may not be uninteresting or useless, seeing that so much is said about holding a caucus of the "democratic members" of Congress, to recommend a sound and undeviating "democrat," to the support of the party, as President of the United States. It is not my intention, at least, at present, either to be deluded, coaxed, or driven into a discussion as to the *persons* put up for the chief magistracy of the republic—but I am willing to do what I can to place certain general subjects before the people, some of whom are too young to know what parties were, others have forgotten their condition, and many find it convenient just now to disremember things, once deemed essential to constitute a "democrat." But if any will use that word, they ought to understand the meaning that it had in primitive times, when the lines between parties were so strictly drawn that no mistake could be made about it. This will not stir up old animosities, and I utterly disavow the most remote intention of the sort—for justice compels me to say, that the "federalists" were not always wrong, nor the "democrats" always right. Some measures were at different times proposed by one party, that were worthy of the support or deserved the reprehension of both parties—but it was too much the practice of one to be continually opposed to the other, no matter what was the subject acted upon, in relation to our foreign or domestic policy.

I shall proceed to detail the prominent points on which parties divided in the United States.

In Washington's administration, partly on account of the neutral policy that he had adopted and maintained, on the breaking out of the French Revolution, (now universally acknowledged to have been a wise one,) but especially concerning the treaty with Great Britain, signed at London in November 1794, and ratified in the following year, and the money to carry it into effect appropriated in 1796.

Previous to the receipt of this treaty, with Great Britain, much feeling had been excited by certain assumptions and arbitrary and unjust proceedings of the British Government, a narrative of which is too long for the present occasion; and an undoubtedly large majority of the people of the United States were willing to come to an open rupture on account of them; and there was a very warm feeling in favor of France, because, having shaken off her regal government, the crowned heads of Europe had entered into an infamous league, to force chains upon her in the manner that the successor of Louis XVI attempted to fasten upon Spain, at a subsequent day—to which proceeding the British were a party. The appointment of Mr. Jay, then chief justice of the United States, to negotiate this treaty, was much objected to on *constitutional* as well as *political* considerations, for he did not resign the office of chief justice, and was regarded by many as being too warmly attached to the interests of those with whom he was to treat. [It is not necessary for *me* to express an opinion on this case, or others of its nature—I only state the facts as I personally know that they were.] When the treaty was received, president Washington laid it before the Senate, who then, as they do now, sat with closed doors, (and the president often attended their secret deliberations.) It was supported and opposed with uncommon ardor—at last, and before the question on its reception was decided, Mr. Mason, a senator from Virginia, in the heat of his indignation at the whole proceeding, furnished a copy of the instrument to the editor of the "Aurora," and thousands of copies were almost instantly published. The shock on the political mind of the people, could be compared to nothing but that of an earthquake on the moral feelings of a society. Meetings were held everywhere to express the public disapprobation of the instrument, and to entreat the president to withhold his signature from it; and, perhaps not less than nine-tenths of the yet surviving soldiers and sages of the revolution were, *at first*, opposed to it. But still the treaty was ratified by the Senate, and Washington firmly signed it. The mighty weight of his character thus thrown into the scale, brought many to a serious pause, and the people began to divide into parties, pretty nearly equal in strength, and out of this mainly grew the late democratic and federal sects—for until then, it had really been chiefly *whig* and *tory*, so far as questions merely political had been regarded. Washington naturally rallied around him a vast amount of the good people of the nation, and all persons believed that he meant what was right; though others, and yet a majority, thought he had done what was wrong. Before the treaty could be fully perfected, certain appropriations of money would have to be made by the house of representatives, and this subject was seriously and very warmly agitated until the meeting of congress late in the year 1795. Those, and those only, who truly *felt* the importance of the "Missouri question," of 1820-21 can apprehend the then existing state of the public mind, unless they saw and felt it at that period. I heard many men say, they were reminded of the awful anxiety that prevailed when the Declaration of Independence was about to be made in 1776—that they never had, except at that season been so moved as they were then. I was yet in my "teens," but accident placed me in certain situations where I had a much better opportunity, perhaps, than most youths of my age, to know what was going on. The papers were filled with essays for and against the treaty. It was discussed before the people by the ablest men in the United States, and attacked or defended by smaller essayists without number; even by myself, without the editor of the paper, who published my articles, ever suspecting the source from whence they came—and here was the date of my "democracy." The most solemn debate took place in Congress that had ever been known, except on the case of Independence. Notwithstanding the senate had ratified and Washington approved of the treaty, there was a clear and decided majority in the house of representatives hostile to it, and apparently resolved to withhold the appropriations necessary to carry it into effect. It was during this discussion that Mr. Fisher Ames delivered his famous speech. I heard a part of it; it was, indeed a most powerfel appeal to the passions. It was said, and perhaps truly, that even WASHINGTON himself exerted his personal influence on the occasion: and thereon, for the first time (that I know of in the United States,) the people were excited to *instruct their representatives*, and claim it as a right. Meetings were extensively held, and many sets of instructions forwarded, that were seemingly in opposition, as to the private opinions of some of the members, as well as a majority of those whom they represented—that opinion and majority being really opposed to the treaty. I believe that I speak understandingly, and might venture to mention particular cases, if I pleased. Many questions of various character, but bearing on the treaty, were decided, and the *right* of the House to withhold the appropriations, if it pleased, was maintained by Mr. Gallatin, and, I well remember, he was severely attacked for his expression, that it was the constitutional principle of the house of representatives "to hold the purse strings," even if "the wheels of government should be stopped," though he was supported in his opinions by the late president Madison, the venerable Macon, and by Mr. Giles, and nearly all the rest of the "democratic" members of congress. The famous *Cobbett*, who then or soon after prided himself on being believed to be in the confidence and pay of the British government, caricatured Mr. Gallatin, in a print prefixed to a periodical work published by him, and called the "Political Censor." The friends of the treaty, [joined by a few who believed it was *expedient* to carry it into effect, *circumstanced as things were*, it having been approved by the president, by and with the advice and consent of the senate, co-ordinate branches of the government,] resorted to several indirect means to operate on the main question, but failed until the thirtieth April, 1796, when the following resolution was decided:

"*Resolved*, As the opinion of the committee, [of the
" whole,] that it is *expedient* to pass the laws necessary for
" carrying into effect the treaty lately negotiated between
" the United States and Great Britain."

This was unexpectedly passed in the affirmative—51 to 48. One or two persons, who had originally opposed the appropriations, were suddenly *indisposed* and could not attend, and several had "*chopped round*," as the sailors say, suddenly, under *cover* of "instructions," professing obedience to the will of the people. Every member present from Maryland, except General *Sprigg*, voted in the affirmative, though at least three of them were counted on as being firmly opposed to the treaty as he was—and there was one vacancy. One of these, was rejected by his constituents at the next election, on account of his vote; a second never regained the confidence of his party or went again to Congress—a third succeeded in reinstating himself. One that was *absent* I happened to have the pleasure of an acquaintance with some years afterwards—he had been a gallant soldier in the revolution, and was one of the most amiable of men, but was not returned to Congress: and to his dying day, that absence "hung heavy at his heart." In the fifty-one yeas there are the names of many afterwards distinguished as "Federalists," but in the forty-eight nays, I cannot call to mind any one who did not retain the reputation of a "democrat." Among them were Madison, Macon, Giles, Gallatin, Baldwin, Dearborn, Livingston, New, Swanwick, Varnum, Hampton and others, equally well known in their day, and all who yet survive of them, are still called "democrats." Notwithstanding the "starting place," of parties was at the adoption of "Jay's treaty," it was a mere difference of opinion with WASHINGTON, on a single point, and a question of *expediency*. No regular opposition was made to the measures of his administration, and the lines of parties were not fairly drawn until the campaign for the next president was opened. It was, no doubt, the fact, that a large majority of the people of the United States was opposed to the treaty; and it was said, by persons who were believed to know, that Washington himself had agreed to receive it with great reluctance; but, having adopted his course, he was not to be diverted from it, and he accomplished what he thought the good of the country required. But surely, he was the *only man* in the nation who could have got that treaty through. The love and reverence of the people for him, induced many to give up their *private* opinions wholly to him: a proceeding that, in this case, was not so important, but which I have no desire to see a recurrence of. It has destroyed the liberties of many nations, for few have had a WASHINGTON at their head.

I believe that this is a faithful political history of the first arrayment of parties in the United States, under the names by which they were long after designated. It is a brief detail—yet it may call up somethings to recollection, and especially impress it on the house of representatives, that that body "holds the purse strings"—that no provision of the constitution will admit of the drawing of one dollar from the public treasury without their approbation. There is safety in this consideration: and, as the senate was wisely designed to act as a check on the haste of the house, so the house may serve as a check on the power of the senate, even in the making of treaties.

In continuing this history, it will be observed that Mr. NILES, from whom we are still quoting largely from "Niles' Register," refers to matters then existing July, 1823. It will also be observed that the Register frequently alludes to the Congressional caucus system. Mr. Niles was a violent opponent of that system, in which he differed with Edwin Croswell of the Albany Argus, and Mr. Ritchie of the Richmond Enquirer, and now of the Union. The Congressional caucus system continued to exist for some considerable time, as also the legislative caucus system, in the State of New-York, until finally it became unpopular with the masses of the people at large, as it was thought that it concentrated too much power in the hands of a few men who were thrown together during a session. It was also thought that the abuse of that power thus delegated was fast destroying all confidence in the caucus or convention system. The result was that that system was superceded by the system of electing delegates from town to county conventions, and from county to state conventions; and for the nomination of candidates to be supported for President and Vice-President, delegates were sent from state to national conventions, thus constituted. In this manner the full and fair expression of the people is supposed to be arrived at. The federalists opposed this scheme for a time, but finally adopted it as the only true mode of making political nominations.

The contest between John Adams *and* Thomas Jefferson, *for the Presidency in 1796, and the subsequent measures of Mr. Adams' administration in regard to the quasi war with France, &c.*

ELECTORAL VOTE:

John Adams received, - - - - -	71
Thomas Jefferson, - - - - - -	69
Thomas Pinckney, - - - - -	59
Aaron Burr, - - - - - -	30
Scattering, - - - - - - -	48

A full table will be appended in the close of the work, showing the vote of each state.

This election was maintained with great warmth, and tended more firmly to fix the lines between parties, which were yet indistinct on account of the personal popularity of Washington, and the well-earned confidence that was reposed in his discretion and zeal for the public good. Mr. Adams was elected, and commenced his administration with a speech to Congress that astonished many who had opposed him, and startled some that had supported him. It had less of party in it than either expected, and some members of his administration, (as was then believed,) went to work to give a higher tone and "energy," as the word was, to the government. They succeeded. Among the measures adopted in 1798, was that of getting up addresses to the president, commending him in the most extravagant terms, and expressing "unlimited confidence in the wisdom and virtue of his administration." These addresses were hawked about from door to door, like petitions in our cities to get a street paved—those who signed them were good citizens, and those who refused were put down as "jocobins." In many places it was like taking the census of the people, to determine how many were "federalists," and how many were "democrats;" and it was believed that many persons were actually dismissed from office as being "disaffected," because they thus refused to send in their ADHESION." I do not magnify facts. Parties were at such a height at that day, that I well recollect to have been personally abused, because I did not mount a black cockade, and once had great difficulty to prevent personal violence on a young man of my acquaintance, because he foolishly braved a set of persons by wearing one. Both parties went so far, that social, family intercourse was destroyed, in thousands of cases—and a gentleman could hardly join a mixed company without being insulted by unsupportable epithets. To receive the "Aurora" at that time, was regarded as the extreme point of political degradation, and so powerful was the persecution, that many obtained and read it secretly, though "Porcupine's Gazette" was openly patronized! People compared the proscription of that and other newspapers to the proceedings of the "holy inquisition," by whom it was made an unpardonable sin to read the Bible! Lists of the subscribers to these offensive papers were obtained at some places and forwarded to the seat of government! Credit was, very generally refused, at some banks to the "opposition," and it was believed that the old bank of the United States at Philadelphia, had closed the accounts, (or caused the closing of them,) of most persons that were not acknowledged "federalists." I recollect one personal instance of this sort. It happened in the bank at Wilmington, Delaware, where I then lived—a note was objected to because the maker of it was an "enemy of the government;" but the good sense of the direction rejected the proposition and the "*legitimate*" was exposed. Further to show the spirit of parties, I will notice a fourth of July celebration that took place in that town, always remarkable for its "republicanism," though then almost broken down by the power of "federalism." It had been agreed to make a joint celebration of the anniversary of independence—that the president of the day should be a "federalist," and the vice president a "democrat," and that the company should in good humor, drink *all* the toasts that they might alternately offer. The dinner party consisted of a number of the most prominent and respectable gentlemen on both sides. When the cloth was removed the president gave "John Adams," &c. The toast was drank by all, though it afforded no small degree of merriment to see what a "hard job" it was for some to get down their wine. The vice president then gave "Thomas Jefferson," &c. It was generally drank as the other had been, but an imprudent young man violently broke his glass and spilled his wine on the table. Every one was on his feet in a moment. The act was deprecated by almost every one present and in the severest terms–yet party feelings were soon so much roused, that a general battle seemed inevitable. All wanted to talk, and none were willing to listen! But the affray was soon settled—a powerful mechanic very deliberately seized the young man by the back of the neck, grasping him as if in a vice by one hand, while with the other he poured a glass of wine down his throat to the manifest danger of suffocating him! This was the act of a moment—but that moment was happily sufficient to restore the company to discretion, and convince both parties of the necessity of an immediate separation—which took place, and each division of the company finished the celebration 'in its own way.' Things of this character were *forced* into the most common transactions of life, from the making of a pair of shoes to the building of a ship, in all places whereat the parties were pretty equally matched. In some, the different political sects met in actual combat, with as much regularity as opposing armies ever did. This was notoriously the case in Maryland, and especially in Baltimore, during a famous electioneering campaign, when *fighting* and *voting* were a common object on both sides! All persons had yet to learn, or at least to attend to the admonition, that "TRUTH IS A VICTOR WITHOUT VIOLENCE." The passage of the alien and sedition laws increased the flame. These two acts of Congress passed in the summer of 1798, which became extremely unpopular with a large portion of the people. The alien law was opposed upon the ground that it was liable to abuse by the president, who had authority to order aliens, who were found, or supposed to be conspiring against the peace and authorities of the United States, to depart from its territories. It is known to all, that the revolutionary war was carried on mainly by foreigners—that is, the battles were mainly fought by men who had repaired to this country, then in its infancy, to better their own condition. These were found in the front ranks, nobly combatting friends and kindred, in maintaining what they considered to be the rights of their adopted country. One apology for the law was, that there were then computed to be thirty thousand Frenchmen in the United States, all of whom were devoted to their native country, and mostly associated through clubs or otherwise. Besides these, there were computed to be fifty thousand who had been subjects of Great Britain, some of whom had found it unsafe to remain at home. It was also contended that the persons who by the law, were liable to be required to leave the country, were not citizens—had no just claim to a continuance here—and that their residence, with the views they had, and the opinions they published, endangered the welfare of the nation. The objection to the sedition law was, that it restricted the liberty of speech and of the press, which was an arbitrary interference with the right of the citizens to express freely their opinions on all public and political measures. Those who justified the law asserted that the grossest falsehoods were uttered and published, tending to deceive the people, and to excite their prejudices unduly, to the danger of the peace of the nation. There were at this period about two hundred newspapers published in the United States, 180 of which were in favor of the federal administration, and about twenty were opposed to the leading measures then adopted; and it was urged that the greater proportion of the twenty were under the control of aliens.

In Virginia and Kentucky particularly, the people were violently opposed to these measures. The legislatures of those States declared them to be direct and gross infractions of the constitution, and appealed to the other states to join in opposition to them. An attempt was made to repeal the measures at the next session of Congress, but without avail. The officers of the provisional army were often very overbearing, and, perhaps, not, at all times treated with the respect that they deserved, on account of a letter said to be written by the secretary of war, Gen. D. of Virginia, in which it was said that persons laboring under a certain hideous political designation, would not be objected to on that account for officers; and many believed that the army was rather intended to operate on the people of the United States, than on the French republic; that it was designed to build up "a strong administration," to support an alliance with England in a crusade against liberty, *destroy the state sovereignties*, and *consolidate the government*. That these were the designs of *some*, there cannot be a doubt. Washington, however, yet lived, and the "federal party" certainly embraced many of the best men of the nation, who had for seven years contended for freedom, and could not be supposed willing to establish such an aristocracy as a faction of that party, (the Hartford conventionists of latter times,) aimed at. Moderate measures were recommended and encouraged, and the election of *Thomas McKean* as governor of the great central state of Pennsylvania, "the key stone of the political arch," had a wonderful effect in suppressing violence. President Adams seemed displeased with the lengths to which parties had proceeded, and he changed his policy, in renewing his attempt to effect, and in bringing about an accommodation with France. This was understood to be against the advice of the heads of departments, and an explosion took place. Immediately after the New-York election was over, Mr. Adams abruptly dismissed two of his Cabinet ministers—Mr. Pickering, Secretary of state, and Mr. McHenry, Secretary of war, an event which caused much sensation, and had much influence in reducing the federalists to a minority. Gen. Hamilton, although of the same party, subsequently came out with a letter censuring the public conduct and character of Mr. Adams; which letter disclosing a determined aversion to the president by so conspicuous a leader of the administration party, was considered as among the operative causes of Mr. Adams' failure at the then approaching election. Mr. Hamilton, it was supposed, designed the pamphlet only for circulation at the south, but it got into the hands of the democrats, and its publication was very general at the north. Mr. Hamilton was favorable to the election of General Pinckney to the Presidency, but did not openly advise the withholding any electoral votes from Mr. Adams. In consequence of this rupture, a party was got up only less hostile to Jefferson and the democrats than to Mr. Adams. Some account of these things were given in several curious pamphlets that appeared at the time—but a friend long since borrowed my collection of them; still the general facts of that political quarrel are pretty fresh in my recollection. The president, it is said, was highly offended, because things had been done by his secretaries, as under his sanction, that he did not approve of; and it seemed as if he had himself really began to apprehend what the "democrats" imputed to him, as the design of his administration—to wit, *a change in the form of government, "a fraternal alliance" with England, and an extinction of the free representative system.* It may be, that it was the idea of the *alliance* that first caused a stir in the blood of the old patriot. He had been worked into what was, perhaps, a too hostile disposition towards France—but to unite with England, and give up the destinies of this country to the will of old George and his ministers, was too much! The *fire of the revolution* again warmed his soul, he penetrated into what he supposed was the ulterior designs of those who had possessed his almost unlimited confidence, and with a burst of his former *spirit of resistance,* cast them all off. I well remember the shock that it produced, and the "long faces," that it made—and it was currently believed, on what then seemed undoubted authority, he said, "*that had all the regiments ordered to be raised been full, and H—— at their head, we should have been compelled to raise another army to preserve the constitution.*" I cannot now refer to the authority for this remarkable declaration as quoted; but I happened to meet with it in a pamphlet written by myself fourteen years ago, called "Things as they are," and have no manner of doubt of its substantial truth. An anecdote may serve to show the probability of these things, which was directly related to me while Mr. Adams was president, and perhaps before the result of the election of 1800 was known. When going from or proceeding to Washington, he met, at one of the public houses on the road, an old revolutionary friend, that he had not seen since the close of the war. They agreed to dine together. Mr. Adams made some observations that evidently manifested a desire to know the politics of his compatriot--who said he had not changed them since 1776; adding, "*but they tell me that you have changed yours.*" The president said, "perhaps it has *appeared* so —but it is not the fact. My predecessor left me surrounded by men that were exceedingly useful to him, and innocent, because they dared not attempt to dictate to or mislead him, but, presuming on their standing with Washington, they have given me inexpressible pain, and, to cast them off, was a most difficult matter. I have relieved myself of them, but it is too late." This is the substance of what, (from particular circumstances,) I remember was told to me sometime in the year 1800, in a way that I believed it. It was well understood that many of the "federalists" were opposed to the taking of Mr. Adams for the presidency, a second time--that they had nearly fixed upon another person; but, having agreed upon him, they supported him to the utmost of their power, as a party--as the "democrats" have supported their candidates. It may here be added, that Mr. Adams was not long out of office before he was a frank and open friend of Mr. Jefferson's administration; and, a few years after, he became a public writer against *impressment* and other hostile acts of the British, under his own name. And it has been stated, I think by himself, that when the first embassy to France was talked of, he was greatly importuned to send Gen. Hamilton as one of the envoys--he yielded to this, on condition that Mr. Madison should be another. This was most decidedly objected to and neither were appointed.

But to return to the subject--the people at large remained nearly as much heated as ever, and it required time for them to get cool. They had been worked into the madness of passion by reported plots and conspiracies—believed on one side to be real, we must hope—and on the other denounced as despicable contrivances to introduce "a reign of terror;" and the approaching election still furnishes materials for inveterate opposition among them, which some of the last acts of Mr. Adam's administration were not calculated to lessen—especially that concerning the judiciary, for this the democrats supposed was designed as a *palladium* of "federal" politics and policy.

In 1784, Mr. Jefferson being in Congress, as chairman of a committee for that purpose, reported the plan for the government of the Northwest Territory, which contained a ***Proviso*** forever inhibiting slavery in the territories of the United States northwest of the Ohio. The measure was carried out three years afterwards, and was sanctioned by the new constitution.

In continuing our remarks, we have thought it not out of place to speak of the life of one who will occupy a conspicuous place in the present number of the "History of Parties."

The life of THOMAS JEFFERSON, the third president of the United States, is one of the most interesting and instructive among those of the distinguished persons whose names are identified with American history. In the character of this extraordinary man, as well as in the events of his life, we are presented with a combination of philosophical attainments and political talents of benevolent feelings, and ambitious aspirations, rarely found united in the same individual, and still more rarely resulting in the popular veneration bestowed upon his name by a large portion of his countrymen; while by others he has been regarded in an unfavorable light as a statesman and a ruler, particularly in the effect of his political principles upon the American people, over whom he acquired such an extraordinary ascendancy.

The family of Jefferson were among the early emigrants from Great Britain to Virginia. Thomas Jefferson was born at Shadwell, in Albemarle county, Virginia, on the 2d of

April 1743. His father, Peter Jefferson, a man of some distinction in the colony, died in 1757, leaving a widow with two sons and six daughters. These children inherited a handsome fortune from their father. Thomas, the eldest received the lands which he called Monticello, on which he resided, when not in public life, and where he died.

Mr. Jefferson by birth, belonged to the aristocracy, but the idle and voluptuous life which marked that order had no charms for a mind like his. He relished better the strong unsophisticated, and racy character of the yeomanry, and attached himself, of choice to that body. He was a republican and a philanthropist, from the earliest dawn of his character. He read with a sort of poetic illusion, which identified him with every scene that his author spread before him. Enraptured with the brighter ages of republican Greece and Rome, he had followed with an aching heart, the march of history which had told him of the desolation of those fairest portions of the earth; and had read with dismay and indignation of that swarm of monarchies, the progeny of the Scandinavian hive, under which genius and liberty were now every where crushed. He loved his country, and with that love, he combined and expanded philanthrophy which encircled the globe. From the working of the strong energies within him, there arose an early vision, which cheered his youth and accompanied him through life —the vision of emancipated man throughout the world.

While a student at law at Williamsburgh, in 1765, Mr. Jefferson heard the celebrated speech of PATRICK HENRY in the Virginia House of delegates, against the stamp-act; and animated by the eloquence of Henry, he from that time stood forward as a champion for his country.

With these brief remarks relative to the early history of Mr. Jefferson, we proceed with the numbers of the "Political Landmarks," it being the second and a very exciting contest between Messrs. Adams and Jefferson:

Second contest between John Adams and Thomas Jefferson for the Presidency, in the year 1800, *in which the latter was successful, and entered upon the duties of his office on the* 4*th of March,* 1801.

ELECTORAL VOTE.

	Thos Jefferson.	John Adams.	Aaron Burr.	C. C. Pinckney.
New-Hampshire, - - -		6		6
Vermont, - - - -		4		4
Massachusetts, - - - -		16		16
Rhode-Island, - - - -		4		3
Connecticut, - - - -		9		9
New-York, - - - -	12		12	
New-Jersey, - - - - -		7		7
Pennsylvania, - - - -	8	7	8	7
Delaware, - - - -		3		3
Maryland, - - - -	5	5	5	5
Virginia, - - - -	21		21	
North-Carolina, - - -	8	4	8	4
South-Carolina, - - -	8		8	
Georgia, - - - -	4		4	
Tennessee, - - - -	3		3	
Kentucky, - - - -	4		4	
	73	65	73	64

Scattering, 1.

Mr. Jefferson commenced the organization of his cabinet by the appointment, with the consent of the Senate, of James Madison, secretary of state; Henry Dearborn of Mass., secretary of war; and Levi Lincoln of Mass., attorney general. The secretaries of the treasury and navy, Samuel Dexter, and Benjamin Stoddert, who had been appointed by Mr. Adams, were continued in office for a brief period of time; but before the meeting of congress, Albert Gallatin of Pennsylvania, was appointed secretary of the treasury, and Robert Smith, of Maryland, secretary of the navy. Gideon Granger, of Connecticut, was appointed post-master general, in place of Mr. Habersham, of Georgia.

The federalists, from the tone of Jefferson's inaugural address, had hopes that he would retain in office the incumbents under Mr. Adams' administration, but they were soon undeceived. In June, 1801, Mr. Jefferson removed Elizur Goodrich, a federalist, from the office of colector of the port of New-Haven, and appointed Samuel Bishop, a democrat, in his place. In reply to a remonstrance from various citizens of New-Haven, in which they asserted the promptness, integrity and ability of Mr. Goodrich, and their belief that he was better qualified for the office than Mr. Bishop, who was nearly eighty years of age, and quite infirm, Mr. Jefferson said among other things, in his answer, dated the 12th of July: "Declarations by myself in favor of political tolerance, exhortations to harmony and affection in social intercourse, and respect for the equal rights of the minority, have, on certain occasions, been quoted and misconstrued into assurances that the tenure of offices was not to be disturbed. But could candor apply such a construction? When it is considered that, during the late administration, those who were not of a particular sect of politics were excluded from all office; when by a steady pursuit of this measure, nearly the whole offices of the United States were monopolized by that sect; When the public sentiment at length disclosed itself, and burst open the door of honor and confidence to those whose opinions they approved; was it to be imagined that this monopoly of office was to be continued in the hands of the minority? Does it violate their *equal rights* to assert some rights in the majority also? Is it *political intolerance* to claim a proportionate share in the direction of public affairs? If a due participation of office is a matter of right, how are vacancies to be obtained? Those by death are few, resignations none. Can any other mode than that of removal be proposed? This is a painful office; but it is made my duty, and I meet it as such. I proceed in the operation with deliberation and inquiry, that it may injure the best men least, and effect the purposes of justice and public utility with the least private distress; that it may be thrown as much as possible on delinquency, on oppression, on intolerance, on anti-revolutionary adherence to our enemies.

"I lament sincerely, that unessential differences of opinion should ever have been deemed sufficient to interdict half the society from the rights and the blessings of self-government, to proscribe them as unworthy of every trust. It would have been to me a circumstance of great relief, had I found a moderate participation of office in the hands of the majority. I would gladly have left to time and accident to raise them to their just share. But this total exclusion calls for prompt correction. I shall correct the procedure; but that done, return with joy to that state of things when the only questions concerning a candidate shall be, *Is he honest? Is he capable? Is he faithful to the constitution?*"

The history of this era embraces a great multitude of facts, but they shall all be noticed with all possible brevity. This election was conducted as violently as the former had been—and the parties abused each other in the most extravagant manner. It was said that if Mr. Jefferson was elected, our churches would be turned into cow stables, the public debt of the United States wiped away, the country become a province of France, and the like; and that if Mr. Adams was chosen, he would do things not much less offensive. Persons of character—some men in the most eminent stations, so far forgot themselves as to become common traducers of public and private reputation. The "federalists" yet had the power, and the "democrats" were struggling to get it; but great principles were maintained and opposed. The first thought, generally, that the constitution was too weak—the latter believed that it was sufficiently strong; and on these leading points hinged many important collaterals, thought to be essential to the well-being of the people.

It is here needful to give some account of the progress and termination of that memorable election in the house of representatives. It was the most awful political contest that ever occurred. Never, perhaps, before had the minds of a whole people been so seriously agitated; and I cannot yet revert to the period without a sensation of horror, when I reflect on the narrow escape that the republic made.

At that time there was no designation on the ballots of the electors whom they designed for president and whom for vice president. They simply contained two names, and the person who had the greatest number of votes was considered as elected president—if no one had a majority, the choice devolved upon the house of representatives of congress, *voting by states.* Thomas Jefferson and Aaron Burr had seventy-three votes each, and Mr. Adams sixty-five. The balloting commenced in the house of representatives on the 11th of February. Eight states voted for Mr. Jefferson, six for Mr. Burr, and two, (Maryland and Vermont,) were divided. It required a majority of the whole number of the states to make a choice, so no determination was had. The balloting, with the same result, continued until the 17th of the same month. In all places, whereat the intelligence of it was received, the people looked as we might have supposed they would do if a civil war was expected, and the agitation at Washington, filled with strangers, was almost beyond bearing. The late estimable Nicholson, of Maryland, though apparently at the point of death, was brought to the capitol in his bed and lodged in one of the committee rooms, that by his vote he might prevent Maryland from being given to Burr. At last, on the thirty-seventh ballot, the following result appeared:

Vermont, New-York, New-Jersey, Pennsylvania, Virginia, North-Carolina, Georgia, Kentucky and Tennessee, *nine* states voted for Mr. Jefferson. Maryland gave 4 votes for him and four blanks, Delaware and South-Carolina declined voting, and New-Hampshire, Massachusetts, Rhode-Island and Connecticut stuck to Burr.

When the issue was known the people were wild with joy—they hugged one another in the streets, and some danced and sung and shouted, not knowing what they did—the old forgot their infirmities—and the young committed many extravagancies. A notice of two little things that happened to myself may illustrate the state of the public feeling. I caught myself, though entirely alone at the time, with my hat in my hand and whirling it round my head, and huzzaing with the whole force of my lungs; and it made me feel very foolish—but I could not help it. Immediately after this I met a friend who begged me to proceed to my office with the least possible delay. I accordingly ran towards it as fast as I could, and there found a large crowd of persons in the very act of forcing a small cannon into the office to give me a grand salute, though I then was a private man like the rest, never having printed a public paper of any sort until several years after. It was with no small difficulty that I diverted them from their design, and, as it was, they were yet so mad as to discharge the gun in a thickly built and populous street, by which a couple of dozen lights of glass were broken in the office alone! In this crowd, a number ofpersons were actors whose common habits were as sober and sedate as those of others in the town in general. It is just to add, that though the "federalists," for a moment, seemed depressed by this event, a common sense of what was right soon caused a large majority of them, (so far as came to my knowledge,) to be satisfied with a result, bottomed on the undoubted will of a majority of the people, though they did not esteem Mr. Jefferson any more on that account.

This act of the "federal" party in Congress can hardly be excused; I never heard it defended. The constitution, true, gave them power to proceed as they did—but if all men should do, on every occasion, what the written law will not prevent them from doing, we should be but little better off than a nation of savages, and, perhaps worse. Take away from society its *moral sense* of decency, justice, mercy, honor, truth, &c., and what remains is not worth contending for, as an improvement over the customs and manners of the rudest aborigines of America. It was just as perfectly known that the people designed Mr. Jefferson for president, and Mr. Burr for vice president, as that an election had been held at all. Some may have quibbled, and said, that members of Congress had no right to know this. It is true they had no *legal right*. But there was a *right far beyond the law*, that should have operated—THE ETERNAL RIGHT OF TRUTH AND JUSTICE: and even the first principle of the constitution under which they acted, "that the will of the people is the supreme law of the land."

The following letter from the late *James A. Bayard*, (then having the vote of a state, being the sole representative from Delaware,) though lately published in the REGISTER, we feel it proper to insert here. It was addressed to one of his friends at Wilmington:

"*Washington*, 17*th February*, 1801.

"DEAR SIR—Mr. Jefferson is our president—Our opposition was continued till it was demonstrated that Burr could not be brought in, and even if he could, he meant to come in as a democrat.

"In such case, to evidence his sincerity, he must have swept every officer in the United States. I have direct in formation that Mr. Jefferson will not pursue that plan. *The New-England gentlemen came out, and declared they meant to go without a constitution, and take the risk of a civil war.* They agreed, that those who would not agree to incur such an extremity ought to recede without loss of time. We pressed them to go with us and preserve unity in our measures.

"After great agitation and much heat, all agreed except one. But in consequence of his standing out, the others refused to abandon their old ground. Mr. J. did not get a *federal* vote. Vermont gave a vote by means of Morris withdrawing. The same thing happened with Maryland. The votes of South-Carolina and Delaware were blank.

Your obedient servant, [Signed] J. A. B."

I have a suspicion of the source from whence this letter was published. I heard of it shortly after its date—and the fact is strongly impressed on my mind, that the writer made a request to withdraw it, *but was assured that it had been destroyed immediately on its receipt, as improper to be kept in existence.* ☞ If he had been living, that letter would not have been published.

[One passing remark on this subject. If I could apprehend the repetition of such a scene and supposed that a congressional caucus would prevent it, liable as it is to many and such serious objections in the present state of affairs—I would support it, *even if it virtually vested the election of president in the senate and house of representatives on their "individual characters."* But I do not believe that an old fashioned caucus, "democratic" or "federal," can now be held, and that if holden, apprehend that it may rather have a tendency to throw the decision into the house of representatives than prevent it—some of the reasons for which I have already assigned.]

The contest being over, and Mr. Jefferson seated, he soon indicated his design of softening down party rage, and he so effected it, that in 1804, he was re-elected almost without opposition! But there were many severe contests in the different states before this unanimity was brought about. I shall notice two of them, that the spirit of the whole may be understood—they are familiar to me, and as applicable to the condition of things elsewhere, as in the little state of Delaware.

In the year 1801, the democrats for the first time since the peace of '83 succeeded in the election of their candidate for governor, and Col. David Hall, who had commanded the justly celebrated Delaware regiment for some time during the revolution, was chosen by a majority of 17 votes. It was the constitutional duty of the senate of that state to count the votes and proclaim the result of such elections. It was currently reported and decidedly believed, that a majority of that body had pre-determined to pronounce the election illegal, and so secure the governorship to the speaker of the senate, a majority of which was "federal." It was deliberately resolved to resist this—and concluded to swear in Col. Hall as governor, *on the green, before the state house*, at Dover, if the senate persisted in its supposed design. Preparatory to this, it was needful to find a willing person who could administer the oath; and after much inquiry, it was discovered, *that only one "democrat" in the whole state had authority to administer a common oath—so perfect had been the proscription;* and how that one had escaped then became a matter of much speculation; it was an honest Irishman who had fought bravely in the revolution, and he promptly agreed to perform the duty requested, for which purpose he proceeded to the seat of government; and in its neighborhood, many resolute persons were located—among them as respectable men as there were in the state, to act as occasion might require. A sort of negotiation was entered into and an understanding had, as to the proceedings that would take place. One of the senators, (who could not "go the whole") gave way and voted against his party; Col. Hall was then declared duly elected and each man departed for his home in peace.

We had another great contest in this small state in the ensuing year, 1802, which I shall briefly notice, and conclude this branch of the subject. Mr. Bayard, who voted thirty-six times for Burr in the house of representatives, vested with the whole power of the state in his own person, was again a candidate. We put up Mr. C. A. Rodney to oppose him. These gentlemen ever were, till the lamented decease of the former, on the most intimate and friendly footing of any two persons that I ever knew, and they nobly maintained their regard for one another, even in this furious rencontre of parties. It was as stubborn a contest as ever took place—but resulted in the election of Mr. Rodney by a majority of fifteen votes! Mr. Bayard was a man of great powers—fearless and brave, almost an idol with his party, and so much the more desired to be put down by the other side. In looking over some old papers, I happened to meet with an extract from the *Baltimore* Federal Gazette, of the 11th October, 1802. This was not the most violent of the papers of that day; it, however said, "Indeed, the death of WASHINGTON could not have given the *enemies of liberty* more satisfaction than that Bayard has lost his election." It was an event deplored by one party, and a cause for triumph in the other, that, perhaps, never had its fellow in the choice of *one* representative in the congress of the United States. Mr. Bayard, surely, was about the strongest man in the "federal" interest—he was privately liberal, yet as a puhlic man, resolved, and sometimes apparently rather austere. Still every one admired his uncommon talents, and all believed him *honest.* His political principles were severely assailed in this contest, but his integrity never impeached; and it is fair to add that Mr. Rodney was treated in the same respectful manner by the other side; but it would sometimes make one smile to see these gentlemen, almost daily arm-in-arm together, while their adverse political friends were seemingly ready to make battle at every corner or cross roads in the state!

Before Mr. Bayard proceeded to Washington in the latter end of the year 1800, he declared, in my hearing, that, if the choice of a president was to be made between Mr. Jefferson and Mr. Burr, no man ought to hesitate. He believed, he said, that the first meant right, but that his scheme of government was not fitted to the state of society, and he pronounced it visionary. Of the latter he spoke in very rough terms, and expressed his surprise that the "democrats" had ever taken him up, saying he was a perfect *Cataline.* The very evening of Mr. Bayard's return home, on the 6th or 7th of March, 1801, we accidentally met, and I took the liberty to remind him of the conversation alluded to, and apply it to his late votes for Mr. Burr in congress. He said that his opinion of the men had not been changed; and then expressed his detestation of the trammels of party; observing, that I could not yet understand their force. He said this in a way that silenced me, for he appeared exceedingly mortified, if not distressed. I do not affect to have had an intimacy with Mr. B. but we were sometimes together at the house of a mutual friend; and then, as on all other occasions, he was polite and communicative—liberal in his remarks, and willing to hear the observations of those that he happened to be in company of. This gentleman's conduct in 1801, has already been mentioned—it was he who then, perhaps, prevented a dreadful calamity; and if the history of a certain meeting that took place between 1808 and '10 is ever brought to light, I apprehend it will appear that he, A SECOND TIME, interposed, and destroyed a scheme that had for its apparent purpose a separation of the states. He was a warm partizan—but a real patriot; a good neighbor and a generous friend. My testimony cannot add any thing to his reputation; but a notice of him seemed fitted to the general subject that I am endeavoring to give a faithful, though imperfect, account of—and when a man such as he was, proceeded to the lengths that he did, *through party,* what must have been the state of the public mind.

In 1803, an amendment of the constitution was proposed relative to the election of president and vice-president, so as to designate which person was voted for as president and which as vice-president. The admendment was proposed by the republicans, to provide against the disappointment which had threatened them at the election in 1801, and which had caused so much bitterness of feeling. The federalists opposed the amendment as an unwise departure from the spirit and design of the constitution, which was, that two persons fully qualified for the office of chief magistrate, should be voted for without a specific and exclusive designation of one to the presidency, and thus in case of death of one, the other who would succeed, would be equal to the discharge of the high trust. The amendment was agreed to by the votes of two-thirds of the members of both branches of Congress, and within the year 1804, it was ratified by three-fourths of the States as required by the constitution. It became a part of the constitution on the 25th September, 1804.

An additional law was passed by Congress on the subject of the naturalization of aliens, and the time of residence required previous to their becoming citizens was placed on its original footing of five years, instead of fourteen. The federalists opposed this law, as they deemed it unreasonable to admit foreigners to all the rights of those born and educated in the United States, until they had resided a longer time in this country, while they were readily allowed protection and equal justice.

The bankrupt law which had been enacted under Mr. Adams' administration was repealed at the first session of the 8th Congress at the instance, it is believed, of Mr. Jefferson, and certainly with his hearty concurrence.

During the contest in the House of Representatives between Jefferson and Burr, the latter was in Albany, and his friends represented that he took no part in the matter ; but strong feelings of dissatisfaction and jealousy grew up between the friends of the president and vice-president, creating quite a schism in the ranks of the democratic party. These feelings were suppressed in a measure ; but the result was the political prostration of Col. Burr, before his term of office expired.

Second election of* THOMAS JEFFERSON, *as President of the United States, and the incidents therewith connected.

In 1803, the zeal of parties was so much softened, that Mr. Jefferson was re-elected in 1804, as before observed, almost unanimously—Connecticut and Delaware being the only states that voted against him, supported however, by two straggling votes from Maryland—14, all told. Matters went on pretty quietly until 1807, though parties were yet strictly divided in Congress, and some agitations took place about " Burr's conspiracy," the purchase of Louisiana, and divers other things—none of them, perhaps, coming into our view as " landmarks,"—the majority was not violent, and the minority submitted as it should do.

In November, 1806, Napoleon, emperor of France issued is Berlin decree. This was followed up by the famous British orders in council, the first dated January 7, 1807, and order was heaped on order, in perfect contempt of neutral rights, Napoleon taking part in the effect by his Milan decree of the 17th December, same year. The British orders in council declared nearly all Europe in a state of blockade, and the American coast was lined with ships to enforce *said blockade,* at the mouth of the *harbor of New-York, and it was done!* Nay, the insolent persons who commanded these ships took the liberty of overhauling even shallops, laden with *cord wood* or *hay,* for the New-York market, and a scoundrel, named Whitby, fired into a sloop and *murdered* a citizen of the United States. At other places, acts nearly as outrageous were committed, and the cup of bitterness was filled by the base attack on the Chesapeake frigate, to support British claims to the " right of search," and to *impress seamen* from our ships, thousands of whom, native American citizens, were then enslaved in her " floating hells." Blessed be heaven!—I never expect to hear of a recurrence of these things—they *cannot* happen in a state of peace; for though Britain thus made war on *us* we were at peace with *her.* Not being prepared for the contest, and for every good reason wishing to avoid a war that would mix our affairs with those of Europe, what were called "restrictive measures" were adopted, and the *embargo* laid in December, 1807, to protect persons and property against the depredations of the British, and nearly two months before the Milan decree was here known to have been passed. It was regarded as the only alternative between submission and war, by the "democrats," though opposed by the "federalists," being, as they asserted, laid at the dictation of France.

A minute account of the proceedings that led to the embargo would be highly interesting—and shew that those who first urged the government to resist British encroachments, were the first to abandon it for having resisted them! The facts are in proof, in the memorials of the merchants and others—and, if collected, would make a curious little volume.

The bill for laying an embargo passed the senate, 22 yeas and 6 nays—and was carried in the house, 82 to 44. On looking over the yeas and nays, I notice the name of one gentleman, at that time holding his seat as a "federalist," who voted for the embargo—and one also, so regarded as a "democrat," who voted against it. Perhaps there never was a more strict drawing of the line between parties than on this occasion. It was the great point or "landmark" of Mr. Jefferson's administration, involving in its practice, the whole of his theory in favor of peace and in opposition to war. But it rekindled the old fire of party. He that was for the embargo was a "democrat"—he that was against it, a "federalist." It was a wall between the parties, to be seen and almost *felt with the hand*, (so strong was it,) in every state, city, county, town, village or hamlet of the United States, and in every class or condition of the people, "high or low, rich or poor." It was the TOUCHSTONE OF PRINCIPLE—as shall be exemplified by familiar events that happened in Maryland, to represent the acts and feelings of the whole people of the United States.

The city and county of Baltimore formed a district that sent two members to congress. The "democrats," resolved to re-elect Major N. R. Moore, a soldier of the revolution, who had voted for the embargo, with Mr. A. McKim, a very respectable merchant and a friend of the embargo as his colleague. The "federalists," or opponents of the embargo, thought they had a better chance of success by taking up one man only, and they fixed on a gentleman that would have succeeded if it had been *possible* to elect one favorable to the policy of his then party; it was Mr. W. H. Winder, since General Winder of the army of the United States, at that time believed and *now* held to be, not only a learned and accomplished gentleman, but as true an American as ever lived. If perseverance, in itself, ever deserved success, he ought to have been elected. The campaign was a very hot one, and each party spent much time, and used all possible exertion, to increase or bring forth its strength. But when the election came on, Messrs. Moore and McKim obtained 6857 votes, and Mr. Winder only 1818. But let us further mark the prevalence of *principles*—this same Major Moore, who obtained such an overwhelming majority in 1808, who had always sustained the character of one of the best of men and soundest of "democrats," was rejected in 1810, and Mr. Peter Little, sent in his place! Little 2604, Moore, 2478. The reason for this was, that Major Moore had voted for a repeal of the embargo law, which Mr. Little said he would not have done; and the old veteran, with all the power of old attachments and faithful services, supported too by three-fourths of the wealthy of the "democratic party," was beaten by a new man, a mechanic, for principle sake; and hundreds who voted against him put in their ballots with serious regret. I was one of these. We all loved the man, but felt it our duty to maintain what we thought a matter of principle. It is notorious that the whole state of Maryland so acted for or against the embargo question; and that because the majority was in favor of that measure Gen. Smith was re-elected to the senate, in 1806.

During the term of Mr. Jefferson's administration, some points were unsuccessfully made by the "federalists," in which subsequent events and increased knowledge have shewn that they were right—and others were made in which they were undoubtedly wrong. But party supported and party opposed, almost every measure suggested by the executive. The *gun boat system*, no doubt proper, useful and efficient in certain cases, but now universally acknowledged as wholly incompetent to a scheme of national defence; and the opposition of the "democrats" to the navy (proper) had also been in the extreme. But I doubt very much whether in the leap we have made from *gun boats* to ships of the *first class* will not be found as inconsistent with sound policy, *if much further extended.* I am fearful that the science and skill of our invaluable seamen, and their exploits on the ocean, may have seduced us into an establishment that will hereafter cause us much trouble. It is an easy thing to build ships of the line—but to man and support them for war, is another affair: and when we call to mind the accidents of storm and battle to which they are liable, perhaps there may be reason to believe that they may become too much a favorite with us. A fleet *may* be defeated—it may be wrecked, and then the naval means for the whole period of a war may be lost. I know that it is the opinion of some of our best naval officers, that if the navy is to be increased beyond the amount of ships now building, attention should be paid exclusively to the erection of strong frigates and sloops of war, to harass an enemy and dissipate his strength.

We must here be permitted to diverge a little from what might be, strictly speaking, our straight path, in order to show up an error, which even in these days, prevails in the minds of many. There are not a few who believe that the difference of party consists merely in the strife of one set of men to obtain offices and posts of honor to the exclusion of others. It is a very great error. The contests between the two great political parties have ever been conducted upon the supposition that in the success of one or the other, a particular line of policy would be adopted in accordance with the views and policy of that majority. To show this more clearly, we place before the reader the following

Extract of a letter from Mr. Jefferson to Mr. Melish, dated

MONTICELLO, Jan. 13, 1813.

DEAR SIR:—I received, duly, your favor of the 15th, and with it the copies of your map and travels, for which be pleased to accept my thanks. The book I have read with extreme satisfaction and information.

* * * * * * *

The candor with which you have viewed the manners and condition of our citizens, is so unlike the narrow prejudices of the French and English travelers preceding you, who, considering each the manners and habits of their own people as the only orthodox, have viewed every thing differing from that test as boorish and barbarous, that your work will be read here extensively and operate great good.

Amidst this mass of approbation which is given to every other part of the work, there is a single sentiment which I cannot help wishing to bring to what I think the correct one; and, on a point so interesting, I value your opinion too highly not to ambition its concurrence with my own. Stating in volume one, page sixty-three, the principle of difference between the two great political parties here, you conclude it to be, "whether the controlling power shall be vested in this or that set of men." That each party endeavors to get into the administration of the government, and to exclude the other from power, is true, and may be stated as a motive of action: but this is only secondary;

the primary motive being a real and radical difference of political principle. I sincerely wish our differences were but personally who should govern, and that the principles of our constitution were those of both parties. Unfortunately, it is otherwise; and the question of preference between monarchy and republicanism, which has so long divided mankind elsewhere, threatens a permanent division here.

Among that section of our citizens called federalists, there are three shades of opinion. Distinguishing between the *leaders* and *people* who compose it, the *leaders* consider the English constitution as a model of perfection, some, with a correction of its vices, others, with all its corruptions and abuses. This last was Alexander Hamilton's opinion, which others, as well as myself, have often heard him declare, and that a correction of what are called its vices, would render the English an impracticable government. This government they wished to have established here, and only accepted and held fast, *at first*, to the present constitution, as a stepping stone to the final establishment of their favorite model. This party has therefore always clung to England, as their prototype, and great auxiliary in promoting and effecting this change. A weighty MINORITY, however, of these *leaders*, considering the voluntary conversion of our government into a monarchy as too distant, if not desperate, wish to break off from our Union its eastern fragment, as being, in truth, the hot bed of American monarchism, with a view to a commencement of their favorite government, from whence the other states may gangrene by degrees, and the whole be thus brought finally to the desired point. For Massachusetts, the prime mover in this enterprise, is the last state in the Union to mean a *final* separation, as being of all the most dependant on the others. Not raising bread for the sustenance of her own inhabitants, not having a stick of timber for the construction of vessels, her principal occupation, nor an article to export in them, where would she be, excluded from the ports of the other states, and thrown into dependance on England, her direct and natural, but now insidious rival? At the head of this MINORITY is what is called the Essex Junto of Massachusetts. But the MAJORITY of these *leaders* do not aim at separation. In this, they adhere to the known principle of General Hamilton, never, under any views, to break the Union. Anglomany, monarchy, and separation, then, are the principles of the Essex federalists; Anglomany and monarchy, those of the Hamiltonians, and Anglomany alone, that of the portion among the *people* who call themselves federalists. These last are as good republicans as the brethren whom they oppose, and differ from them only in the devotion to England and hatred of France, which they have imbibed from their leaders. The moment that these leaders should avowedly propose a separation of the Union, or the establishment of regal government, their popular adherents would quit them to a man, and join the republican standard; and the partisans of this change, even in Massachusetts, would thus find themselves an army of officers without a soldier.

The party called republican is steadily for the support of the present constitution. They obtained, at its commencement, all the amendments to it they desired. These reconciled them to it perfectly, and if they have any ulterior view, it is only, perhaps, to popularise it further, by shortning the senatorial term, and divising a process for the responsibility of judges, more practicable than that of impeachment. They esteem the people of England and France equally, and equally detest the governing powers of both.

This I verily believe, after an intimacy of forty years with the public councils and characters, is a true statement of the grounds on which they are at present divided, and that it is not merely an ambition for power. An honest man can feel no pleasure in the exercise of power over his fellow citizens. And considering as the only offices of power those conferred by the people directly, that is to say, the executive and legislative functions of the general and state governments, the common refusal of these, and multiplied resignations, are proofs sufficient that power is not alluring to pure minds, and is not, with them, the primary principle of contest. This is my belief of it; it is that on which I have acted; and had it been a mere contest who should be permitted to administer the government according to its genuine republican principles, there has never been a moment of my life, in which I should have relinquished for it the enjoyments of my family, my farm, my friends and books.

You expected to discover the difference of our party principles in General Washington's valedictory, and my inaugural address. Not at all. General Washington did not harbor one principle of federalism. He was neither an Angloman, a monarchist, nor a separatist. He sincerely wished the people to have as much self-government as they were competent to exercise themselves. The only point in which he and I ever differed in opinion, was, that I had more confidence than he had in the natural integrity and discretion of the people, and in the safety and extent to which they might trust themselves with a control over their government. He has asseverated to me a thousand times his determination that the existing government should have a fair trial, and that in support of it he would spend the last drop of his blood. He did this the more repeatedly, because he knew General Hamilton's political bias, and my apprehensions from it. It is a mere calumny, therefore, in the monarchists, to associate General Washington with their principles. But that may have happened in this case which has been often seen in ordinary cases, that, by often repeating an untruth, men come to believe it themselves. It is a mere artifice in this party, to bolster themselves up on the revered name of that first of our worthies. If I have dwelt longer on this subject than was necessary, it proves the estimation in which I hold your ultimate opinions, and my desire of placing the subject truly before them. In so doing, I am certain I risk no use of the communication which may draw me into contention before the public. Tranquility is the *summum bonum* of a Septagenaire.

To return to the merits of your work: I consider it as so lively a picture of the real state of our country, that if I can possibly obtain opportunities of conveyance, I propose to send a copy to a friend in France, and another to one in Italy, who, I know, will translate and circulate it as an antidote to the misrepresentations of former travelers. But whatever effect my profession of political faith may have on your general opinion, a part of my object will be obtained, if it satisfies you as to the principles of my own action, and of the high respect and consideration with which I tender you my salutations. TH: JEFFERSON.

The election of JAMES MADISON to the Presidency in 1808 was incidental to the *embargo policy*, and not in itself a landmark. His opponent CHARLES C. PINCKNEY, of South-Carolina, only received 47 votes, while Mr. Madison received 122, as follows:

	Madison,	*Pinckney.*
New-Hampshire, - - -		7
Vermont, - - - - -	6	
Massachusetts, - - -		19
Rhode-Island, - - -		4
Connecticut, - - - -		9
New-York, - - - -	13	
New-Jersey, - - - -	8	
Pennsylvania, - - -	20	
Delaware, - - - -		3
Maryland. - - - -	9	2
Virginia, - - - - -	24	
North-Carolina, - - -	11	3
South-Carolina, - - -	10	
Georgia, - - - -	6	
Tennessee, - - - -	5	
Kentucky, - - - -	7	
Ohio, - - - - -	3	
	122	47

George Clinton was the democratic candidate running with Mr. Madison, and Rufus King was the federal candidate running with Mr. Pinckney, receiving of course the same vote.

Mr. Madison selected for his cabinet, Robert Smith, of Maryland, as secretary of state; William Eustis, of Massachusetts, secretary of war; Paul Hamilton, of South-Carolina, secretary of the navy; Mr. Gallatin was continued as secretary of the treasury, as was Cesar Rodney, of Delaware, attorney-general.

The eleventh Congress met on the 22d of May, 1809, agreably to a law passed by the previous congress, in consequence of the critical state of the nation, and the apprehension of a war with Great Britain or France.

At this session the non-intercourse act with Great Britain and France, which had been substituted for the embargo, by the last congress, was continued, with some modifications.

Soon after this there was a tolerable political calm.

The next great political struggle was upon the attempt to renew the charter of the old Bank of the United States, in 1811. The federalists, regarded that institution as a "Sheet Anchor," and the "democrats" deprecated it as an oppression; unconstitutional in organization, and pernicious in its operation.

That some cases of *political* persecution, at least, seemed to appear in the conduct of the bank of the United States, was undoubted—perhaps, they were magnified; but the fact was, that the management of its concerns, during the most ardent of our contests, was *exclusively* vested in "federalists," as was stated at the time, and now believed to have been the case. The boards of directors were generally made up of the most active *politicians*. From the period of the election of Mr. Jefferson, in 1800, it seemed as if it was the common purpose of *all* the "democrats" to refuse to re-charter that institution. Its establishment had been opposed by Mr. Madison and other men, of the highest standing, as unconstitutional, and so it was accepted to be by the democratic party, whose opinion, it may be, was strenghtened by party hostility to it; but, when the time to act arrived, some flew the course, on the ground of expediency, or an honest apprehension of the great injury that would result from the natural death of the institution: but the body of the party held its ground, and, for their maintaining it, the "*democratic*" papers were severely alluded to in the senate, when the subject was under discussion, as may be seen by a reference to the speeches then delivered. Still, the vote in both houses was, (taken together,) unprecedentedly close.

Nothing like it before, perhaps, had ever taken place. A bill to renew the charter was first introduced in the house—and, after much debate, the first section was struck out, (or, in other words, the bill was rejected,) by sixty-five votes against sixty-four—majority *one.* This vote was taken on the 24th January, 1811. A bill with some new provisions, but to effect the same general purpose, was introduced into the senate, and a motion made therein to strike out the first section. A long and very able debate followed —the vote was taken on the 20th of February and stood *seventeen* to *seventeen!* The vice-president of the United States, the venerable *George Clinton,* then rose, and, having assigned his reasons, directed that his vote should be entered in the affirmative.

It was an exciting moment when it was discovered that "to be or not to be," depended upon one man—the casting vote of the vice-president—but he discharged his duty manfully.

The bill pending before the Senate was to renew the charter of the United States Bank, which was so odious to the democratic party, when a motion was made to strike out the first section; the effect of which would be to destroy the bill, the vote stood as follows:

YEAS.—Messrs. Anderson, Campbell, Clay, Cutts, Gaillard, German, Giles, Gregg, Franklin, Lambert, Leib, Mathewson, Reed, Robinson, S. Smith, Whiteside, Worthington, 17.

NAYS.—Messrs. Bayard, Bradley, Brent, Champlin, Condit, Crawford, Dana, Gilman, Godrich, Horsey, Lloyd, Pickering, Pope, J. Smith, Tait, Taylor, Turner, 17.

It will be observed that WILLIAM H. CRAWFORD was one of the *expediency* democrats who voted in the negative. HENRY CLAY, then a member of the United States Senate, voted in the affirmative, and was then a democrat. He made a powerful speech against the bank at the same time. It has been regarded as one of the most argumentative speeches ever made upon that subject. Subsequently Mr. Clay left the "democrats," which fact alone has probably kept him from the presidential chair, as he stood high as a statesman, and the democracy retained the ascendancy for years afterwards. He became an advocate of the re-charter of the bank in 1816, and during the discussions incident to the attempt to re-charter the same in 1832, he was the main champion of the whigs upon that question in favor of such re-charter.

The position taken by Mr. Crawford upon the bank question in 1811 injured him very materially with democrats in 1824, when his name was brought into the presidential canvass. He had many warm supporters, and among the rest THOMAS RITCHIE, then of the Richmond Enquirer, and now of the "Union," who, in his devotion to Mr. Crawford, allowed himself to deal in rather unwarranted language towards ANDREW JACKSON, who was always a democrat, and one who never deviated from a straight forward course for expediency sake, or any other cause.

Both houses resolved that they would not re-establish the bank, *on any conditions whatever.* That the federalists regarded this as a great party measure is to be ascertained from the fact, that *every one of them, in both houses,* voted for a renewal of the bank; and they were joined by a number of members, who were regarded as "democrats," not believing the bank to be unconstitutional, and thinking it expedient to re-instate it, for various reasons. The decease of this bank afforded much joy to the party.

The twelfth Congress assembled on the 4th of November, 1811, when Henry Clay of Kentucky, an ardent supporter of the administration, was elected speaker of the house of representatives, it being the first time in which he had taken a seat in that body, although he had previously been a member of the United States Senate at two short sessions, when he had acquired considerable reputation as a ready and eloquent debater, and exhibited some of those traits of character which have since distinguished him in the annals of the country, as a statesman.

The next landmark was laid down in the declaration of war, in June 1812.

The main question was carried in the House of Representatives of Congress on the 4th of June, yeas 78—nays, 45. All the yeas were "democrats." In the Senate, yeas 19, nays, 13. All the "federalists" in both houses were against it,—one who had rather been considered as such, excepted.

The war was successfully prosecuted and resulted favorably, in the winding up scene, being the great achievements of ANDREW JACKSON at New-Orleans, on the 8th day of January, 1815. The embarassments thrown in the way of the party in power in the prosecution of the war were very great on the part of the "federalists."

History furnishes the particulars of that war and its results, and we have not space to refer to it at length.

Attempt made in 1812 *to defeat the re-election of Mr. Madison by putting up a "democrat," De Witt Clinton, against him.*

The result of the matter was, that Mr. Madison received 128 votes, and Mr. Clinton 89 votes, as follows:

	Madison.	Clinton.
New-Hampshire, - - - -		8
Vermont, - - - - -	8	
Massachusetts, - - - -		22
Rhode-Island, - - - -		4
Connecticut, - - - -		9
New-York, - - - -		29
New-Jersey, - - - - -		8
Pennsylvania, - - - -	25	
Delaware, - - - - -		4
Maryland, - - - - -	6	5
Virginia, - - - - -	25	
North-Carolina, - - - -	15	
South-Carolina, - - - -	11	
Georgia, - - - - -	8	
Louisiana, - - - - -	3	
Tennessee, - - - -	8	
Kentucky, - - - - -	12	
Ohio, - - - - - - -	7	
	128	89

Elbridge Gerry, of Massachusetts was the democratic candidate for Vice-President, and Jared Ingersoll, the candidate of the federal party. The vote stood 131 to 86.

The declaration of war against Great Britain gave full force again to parties, and a re-organization of the "federal" strength took place.

Mr. Clinton had been regarded as a most decided " dem ocrat," but the opposition, knowing that they could not displace Mr. Madison by one of *their own men*, agreed on Mr. Clinton, that they might secure the important state of New-York, at that time of doubtful politics, or indeed " federal." He was known to be a man of energy and talents—there were strong attachments to him among the " democrats," and it is morally certain that, if he had not been pushed forward in 1812, he would have received the unanimous support of the party in 1816. Local feelings, it may be, had some influence in New-York and New-Jersey, but almost every where else, *it was the old question of democracy and federalism.* The friends of the war generally thought that a change of the administration would have a fatal effect on its results, and shew a wavering policy highly prejudicial to the national character—still there were some few in Maryland, supporters of the war, who advocated the election of Mr. Clinton, on the alleged incompetency of Mr. Madison to carry it on with spirit, and bring it to a successful termination. Some of us, nevertheless, thought, at the same time, that *personal* considerations had as much to do in this proceeding as national feelings. I do not believe that we were greatly mistaken—and it is probable that most of us had respected Mr. Clinton as sincerely as any of those opposed to Mr. Madison. They had not influence enough to obtain an election in either of the districts. All the "democrats" chosen in Maryland voted for Mr. Madison—all the "federalists" for Mr. Clinton.

The congressional elections in 1810-11, proved that the policy of Mr. Madison's administration was sustained by a large majority of the American people; the preponderance of the democratic party being kept up in both branches of congress.

Many divisions of parties took place before the termination of Mr. Madison's second period of service—but they were all incidental to or depending upon the great points already laid down; and before he retired we had arrived at a state of things not materially different from that which existed in the first part of Mr. Jefferson's second period of service. The nation had acquired a character of which all real Americans were proud, though called by different names.

THE HARTFORD CONVENTION.

Theodore Dwight, in his history of the Hartford Convention, makes an attempt to vindicate the character of those engaged in that matter, from the denunciations of the American people. In this work Mr. JEFFERSON is unmercifully handled. He is denounced as being the leader of the "anti-federal party." Among other objections urged by Mr. Dwight against Mr. Jefferson, was, that he "strongly disapproved of the assumption of the state debts" by the General Government, was opposed to the United States Bank, &c. &c.

We now proceed to give the Secret Journal of the Hartford Convention, as made out by Theodore Dwight, the Secretary of the Convention. It is quite lenghty, but as it embraces a very important branch of the history of parties, we publish it entire, in his own language.

SECRET JOURNAL OF THE HARTFORD CONVENTION.

"HARTFORD, Thursday, Dec. 15, 1814.

"This being the day appointed for the meeting of the convention of delegates from the New England States, assembled for the purpose of conferring on such subjets as may come before them, the following persons from those states, met in the council chamber of the state house, in Hartford, in the state of Connecticut, viz:

"*From the state of Massachusetts*, Messrs. George Cabot, William Prescott, Harrison Gray Otis, Timothy Bigelow, Nathan Dane, George Bliss, Joshua Thomas, Hodijah Baylies, Daniel Waldo, Joseph Lyman, Samuel S. Wilde, and Stephen Longfellow, Jun.

"*From the state of Rhode-Island*, Messrs. Daniel Lyman, Benjamin Hazard, and Edward Manton.

From the state of Connecticut, Messrs. Chauncey Goodrich, James Hillhouse, John Treadwell, Zephaniah Swift, Nath'l Smith, Calvin Goddard, and Roger M. Sherman.

"*From the State of New-Hampshire*, Messrs. Benjamin West, and Mills Olcott.

"Upon being called to order by Mr. Cabot, the persons present proceeded to choose, by ballot, a president. Messrs.

Bigelow and Goodrich were appointed to receive and count the votes given for that purpose, who reported that Mr. George Cabot, a Member from Massachusetts was unanimously chosen.

"On motion, voted, that the Convention proceed to the choice of a person to be their secretary, who is not a member of the Convention; and the votes having been received and counted, Theodore Dwight of Hartford, was declared to be chosen unanimously.

"Messrs. Otis, Hillhouse, and Lyman were appointed a committee to examine the credentials of the members returned to serve in the convention, and report the names of such as they should find duly qualified; who, having attended to the subject of their said appointment, made the following report:

"The committee appointed to examine the credentials of the members returned to serve in the convention now assembled at Hartford, have attended to that service, and find the following persons to have been elected members thereof by the respective legislatures of the following states: From *Massachusetts*, Geo. Cabot, William Prescott, Harrison Gray Otis, Timothy Bigelow, Stephen Longfellow, Jun., Daniel Waldo, George Bliss, Nathan Dane, Hodijah Baylies, Joshua Thomas, Joseph Lyman, and Samuel S. Wilde. From *Rhode Island*, Daniel Lyman, Samuel Ward, Benjamin Hazard, and Edward Manton. From *Connecticut*, Chauncy Goodrich, James Hillhouse, John Treadwell, Zephaniah Swift, Calvin Goddard, Nathaniel Smith, and Roger Minot Sherman.

"The committee also report, that at a conventional meeting of twenty towns in the county of Cheshire, in the state of New-Hampshire, Hon. Benjamin West was elected to meet in this convention; and at a conventional meeting of delegates from most of the towns in the county of Grafton, and from the town of Lancaster in the county of Coos, Mills Olcott, Esq., was Elected to meet in this convention;

3

and the committee are of opinion that the above named persons are entitled to take their seats as members of this convention.

"On motion, voted, that the report be accepted and approved.

"On motion of Mr. Otis, voted, that the convention be opened with prayer, and that the delegates from the state of Connecticut be requested to invite a clergyman belonging to the town of Hartford to perform such service.

"On motion voted that Messrs. Goddard, Bigelow, and Lyman be a committee to prepare rules of proceeding for this convention.

"The convention was opened with prayer by the Rev. Dr. Strong of Hartford.

On motion, voted, that this convention be adjourned to 3 o'clock, P. M. of this day, then to meet at this place.

THURSDAY, Dec. 15, 3 o'clock P. M.

"The convention met agreeably to adjournment.

"The committee appointed to prepare rules of proceeding, proper to be observed by this convention, &c., made the following report:

"The committee appointed to prepare rules and orders, proper to be observed by this convention, during its continuance, ask leave to report the following; which are respectfully submitted.

CALVIN GODDARD, *per order*.

"1. The meetings of this convention shall be opened each morning by prayer, which it is requested may be performed, alternately, by the chaplains of the legislature of Connecticut, residing in Hartford.

"2. The most inviolable secrecy shall be observed by each member of this convention, including the secretary, as to all propositions, debates, and proceedings thereof, until this injunction shall be suspended or altered.

"3. The secretary of this convention is authorized to employ some suitable person to serve as a doorkeeper and messenger, together with a suitable assistant, if necessary, neither of whom are at any time to be made acquainted with any of the debates or proceedings of the board.

"4. That the president of this convention be authorized to regulate and direct the debates and proceedings thereof, in such a manner as to him may seem discreet and proper, and to name all their committees.

"On motion, voted, that said report be accepted and approved.

"On motion, voted, that a committee of five be appointed to inquire what subjects will be proper to be considered by this convention; and report such propositions for that purpose, as they may think expedient, to the convention, to-morrow morning.

"The following persons were appointed on that committee: Messrs. Goodrich, Otis, Lyman, of Rhode-Island, Swift and Dane.

"On motion, voted, that this convention be adjourned to ten o'clock to-morrow morning; then to meet at this place.

FRIDAY, December 16, 1814.

"The convention met agreeably to adjournment.

The convention was opened with prayer by the Rev. Dr. Strong.

"Mr. Ward, a member from Rhode-Island, attended and took his seat in the convention.

"The committee appointed to inquire what subjects will be proper to be considered by the convention, and to report such propositions for that purpose, as they may think expedient, respectfully report:

"That your committee deem the following to be proper subjects for the consideration of the convention: The powers claimed by the executive of the United States, to determine, conclusively, in respect to calling out the militia of the states into the service of the United States; and the dividing the United States into military districts, with an officer of the army in each thereof, with discretionary authority from the executive of the United States, to call for the militia to be under the command of such officer. The refusal of the executive of the United States to supply, or pay the militia of certain states, called out for their defence, on the grounds of their not having been called out under the authority of the United States, or not having been, by the executive of the state, put under the command of the commander over the military district. The failure of the government of the United States to supply and pay the militia of the states by them admitted to have been in the United States' service. The report of the secretary of war to Congress, on filling the ranks of the army, together with a bill, or act on that subject. A bill before Congress providing for classing and drafting the militia. The expenditure of the revenue of the nation in offensive operations on the neighboring provinces of the enemy. The failure of the government of the United States to provide for the common defence; and the consequent obligations, necessity and burdens, devolved on the separate states to defend themselves; together with the mode, and the ways and means, in their power for accomplishing the object.

"On motion, voted, that said report be accepted and approved. On motion, voted, that a committee of three be appointed to obtain such documents and information as may be necessary for the use and consideration of the convention, and may be connected with their proceedings. Mr. Hillhouse, Mr. Bliss, and Mr. Hazard, were appointed on that committee. On motion, voted, that the Rev. Dr. Perkins be invited to attend in turn with the other gentlemen already invited, as chaplains. On motion, voted, that the injunction of secrecy, as to the proceedings of yesterday, be removed. On motion, voted, that the convention be adjourned to 3 o'clock, P. M. of this day, then to meet in this place.

"*Three o'clock P. M.*—The Convention met agreeably to adjournment. After spending the afternoon in various discussions of important subjects, on motion, voted, that this Convention be adjourned till to-morrow, 10 o'clock A. M., then to meet at this place.

SATURDAY, December 17, 1814.

"The Convention met, agreeably to adjourment.

"The Convention was opened with prayer, by the Rev. Dr. Strong. After spending the forenoon in discussing the first section of the report of the committee made on Friday, on motion, voted, that when this Convention adjourn, it be adjourned till Monday next. On motion, voted, that this Convention be adjourned till Monday next, at 10 o'clock, A. M. then to meet at this place.

"MONDAY, December 19, 1814.

"The Convention met, agreeably to adjournment. The Convention was opened with prayer, by the Rev. Mr. Chase.

"On motion, voted, that a committee of five be appointed to prepare a general project of such measures as it may be proper for this Convention to adopt.

"Messrs. Smith, Otis, Goddard, West and Hazard, were appointed to be of that committee.

"On motion, voted, that this convention be adjourned till 3 o'clock this afternoon then to meet at this place.

"*Three o'clock P. M.*—The Convention met agreeably to adjournment. On motion, voted, that the Rev. Mr. Cushman be invited to attend in turn with the other gentlemen already invited, as chaplains.

"After spending the afternoon in discussing the report, the committee, on motion, voted, that this convention be adjourned till to-morrow morning, 10 o'clock, then to be held at this place.

"TUESDAY, Dec. 20, 1814.

"The Convention met agreeably to adjournment. The Convention was opened with prayer, by the Rev. Dr. Strong. The committee appointed to prepare and report a general project of such measures as it may be proper for this Convention to adopt, made a report, which was laid in and read. After discussing several articles of the said report, the further consideration of it was postponed until the afternoon. On motion, voted, that this Convention be adjourned till 3 o'clock this afternoon, then to meet at this place.

Three o'clock P. M.—The Convention met pursuant to adjournment. The Convention resumed the consideration of the report of the committee, which was postponed in the forenoon; and after discussion through the afternoon, the same was postponed until the morning. On motion, voted, that this Convention be adjourned until to-morrow morning, 10 o'clock A. M. then to meet at this place.

"WEDNESDAY, Dec. 21, 1814.

"The Convention met pursuant to adjournment. The Convention was opened with prayer, by the Rev. Mr. Chase. The Convention resumed the consideration of the report postponed yesterday. After spending the time of the forenoon in the discussion of the report of the committe, the further consideration was postponed to the afternoon. On motion, voted, that this Convention be adjourned to 3 o'clock this afternoon then to meet at this place.

Three o'clock P. M.—The Convention met pursuant to adjournment. The Convention resumed the consideration of the report of the committee, which was postponed in the forenoon. On motion, voted, that a committee of seven be raised to prepare a report illustrative of the principles and reasons which have induced the Convention to adopt the results to which they have agreed. Mr. Otis, Mr. Smith, Mr. Sherman, Mr. Dane, Mr. Prescott, Mr. West, and Mr. Hazard, were appointed on that committee. On motion, voted, that this Convention be adjourned till to-morrow morning, 10 o'clock.

"THURSDAY, Dec. 22, 1814.

"The Convention met pursuant to adjournment. The Convention was opened with prayer, by the Rev. Dr. Perkins. The Convention resumed the consideration of the report of the committee, postponed last evening. After spending the forenoon in discussing said report, further consideration was postponed till this afternoon. On motion, voted, that this Convention be adjourned till 3 o'clock then to meet at this place.

"*Three o'clock P. M.*—The Convention met agreeably to adjournment. The Convention resumed the consideration of the report of the committee, which was postponed in the forenoon. After spending the afternoon in discussing said report, the further consideration thereof was postponed. On motion, voted, that this Convention be adjourned till to-morrow morning, 10 o'clock, then to meet at this place.

"FRIDAY, Dec. 23, 1814.

"The Convention met pursuant to adjournment. The Convention was opened with prayer by the Rev. Mr. Chase. The Convention resumed the consideration of the report of the committee, which was postponed yesterday. After spending the forenoon in discussing the report of the committee, the further consideration thereof was postponed until to-morrow. On motion, voted, that this Convention be adjourned until to-morrow morning, 10 o'clock, then to meet at this place.

"SATURDAY, Dec. 24, 1814.

"The Convention met pursuant to adjournment. The Convention was opened with prayer, by the Rev. Dr. Perkins. The president communicated an address from a number of citizens belonging to the county of Washington, in the state of New-York, which was read. On motion, voted, that the said address be referred to the committee appointed on the 21st instant.

"The Convention resumed the consideration of the report of the committee, which was postponed yesterday. On motion, voted, that another member be added to the committee appointed on the 21st, Mr. Sherman being necessarily absent. Mr. Swift was appointed on said committee.

"The report of the committee which was laid in on the 20th instant, having been under discussion at the several meetings of the Convention, and having been amended, was adopted, and referred to the committee appointed on the 21st to report, which report is as follows, viz:

"The committee appointed to prepare and report a general project of such measures as it may be proper for this Convention to adopt, respectfully report:

"1. That it will be expedient for this convention to prepare a general statement of the unconstitutional attempts of the executive government of the United States to infringe upon the rights of the individual states, in regard to the militia, and of the still more alarming claims to infringe upon the rights of the individual states, manifested in the letter of the secretary of war, and in the bills pending before Congress, or acts passed by them, and also to recommend to the legislatures of the states, the adoption of the most effectual and decisive measures, to protect the militia and the states from the usurpations contained in these proceedings.

"2. That it will be expedient, also, to prepare a statement exhibiting the necessity which the improvidence and inability of the general government have imposed upon the several states, of providing for their own defence, and the impossibility of their discharging this duty, and at the same time fulfilling the requisitions of the general government; and also, to recommend to the legislatures of the several states, to make provision for mutual defence, and to make an earnest application to the government of the United States, with a view to some arrangement, whereby the states may be enabled to retain a portion of the taxes levied by Congress, for the purpose of self-defence, and for the reimbursement of expenses already incurred, on account of the United States.

"3. That it is expedient to recommend to the several state legislatures, certain amendments to the constitution of the United States, hereafter enumerated, to be by them adopted and proposed. (The remainder of this article in the report was postponed).

"1. That the power to declare or make war, by the Congress of the United States, be restricted.

"2. That it is expedient to attempt to make provision for restraining Congress in the exercise of an unlimited power, to make new states, and admit them into this Union.

"3. That the powers of Congress be restrained in laying embargoes, and restrictions on commerce.

"4. That a president shall not be elected from the same state two terms successively.

"5. That the same person shall not be elected president a second time.

"6. That an amendment be proposed, respecting slave representation, and slave taxation.

"On motion, voted, that this Convention be adjourned to Monday afternoon, three o'clock, then to meet at this place.

MONDAY, December 26, 1814.

"The convention met pursuant to adjournment. The convention was opened with prayer, by the Rev. Mr. Woodbridge, of Hadley, Massachusetts. The committee not being prepared to lay in their report, on motion, voted, that this convention be adjourned till to-morrow morning, 10 o'clock, then to meet at this place.

TUESDAY, December 27, 1814.

"The convention met pursuant to adjournment. The convention was opened with prayer, by the Rev. Dr. Perkins. The committee not being prepared to lay in their report, on motion, voted that this convention be adjourned to 3 o'clock this afternoon, then to meet at this place.

Three o'clock P. M.—The convention met pursuant to adjournment. The committee not being prepared to lay in their report, on motion, voted, that this convention be adjourned to 10 o'clock to-morrow morning, then to meet at this place.

WEDNESDAY, December 28, 1814.

"The convention met pursuant to adjournment. The convention was opened with prayer, by the Rev. Mr. Chase.

A certificate of the proceedings of a convention in the county of Windham, in the state of Vermont, appointing Hon. William Hall, Jun., to represent the people of that county in this convention, was read. On motion, voted, that the Hon. William Hall Jun., is entitled to a seat in this convention; and that the Hon. Mr. Olcott, of New-Hampshire be requested to introduce Mr. Hall for the purpose of taking his seat.

" Mr. Hall, a member from the county of Windham, in the state of Vermont, attended and took his seat in the convention. The report of the committee not being prepared, on motion, voted, that this convention be adjourned to 3 o'clock this afternoon; then to meet at this place.

" *Three o'clock P. M.*—The convention met pursuant to adjournment. The report of the committee not being prepared, upon motion, voted, that this convention be adjourned till to-morrow morning at 10 o'clock.

THURSDAY, December 29, 1814.

The convention met pursuant to adjourment. The convention was opened with prayer by the Rev. Dr. Strong. On motion, voted that the following proposition be referred to the committee appointed on the 21st inst:

" That the capacity of naturalized citizens to hold offices of trust, honor or profit ought to be restrained; and that it is expedient to propose an amendment to the Constitution of the United States, in relation to that subject.

" The report of the committee not being prepared, on motion, voted that this convention be adjourned till 3 o'clock this afternoon, then to meet at this place.

FRIDAY, December 30, 1814.

The convention met pursuant to adjournment. The convention was opened with prayer by the Rev. Dr. Perkins. The committee appointed on the 21st instant presented their report, which was read twice. The forenoon having been spent in reading the report, on motion, voted, that this convention be adjourned till three o'clock this afternoon, then to meet at this place.

Three o'clock P. M.—The convention met pursuant to adjournment. After spending the afternoon in discussing the report, the subject was postponed. On motion, voted, that this convention be adjourned till to-morrow morning, 10 o'clock, then to meet at this place.

SATURDAY, December 31, 1814.

"The convention met pursuant to adjournment. The convention was opened with prayer by the Rev. Mr. Chase. The convention resumed the consideration of the report, postponed yesterday. On motion, voted, that a committee to consist of three, be appointed to procure that part of the report which relates to the militia, printed confidentially. Messrs. Goodrich, Lyman, of Massachusetts, and Goddard, were appointed on that committee. After spending the forenoon in considering the report of the committee, the further consideration thereof was postponed. On motion, voted, that this convention be adjourned till half-past two o'clock this afternoon, then to meet at this place.

Half-past two o'clock P. M.—The convention met pursuant to adjournment. The convention resumed the consideration of the report of the committee, which was postponed in the forenoon. After spending the afternoon in discussing the report of the committee the further consideration thereof was postponed. On motion, voted, that a com mittee of three persons be appointed to ascertain what expenses have been incurred in this convention, which it is necessary for them to defray, and to report the mode of discharging them. On motion, voted, that the first eight pages of the report be recommitted to the committe which reported it, to reconsider the same. On motion, voted, that the same committee report such documents and articles as they may think proper, to compose an appendix to the report.

"On motion, voted, that this convention be adjourned till Monday morning at 10 o'clock, to meet at this place.

MONDAY, January 2, 1815.

"The convention met pursuant to adjournment. The

convention was opened with prayer by the Rev. Mr. Chase. The convention resumed the consideration of the report of the committee which was postponed from Saturday. After spending the forenoon in discussing the report, the farther consideration thereof was postponed. On motion, voted, that this convention be adjourned till half-past two o'clock this afternoon, then to meet at this place.

"*Half past two o'clock, P. M.*—The convention met pursuant to adjournment. The convention resumed the consideration of the report of the committee, which was postponed in the forenoon. After spending the afternoon in discussing the report of the committee, the further consideration thereof was postponed. On motion, voted, that this convention be adjourned till to-morrrow morning, nine o'clock, then to meet at this place.

"TUESDAY, January 3, 1815.

"The convention met pursuant to adjournment. The convention was opened with praper by the Rev. Dr. Perkins. The convention resumed the consideration of the report of the committee, which was postponed yesterday. After spending the forenoon in discussing the report of the committee, the same was posptoned till afternoon. On moion, voted, that this convention be adjourned till three o'clock this afternoon, then to meet at this place.

"*Three o'clock P. M.*—The convention met pursuant to adjournment. The convention resumed the consideration of the report of the committee, which was postponed in the forenoon. After discussing and amending the report of the commitee, voted, that the same be accepted and approved. On motion, resolved, that the injunction of secresy, in regard to all the debates and proceedings of this convention, except in so far as relates to the report finally adopted, be, and hereby is continued. On motion, voted, that a committee of three persons be appointed to consider and report what measures it will be expedient to recommend to the states, for their mutual defence. Mr. Prescott, Mr. Wilde, and Mr. Manton, were appointed on that committee.

"On motion, voted, that Mr. Sherman be added to the committee for superintending the printing of the report. On motion, voted, that this convention be adjourned till to-morrow morning, ten o'clock, then to meet in this place.

WEDNESDAY, January 4, 1815.

"The convention met pursuant to adjournment. The convention was opened with prayer by the Rev. Mr. Chase. On motion, voted, that certain documents before the convention be published, with the following title: 'Statements prepared and published, by order of the convention of delegates, held at Hartford, December 15, 1814, and printed by their order.

"On motion, voted, that Mr. Goodrich be discharged from any further services on the committee to superintend the printing of the report, &c. On motion, voted that another member be added to that committee. Mr. Otis was appointed to that place. The committee appointed to report what measures it will be expedient to recommend to the states, for their mutual defence, presented a report, which was read. On motion, voted, that the said report be accepted and approved. On motion, voted, that this convention be adjourned till three o'clock this afternoon, then to meet at this place.

"*Three o'clock P. M.*—The convention met pursuant to adjournment. On motion, voted, that two copies of the report of the couvention, subscribed by all the members who shall be disposed to sign the same, be forwarded to each of the governors of the states of Massachusetts, Connecticut, Rhode-Island, New-Hampshire, and Vermont; one of which to be for the private use of the said governors, and with a request that the other, at some proper time, may be laid before the legislatures of the states aforesaid.

"Mr. Goodrich submitted the following resolution to the convention: Resolved, That the thanks of the convention be presented to the Hon. George Cabot, in testimony of the respectful sense they entertain of his conduct while presiding over their deliberations.

"On the question being put by the secretary, it passed in the affirmative unanimously. On motion, voted, that the convention be adjourned till seven o'clock this evening, then to meet at this place.

"*Seven o'clock P. M.*—The convention met pursuant to adjournment. On, motion, voted, that the report as amended, and the resolves accompanying the same, be accepted and approved. On motion, voted, that the delegates from Massachusetts, Connecticut, and Rhode-Island, take two copies of the report of the convention, and deliver the same to the governors of those states, agreeably to the vote of the convention passed this day, and that the president be requested to transmit two copies of the report to the governors of the states of New-Hampshire and Vermont, together with a copy of the vote of the Convention aforesaid.

"On motion, voted, that at the close of the convention, the journal be committed to the care of the president. On motion, voted, that the convention be adjourned till to-morrow morning, nine o'clock, then to meet at this place.

THURSDAY, January 5, 1815—9 o'clock A. M.

"The convention met pursuant to adjournment—after solemn prayer, by the Rev. Dr. Strong, on motion, voted, that this convention be adjourned without day.

"Attest, THEODORE DWIGHT, *Secretary.*"

—

It will be borne in mind that the convention was adjourned for future action, without the accomplishment of any thing save sending forth a report, which we proceed to publish, it being closely interwoven with the history of parties. The author of the work from which we extract, was a "federalist" and secretary of the convention, and the object of the work appears to be to satisfy the world that the designs of those comprising that convention were not so revolutionary or disgraceful as common reports ascribed to them.

Soon after the adjournment of the convention the news of peace arrived, which put a quietus upon their revolutionary movements.

SECRET JOURNAL OF THE HARTFORD CONVENTION.

REPORT.

' *The delegates from the legislatures of the states of Massachusetts, Connecticut and Rhode Island, and from the counties of Grafton and Cheshire, in the state of New-Hampshire and the county of Windham in the state of Vermont, assembled in convention, beg leave to report the following result of their conference:*

"The convention is deeply impressed with a sense of the arduous nature of the commission which they were appointed to execute, of devising the means of defence against dangers, and of relief from oppressions proceeding from the acts of their own government, without violating constitutional principles, or disappointing the hopes of a suffering and injured people. To prescribe patience and firmness to those who are already exhausted by distress, is sometimes to drive them to despair, and the progress towards reform by the regular road, is irksome to those whose imaginations discern, and whose feelings prompt, to a shorter course. But when abuses, reduced to system, and accumulated through a course of years, have pervaded every department of government, and spread corruption through every region of the state; when these are clothed with the forms of law, and enforced by an executive whose will is their source, no summary means of relief can be applied without resource to direct and open resistance. This experiment, when justifiable, cannot fail to be painful to the good citizen; and the success of the effort will be no security against the danger of the example. Precedents of resistance to the worst administration, are eagerly seized by those who are naturally hostile to the best. Necessity alone can sanction a resort to this measure; and it should never be extended in duration or degree beyond the exigency, until the people, not merely in the fervor of sudden excitement, but after full deliberation, are determined to change the constitution.

"It is a truth not to be concealed, that a sentiment prevails to no inconsiderable extent, that administration have given such constructions to that instrument, and practised so many abuses under color of its authority, that the time for a change is at hand. Those who so believe, regard the evils which surround them as intrinsic and incurable defects in the constitution. They yield to a persuasion, that no change, at any time, or on any occasion, can aggravate the misery of their country. This opinion may ultimately prove to be correct. But as the evidence on which it rests is not yet conclusive, and as measures adopted upon the assumption of its certainty might be irrevocable, some general considerations are submitted, in the hope of reconciling all to a course of moderation and firmness, which may save them from the regret incident to sudden decisions, probably avert the evil, or at least insure consolation and success in the last resort.

"The constitution of the United States, under the auspices of a wise and virtuous administration, proved itself competent to all the objects of national prosperity comprehended in the views of its framers. No parallel can be found in history, of a transition so rapid as that of the United States from the lowest depression to the highest felicity—from the condition of weak and disjointed republics, to that of a great, united, and prosperous nation.

"Although this high state of public happiness has undergone a miserable and afflicting reverse, through the prevalence of a weak and profligate policy, yet the evils and afflictions which have thus been induced upon the country, are not peculiar to any form of government. The lust and caprice of power, the corruption of patronage, the oppression of the weaker interests of community by the stronger, heavy taxes, wasteful expenditures, and unjust and ruinous wars, are the natural offspring of bad administrations, in all ages and countries. It was indeed to be hoped, that the rulers of these states would not make such disastrous haste to involve their infancy in the embarrassments of old and rotten institutions. Yet all this have they done; and their conduct calls loudly for their dismission and disgrace. But to attempt upon every abuse of power to change the constitution would be to perpetuate the evils of revolution.

"Again the experiment of the powers of the constitution to regain its vigor, and of the people to recover from their delusions, has been hitherto made under the greatest possible disadvantages arising from the state of the world. The fierce passions which have convulsed the nations of Europe, have passed the ocean, and finding their way to the bosoms of our citizens, have afforded to administration the means of perverting public opinion, in respect to our foreign relations, so as to acquire its aid in the indulgence of their animosities, and the increase of their adherents. Further, a reformation of public opinion, resulting from dear-bought experience, in the southern Atlantic states, at least, is not to be despaired of. They will have felt, that the eastern states cannot be made exclusively the victims of a capricious and impassioned policy. They will have seen that the great and essential interests of the people are common to the south and to the east. They will realize the fatal errors of a system which seeks revenge for commercial injuries in the sacrifice of commerce, and aggravates by needless wars, to an immeasurable extent, the injuries it professes to redress. They may discard the influence of visionary theorists, and recognize the benefits of a practical policy. Indications of this desirable revolution of opinion, among our brethren in those states, are already manifested. While a hope remains of its ultimate completion, its progress should not be retarded or stopped, by exciting fears which must check these favorable tendencies, and frustrate the efforts of the wisest and best men in those states, to accelerate this propitious change.

"Finally, if the union be destined to dissolution, by reason of the multiplied abuses of bad administrations, it should, if possible, be the work of peaceable times, and deliberate consent. Some new form of confederacy should be substituted among those states which shall intend to maintain a federal relation to each other. Events may prove that the causes of our calamities are deep and permanent. They may be found to proceed, not merely from the blindness of prejudice, pride of opinion, violence of party spirit, or the confusion of the times; but they may be traced to implacable combinations of individuals, or of states, to monopolize power and office, and to trample without remorse upon the rights and interests of commercial sections of the Union. Whenever it shall appear that these causes are radical and permanent, a separation, by equitable arrangement, will be preferable to an alliance by constraint, among nominal friends, but real enemies, inflamed by mutual hatred and jealousy, and inviting by intestine divisions, contempt and aggression from abroad. But a severance of the union by one or more states, against the will of the rest, and especially in a time of war, can be justified only by absolute necessity. These are among the principal objections against precipitate measures tending to disunite the states, and when examined in connection with the farewell address of the Father of his country, they must, it is believed, be deemed conclusive.

"Under these impressions, the convention have proceeded to confer and deliberate upon the alarming state of public affairs, especially as affecting the interests of the people who have appointed them for this purpose, and they are naturally led to a consideration, in the first place, of the dangers and grievances which menace an immediate or speedy pressure, with a view of suggesting means of present relief; in the next place, of such as are of more remote and general description, in the hope of attaining future security.

"Among the subjects of complaint and apprehension which might be comprised under the former of these propositions, the attention of the convention has been occupied with the claims and pretensions advanced, and the authority exercised over the militia, by the executive and legislative departments of the national government. Also, upon the destitution of the means of defence in which the eastern states are left; while at the same time they are doomed to heavy requisitions of men and money for national objects.

"The authority of the national government over the militia is derived from those clauses in the constitution which give power to Congress "to provide for calling forth the militia to execute the laws of the Union, suppress insurrections and repel invasions;"—Also "to provide for organizing, arming and disciplining the militia, and for governing such parts of them as may be employed in the service of the United States, reserving to the states respectively, the appointment of the officers, and the authority of training the militia according to the discipline prescribed by Congress." Again, "the President shall be the commander-in-chief of the army and navy of the United States, and of the militia of the several states, when called into the actual service of the United States." In these specified cases only, has the national government any power over the militia; and it follows conclusively, that for all general and ordinary purposes, this power belongs to the states respectively, and to them alone. It is not only with regret, but with astonishment, the convention perceive that under color of an authority conferred with such plain and precise limitations, a power is arrogated by the executive government, and in some instances sanctioned by the two houses of Congress, of control over the militia, which, if conceded, will render nugatory the rightful authority of the individual states over that class of men, and by placing at the disposal of the national government the lives and services of the great body of the people, enabled it at pleasure to destroy their liberties, and erect a military despotism on the ruins.

"An elaborate examination of the principles assumed for the basis of these extravagant pretensions, of the consequences to which they lead, and the unsurmountable objections to their admission, would transcend the limits of this report. A few general observations, with an exhibition of the character of these pretensions, and a recommendation of a strenuous opposition to them, must not, however, be omitted.

"It will not be contended that by the terms used in the constitutional compact, the power of the national government to call out the militia is other than a power expressly limited to three cases. One of these must exist, as a condition precedent to the exercise of that power. Unless the laws shall be opposed, or an insurrection shall exist, or an invasion shall be made, Congress, and of consequence the Presidentas their organ, has no more power over the militia than over the armies of a foreign nation.

"But if the declaration of the President should be admitted to be an unerring test of the existence of these cases, this important power would depend, not upon the truth of the fact, but upon executive infallibility. And the limitation of the power would consequently be nothing more than merely nominal, as it might always be eluded. It follows, therefore, that the decision of the President in this particular cannot be conclusive. It is as much the duty of the state authorities to watch over the rights reserved, as of the United States to exercise the powers which are delegated.

"The arrangement of the United States into military districts, with a small portion of the regular force, under an officer of high rank of the standing army, with a power to call for the militia, as circumstances in his judgment may require; and to assume the command of them, is not warranted by the constitution or any law of the United States. It is not denied that Congress may delegate to the President of the United States the power to call forth the militia in the cases which are within their jurisdiction—but he has no authority to substitute military prefects throughout the Union, to use their own discretion in such instances. To station an officer of the army in a military district without troops corresponding to his rank, for the purpose of taking command of the militia that may be called into service, is a manifest evasion of that provision of the constitution which expressly reserves to the states the appointment of the officers of the militia; and the object of detaching such officer cannot well be concluded to be any other than that of superseding the governor or other officers of the militia in their right to command.

"The power of dividing the militia of the states into classes, and obliging such classes to furnish, by contract or draft, able-bodied men, to serve for one or more years for the defence of the frontier, is not delegated to Congress. If a claim to draft the militia for one year for such general object be admissible, no limitation can be assigned to it, but the discretion of those who make the law. Thus, with a power in Congress to authorize such a draft or conscription, and in the executive to decide conclusively upon the existence and continuance of the emergency, the whole militia may be converted into a standing army disposable at the will of the President of the United States.

"The power of compelling the militia, and other citizens of the United States, by a forcible draft or conscription, to serve in the regular armies, as proposed in a late official letter of the secretary of war, is not delegated to Congress by the constitution, and the exercise of it would be not less dangerous to their liberties, than hostile to the sovereignty of the states. The effort to deduce this power from the right of raising armies, is a flagrant attempt to pervert the sense of the clause in the constitution which confers that right, and is incompatible with other provisions in that instrument. The armies of the United States have always been raised by contract, never by conscription, and nothing more can be wanting to a government possessing the power thus claimed to enable it to usurp the entire control of the militia, in derogation of the authority of the state, and o convert it by impressment into a standing army.

"It may be here remarked, as a circumstance illustrative of the determination of the executive to establish an absolute control over all descriptions of citizens, that the right of impressing seamen into the naval service is expressly asserted by the secretary of the navy, in a late report. Thus a practice, which in a foreign government has been regarded with great abhorrence by the people, finds advocates among those who have been the loudest to condemn it.

"The law authorizing the enlistment of minors and apprentices into the armies of the United States, without the consent of parents and guardians is also repugnant to the spirit of the constitution. By a construction of the power to raise armies, as applied by our present rulers, not only persons capable of contracting are liable to be impressed into the army, but those who are under legal disabilities to make contracts, are to be invested with the capacity, in order to enable them to annul at pleasure contracts made in their behalf by legal guardians. Such an interference with the municipal laws and rights of the several states, could never have been contemplated by the framers of the constitution. It impairs the salutary control and influence of the parent over his child—the master over his servant—the guardian over his ward—and thus destroys the most important relations in society, so that by the conscription of the father, and the seduction of the son, the power of the executive over all the effective male population of the United States is made complete.

"Such are some of the odious features of the novel system proposed by the rulers of a free country, under the limited powers derived from the constitution. What portion of them will be embraced in acts finally to be passed, is yet impossible to determine. It is, however, sufficiently alarming to perceive, that these projects emanate from the highest authority, nor should it be forgotten, that by the plan of the secretary of war, the classificatiou of the militia embraced the principle, of direct taxation upon the white population only; and that, in the house of representatives, a motion to apportion the militia among the white population exclusively, which would have been in its operation a direct tax was strenuously urged and supported.

"In this whole series of devices and measures for raising men, this convention discern a total disregard for the constitution, and a disposition to violate its provisions, demanding from the individual states firm and decided opposition. An iron despotism can impose no harder servitude upon the citizen, than to force him from his home and his occupation, to wage offensive wars, undertaken to gratify the pride or passions of his master. The example of France has recently shown that a cabal of individuals assuming to act in the name of the people, may transform the great body of citizens into soldiers, and deliver them over into the hands of a single tyrant. No war, not held in just abhorrence by the people, can require the aid of such stratagems to recruit an army. Had the troops already raised, and in great numbers sacrificed upon the frontier of Canada, been employed for the defence of the country, and had the millions which have been squandered with shameless profusion, been appropriated to their paymeut, to the protection of the coast, and to the naval service, there would have been no occasion for unconstitutional expedients. Even at this late hour, let government leave to New-England the remnant of her resources, and she is ready and able to defend her territory, and to resign the glories and advantages of the border war to those who are determined to persist in its prosecution.

"That acts of congress in violation of the constitution are absolutely void, is an undeniable position. It does not, however, consist with the respect and forbearance due from a confederate state towards the general government, to fly to open resistance upon every infraction of the constitution. The mode and the energy of the opposition, should always conform to the nature of the violation, the intention of its authors, the extent of the injury inflicted, the determination manifested to persist in it, and the danger of delay. But in cases of deliberate, dangerous, and palable infractions of the constitution, affecting the sovereignty of the state, and liberties of the people; it is not only the right but the duty of such a state to interpose its authority for their protection in the manner best calculated to secure that end. When emergencies occur which are either beyond the reach of the judicial tribunals, or too pressing to admit of the delay incident to their forms, states which have no common umpire, must be their own judges, and execute their own decisions. It will thus be proper for the several states to await the ultimate disposal of the obnoxious measures recommended by the secretary of war, or pending before Congress, and so to use their power according to the character these measures shall finally assume, as effectually to protect their own sovereignty, and the rights and liberties of their citizens.

"The next subject which has occupied the attention of the convention, is the means of defence against the common enemy. This naturally leads to the inquiries, whether any expectation can be reasonably entertained, that adequate provision for the defence of the eastern states will be made by the national government? Whether the several states can, from their own resources, provide for self-defence and fulfil the requisitions which are to be expected for the national treasury? and, generally, what course of conduct ought to be adopted by those states, in relation to the great object of defence.

"Without pausing at present to comment upon the causes of the war, it may be assumed as a truth, officially announced, that to achieve the conquest of Canadian territory, and to hold it as a pledge for peace, is the deliberate purpose of administration. This enterprise, commenced at a period when government possessed the advantage of selecting the time and occasion for making a sudden descent upon an unprepared enemy, now languishes in the third year of the war. It has been prosecuted with various fortune, and occasional brilliancy of exploit, but without any solid acquisition. The British armies have been recruited by veteran regiments. Their navy commands Ontario. The American ranks are thinned by the casualties of war. Recruits are discouraged by the unpopular character of the contest, and by the uncertainty of receiving their pay.

"In the prosecution of this favorite warfare, administration have left the exposed and vulnerable parts of the country destitute of all the efficient means of defence. The main body of the regular army has been marched to the frontier. The navy has been stripped of a great part of its sailors for the service of the lakes. Meanwhile the enemy scours the sea-coast, blockades our ports, ascends our bays and rivers, makes actual descents in various and distant places, holds some by force, and threatens all that are assailable with fire and sword. The sea-board of four of the New-England states, following its curvatures, presents an extent of more than seven hundred miles, generally occupied by a compact population, and accessible by a naval force, exposing a mass of people and property to the devastation of the enemy, which bears a great proportion to the residue of the maritime frontier of the United States. This extensive shore has been exposed to frequent attacks, repeated contributions, and constant alarms. The regular forces detached by the national government for its defence are mere pretexts for placing officers of high rank in command. They are besides confined to a few places, and are too insignificant in number to be included in any computation.

"These states have thus been left to adopt measures for their own defence. The militia have been constantly kept on the alert, and harrassed by garrison duties, and other hardships, while the expenses, of which the national government decline the re-imbursement, threaten to absorb all the resources of the states. The President of the United States has refused to consider the expense of the militia detached by state authority, for the indispensable defence of the state, as chargeable to the Union, on the ground of a refusal by the Executive of the state to place them under the command of officers of the regular army. Detachments of militia placed at the disposal of the general government, have been dismissed either without pay, or with depreciated paper. The prospect of the ensuing campaign is not enlivened by the promise of any alleviation of these grievances. From authentic documents, extorted by necessity from those whose inclination might lead them to conceal the embarrassments of the government, it is apparent that the treasury is bankrupt, and its credit prostrate. So deplorable is the state of the finances, that those who feel for the honor and safety of the country, would be willing to conceal the melancholy spectacle, if those whose infatuation has produced this state of fiscal concerns had not found themselves compelled to unveil it to public view.

"If the war be continued, there appears no room for reliance upon the national government for the supply of those means of defence which must become indispensable to secure these states from desolation and ruin. Nor is it possible that the states can discharge this sacred duty from their own resources, and continue to sustain the burden of the national taxes. The administration, after a long perseverance in plans to baffle every effort of commercial enterprize, had fatally succeeded in their attempt at the epoch of the war. Commerce, the vital spring of New-England's prosperity was annihilated. Embargoes, restrictions, and the rapacity of revenue officers, had completed its destruction. The various objects for the employment of productive labor in the branches of business dependent on commerce, have disappeared. The fisheries have shared its fate. Manufactures, which government has professed an intention to favor and cherish, as an indemnity for the failure of these branches of business, are doomed to struggle in their infancy with taxes and obstructions, which cannot fail most seriously to affect their growth. The specie is wilhdrawn from circulation. The landed interest, the last to feel these burdens, must prepare to become their principal support, as all other sources of revenue must be exhausted. Under these circumstances, taxes, of a description and amount unprecedented in this country, are in a train of imposition, the burden of which must fall with the heaviest pressure upon the states east of the Potomac. The amount of these taxes for the ensuing year cannot be estimated at less than five millions of dollars upon the New-England states, and the expenses of the last year for defence, in Massachusetts alone, approaches to one million of dollars.

"From these facts, it is almost superfluous to state the irresistible inference that these states have no capacity of defraying the expense requisite for their own protection, and, at the same time, of discharging the demands of the national treasury.

"The last inquiry, what course of conduct ought to be adopted by the aggrieved states, is in a great degree momentous. When a great and brave people shall feel themselves deserted by their government, and reduced to the necessity either of submission to a foreign enemy, or of appropriating to their own use those means of defence which are indispensable to self-preservation, they cannot consent to wait passive spectators of approaching ruin, which it is in their power to avert, and to resign the last remnant of their industrious earnings to be dissipated in support of measures destructive of the best interests of the nation.

"The convention will not trust themselves to express their conviction of the catastrophe to which such a state of things inevitably tends. Conscious of their high responsibility to God and their country, solicitous for the continuance of the Union, as well as the sovereignty of the states, unwilling to furnish obstacles to peace—resolute never to submit to a foreign enemy, and confiding in the Divine care and protection, they will, until the last hope shall be extinguished, endeavor to avert such consequences.

"With this view they suggest an arrangement, which may be at once consistent with the honor and interest of the national government, and the security of these states. This it will not be difficult to conclude, if that government should be so disposed. By the terms of it these states might be allowed to assume their own defence, by the militia or other troops. A reasonable portion, also, of the taxes raised in each state might be paid into its treasury, and credited to the United States, but to be appropriated to the defence of such state, to be accounted forwith the United States. No doubt is entertained that by such an arrangement, this portion of the country could be defended with greater effect, and in a mode more consistent with economy, and the public convenience, than any which has been practised.

"Should an application for these purposes, made to Congress by the state legislatures, be attended with success, and should peace upon just terms appear to be unattainable, the people would stand together for the common defence, until a change of administration, or of disposition in the enemy, should facilitate the occurrence of that auspicious event. It would be inexpedient for this Convention to diminish the hope of a successful issue to such an application, by recommending, upon supposition of a contrary event, ulterior proceedings. Nor is it indeed within their province. In a state of things so solemn and trying as may then arise, the legislatures of the states, or conventions of the whole people, or delegates appointed by them for the express purpose in another Convention, must act as such urgent circumstances may then require.

"But the duty incumbent on this Convention will not have been performed, without exhibiting some general view of such measures as they deem essential to secure the nation against a relapse into difficulties and dangers, should they, by the blessing of Providence, escape from their present condition, without absolute ruin. To this end a concise retrospect of the state of this nation under the advantages of a wise administration, contrasted with the miserable abyss into which it is plunged by the profligacy and folly of political theorists, will lead to some practical conclusions. On this subject, it will be recollected, that the immediate influence of the Federal Constitution upon its first adoption, and for twelve succeeding years, upon the prosperity and happiness of the nation, seemed to countenance a belief in the transcendency of its perfection over all other human institutions. In the catalogue of blessings which have fallen to the lot of the most favored nations, none could be enumerated from which our country was excluded—a free Constitution, administered by great and incorruptible statesmen, realized the fondest hopes of liberty and independence. The progress of agriculture was stimulated by the certainty of value in the harvest—and commerce, after traversing every sea, returned with the riches of every clime. A revenue, secured by a sense of honor, collected without oppression, and paid without murmurs, melted away the national debt; and the chief concern of the public creditor arose from its too rapid diminution. The wars and commotions of the European nations, and their interruptions of the commercial intercourse afforded to those who had not promoted, but who would have rejoiced to alleviate their calamities, a fair and golden opportunity, by combining themselves to lay a broad foundation for national wealth. Although occasional vexations to commerce arose from the furious collisions of the powers at war, yet the great and good men of that time conformed to the force of circumstances which they could not control, and preserved their country in security from the tempests which overwhelmed the old world, and threw the wreck of their fortunes on these shores. Respect abroad, prosperity at home, wise laws made by honored legislators, and prompt obedience yielded by a contented people, had silenced the enemies of republican institutions. The arts flourished—the sciences were cultivated—the comforts and conveniences of life were universally diffused—and nothing remained for succeeding administrations but to reap the advantages and cherish the resources flowing from the policy of their predecessors.

"But no sooner was a new administration established in the hands of the party opposed to the Washington policy, than a fixed determination was perceived and avowed of changing a system which had already produced these substantial fruits. The consequence of this change, for a few years after its commencement, were not sufficient to counteract the prodigious impulse towards prosperity, which have been given to the nation. But a steady perseverance in the new plans of administration, at length developed their weakness and deformity, but not until a majority of the people had been deceived by flattery, and inflamed by passion, into blindness to their defects. Under the withering influence of this new system, the declension of the nation has been uniform and rapid. The richest advantages for securing the great objects of the constitution have been wantonly rejected. While Europe reposes from the convulsions that had shaken down her ancient institutions, she beholds with amazement this remote country, once so happy and so envied, involved in a ruinous war, and excluded from intercourse with the rest of the world.

"To investigate and explain the means whereby this fatal reverse has been effected, would require a voluminous discussion. Nothing more can be attempted in this report than a general allusion to the principal outlines of the policy which has produced this vicissitude. Among these may be erumerated—

"*First.*—A deliberate and extensive system for effecting a combination among certain states, by exciting local jealousies and ambition, so as to secure to popular leaders in one section of the Union, the control of public affairs, in perpetual succession. To which primary objects most other characteristics of the system may be reconciled.

"*Secondly.*—The political intolerance displayed and avowed in excluding from office men of unexceptionable merit, for want of adherence to the executive creed.

"*Thirdly.*—The infraction of the judiciary authority and rights, by depriving judges of their offices in violation of the constitution.

"*Fourthly.*—The abolition of existing taxes, requisite to prepare the country for those changes to which nations are always exposed, with a view to the acquisition of popular favor.

"*Fifthly.*—The influence of patronage in the distribution of offices, which in these states has been almost invariably made among men the least entitled to such distinction, and who have sold themselves as ready instruments for distracting public opinion, and encouraging administration to hold in contempt the wishes and remonstrances of a people thus apparently divided.

"*Sixthly.*—The admission of new states into the Union formed at pleasure in the western region, has destroyed the balance of power which existed among the original States, and deeply affected their interest.

"*Seventhly.*—The easy admission of naturalized foreigners, to places of trust, honor or profit, operating as an inducement to the malcontent subjects of the old world to come to these States, in quest of executive patronage, and to repay it by an abject devotion to executive measures.

"*Eightly.*—Hostility to Great Britain, and partiality to the late government of France, adopted as coincident with popular prejudice, and subservient to the main object, party power. Connected with these must be ranked erroneous and distorted estimates of the power and resources of those nations, of the probabal results of their controversies, and of our political relations to them respectively.

"*Lastly and Principally.*—A visionary and superficial theory in regard to commerce, accompanied by a real hatred but a feigned regard to its interests, and a ruinous perse verance in efforts to render it an instrument of coercion and war.

"But it is not conceivable that the obliquity of any administration could, in so short a period, have so nearly consummated the work of national ruin, unless favored by defect in the constitution.

"To enumerate all the improvements of which that instrument (the Constitution) is susceptible, and to propos such amendments as might render it in all respects perfect would be a task which this convention has not thought proper to assume. They have confined their attention to such as experience has demonstrated to be essential, and even among these, some are considered entitled to a more serious attention than others. They are suggested without any intentional disrespect to other states and are meant to be such as all shall find an interest in promoting. Their object is to strengthen, and if possible to perpetuate, the union of the states, by removing the grounds of existing jealousies, and providing for a fair and equal representation, and a limitation of powers, which have been misused.

"The first amendment proposed, relates to the apportionment of representatives among the slaveholding states. The cannot be claimed as a right. Those states are entitled to the slave representation by a constitutional compact. It is herefore merely a subject of agreement, which should be conducted upon principles of mutual interest and accommodation, and upon which no sensibility on either side should be permitted to exist. It has proved unjust and unequal in its operation. Had this effect been foreseen, the privilege would probably not have been demanded; certainly not conceded. Its tendency in future will be adverse to that harmony and mutual confidence which are more conducive to the happiness and prosperity of every confederated state, than a mere preponderance of power, the prolific source of jealousies and controversy, can be to any one of them. The time may therefore arrive, when a sense of magnanimity and justice will reconcile those states to acquiesce in a revision of this article, especially as a fair equivalent would result to them in the apportionment of taxes.

"The next amendment relates to the admission of new states into the Union.

"This amendment is deemed to be highly important, and in fact, indispensable. In proposing it, it is not intended to recognize the right of congress to admit new states without the original limits of the United States, nor is any idea entertained of disturbing the tranquility of any state already admitted into the Union. The object is merely to restrain the constitutional power of congress in admitting new states. At the adoption of the constitution, a certain balance of power among the original parties was considered to exist, and there was at that time, and yet is among those parties, a strong affinity between their great and general interests. By the admission of these states that balance has been materially affected, and unless the practice be modified, must ultimately be destroyed. The southern states will first avail themselves of their new confederates to govern the east, and finally the western states, multiplied in number, and augmented in population, will control the interests of the whole. Thus for the sake of present power, the southern states will be common sufferers with the east, in the loss of permanent advantages. None of the old states can find an interest in creating prematurely an overwhelming western influence, which may hereafter discern (as it has heretofore) benefits to be derived to them by wars and commercial restrictions.

"The next amendments proposed by the convention, relate to the powers of Congress, in relation to embargo and the interdiction of commerce.

"Whatever theories upon the subject of commerce have hitherto divided the opinions of statesmen, experience has at last shown that it is a vital interest in the United States, and that its success is essential to the encouragement of agriculture and manufactures, and to the wealth, finances, defence, and liberty or the nation. Its welfare can never interfere with the other great interests of the state, but must promote and uphold them. Still those who are immediately concerned in the prosecution of commerce, will of necessity be always a minority of the nation. They are, however, best qualified to manage and direct its course by the advantages of experience, and the sense of interest. But they are entirely unable to protect themselves against the sudden and injudicious decisions of bare majorities, and the mistaken or oppressive projects of those who are not actively concerned in its persuits. Of consequence, this interest is always exposed to be harrassed, interrupted, and entirely destroyed, upon pretence of securing other interests. Had the merchants of this nation been permitted by their own government to pursue an innocent and lawful commerce, how different would have been the state of the treasury and of public credit! How short-sighted and miserable is the policy which has annihilated this order of men, and doomed their ships to rot in the docks, their capital to waste unemployed, and their affections to be alienated from the government which was formed to protect them! What security for an ample and unfailing revenue can ever be had, comparable to that which once was realized in the good faith, punctuality and sense of honor, which attached the mercantile class to the interests of the government! Without commerce, where can be found the aliment for a navy; and without a navy, what is to constitute the defence, and ornament, and glory of this nation! No union can be durably cemented, in which every great interest does not find itself reasonably secured against the encroachment and combinations of other interests. When, therefore, the past system of embargoes and commercial restrictions shall have been reviewed—when the fluctuation and inconsistency of public measures, betraying a want of information as well as feeling in the majority, shall have been considered, the reasonableness of some restrictions upon the power of a bare majority to repeat these oppressions, will appear to be obvious.

"The next amendment proposes to restrict the power of making offensive war. In the consideration of this amendment, it is not necessary to inquire into the justice of the present war. But one sentiment now exists in relation to its expediency, and regret for its delaration is nearly universal. No indemnity can ever be attained for this terrible calamity, and its only palliation must be found in obstacles to its future recurrence. Rarely can the state of this country call for or justify offensive war. The genius of our institutions is unfavorable to its successful prosecution; the felicity of our situation exempts us from its necessity. In this case, as in the former, those more immediately exposed to its fatal effects, are a minority of the nation. The commercial towns, the shores of our seas and rivers, contain the population whose vital interests are most vulnerable by a foreign enemy. Agriculture, indeed, must feel at last, but this appeal to its sensibility comes too late. Again, the immense population which has swarmed into the west, remote from immediate danger, and which is constantly augmenting, will not be averse from the occasional disturbances of the Atlantic states. Thus interest may not unfrequently combine with passion and intrigue, to plunge the nation into needless wars, and compel it to become a military, rather than a happy and flourishing people. These considerations, which it would be easy to augment, call loudly for the limitation proposed in the amendment.

"Another amendment, subordinate in importance, but still in a high degree expedient, relates to the exclusion of foreigners hereafter arriving in the United States from the capacity of holding offices of trust, honor, or profit.

"That the stock of population already in these states is amply sufficient to render this nation in due time sufficiently great and powerful, is not a controvertible question. Nor will it be seriously pretended, that the national deficiency wisdom, arts, science, arms, or virtue, needs to be replenished from foreign countries. Still, it is agreed, that a liberal policy should offer the rights of hospitality, and the choice of settlement, to those who are disposed to visit the country. But why admit to a participation in the government,aliens who where no parties to the compact—who are ignorant of the nature of our institutions, and have no stake in the welfare of the country but what is recent and transitory? It is surely a privilege sufficient, to admit them after due probation to become citizens, for all but political purposes. To extend it beyond these limits, is to encourage foreigners to come to these states as oandidates for preferment. The Convention forbear to express their opinion upon the inauspicious effects which have already resulted to the honor and peace of this nation, from this misplaced and indiscriminate liberality.

"The last amendment respects the limitation of office of President to a single constitutional term, and his eligibility from the same state two terms in succession.

"Upon this topic it is superfluous to dilate. The love of power is a principle in the human heart which too often impels to the use of all practicable means to prolong its duration. The office of President has charms and attractions which operate as powerful incentives to this passion. The first and most natural exertion of a vast patronage is directed towards the security of a new election. The interest of the country, the welfare of the people, even honest fame and respect for the opinion of posterity, are secondary considerations. All the engines of intrigue, all the means of corruption are likely to be employed for this object. A President whose political career is limited to a single election, may find no other interest than will be prompted to make it glorious to himself, and beneficial to his country. But the hope of re-election is prolific of temptations, under which these magnanimous motives are deprived of their principal force. The repeated election of the President of the United States from any one state, affords inducements and means for intrigues, which tend to create an undue local influence, and to establish the domination of particular states. The justice, therefore, of securing to every state a fair and equal chance for the election of this officer from its own citizens is apparent, and this object will be essentially promoted by preventing an election from the same state twice in succession.

"Such is the general view which this Convention has thought proper to submit, of the situation of these states, of their dangers and their duties. Most of the subjects which it embraces have separately received an ample and luminous investigation, by the great and able assertors of the rights of their country, in the national legislature; and nothing more could be attempted on this occasion than a digest of general principles, and of recommendations suited to the present state of public affairs. The peculiar difficulty and delicacy of performing even this undertaking, will be appreciated by all who think seriously upon the crisis. Negotiations for peace are at this hour supposed to be pending, the issue of which must be deeply interesting to all. No measures should be adopted which might unfavorably affect that issue; none which should embarrass the administration, if their professed desire for peace is sincere; and none which on supposition of their insincerity, should afford them pretexts for prolonging the war, or relieving themselves from the responsibility of a dishonorable peace. It is also devoutly to be wished, that an occasion may be afforded to all friends of the country, of all parties, and in all places, to pause and consider the awful state to which pernicious councils and blind passions have brought this people. The number of those who preceive, and who are ready to retrace errors, must it is believed, be yet sufficient to redeem the nation. It is necessary to rally and unite them by the assurance that no hostility to the Constitution is meditated, and to obtain their aid in placing it under guardians who alone can save it from destruction. Should this fortunate change be effected, the hope of happiness and honor may once more dispel the surrounding gloom.—Our nation may yet be great, our union durable. But should this prospect be utterly hopeless, the time will not have been lost which shall have ripened a general sentiment of the necessity of more mighty efforts to rescue from ruin, at least some portion of our beloved country.

"THEREFORE RESOLVED,

"That it be and hereby is recommended to the legislatures of the several states represented in this Convention, to adopt all such measures as may be necessary effectually to protect the citizens of said states from the operation and effects of all acts which have been or may be passed by the Congress of the United States, which shall contain provisions, subjecting the militia or other citizens to forcible drafts, conscriptions, or impressments, not authorised by the constitution of the United States.

Resolved, That it be and hereby is recommended to the said legislatures, to authorize an immediate and earnest application to be made to the government of the United States, requesting their consent to some arrangement, whereby the said states may, separately or in concert, be empowered to assume upon themselves the defence of their territory against the enemy; and a reasonable portion of the taxes collected within the said states, may be paid into the respective treasuries thereof, and appropriated to the payment of the balance due said states, and the future defence of the same. The amount so paid into the said treasuries to be credited, and the disbursements made as aforesaid, to be charged to the United States.

"*Resolved,* That it be, and hereby is, recommended to the legislatures of the aforesaid states to pass laws (where it has not already been done) authorizing the governors or commanders-in-chief of their militia to make detachments from the same, or to form voluntary corps, as shall be most convenient and comformable to their constitutions, and to cause the same to be well armed, equipped, and disciplined, and held in readiness for service; and upon the request of the governor of either of the other states to employ the whole of such detachment or corps, as well as the regular forces of the state, or such part thereof as may be required and can be spared consistently with the safety of the state, in assisting the state, making such requests to repel any invasion thereof which shall be made or attempted by the public enemy.

"*Resolved,* That the following amendments of the constitution of the United States be recommended to the states represented as aforesaid, to be proposed by them for adoption by the state legislatures, and in such cases as may be deemed expedient by a convention chosen by the people of each state.

"And it is further recommended, that the said states shall persevere in their efforts to obtain such amendments, until the same shall be effected.

"*First.* Representatives and direct taxes shall be apportioned among the several states which may be included within this Union, according to their respective numbers of free persons, including those bound to serve for a term of years, and excluding Indians not taxed, and all other persons.

"*Second.* No new state shall be admitted into the Union by congress, in virtue of the power granted by the constitution, without the concurrence of two-thirds of both houses.

"*Third.* Congress shall not have power to lay any embargo on the ships or vessels of the citizens of the United

States, in the ports or harbors thereof for more than sixty days.

" *Fourth.* Congress shall not have power, without the concurrence of two-thirds of both houses, to interdict the commercial intercourse between the United States and any foreign nation, or the dependencies thereof.

" *Fifth.* Congress shall not make or declare war, or authorize acts of hostility against any foreign nation, without the concurrence of two-thirds of both houses, except such acts of hostility be in defence of the territories of the United States when actually invaded.

" *Sixth.* No person who shall hereafter be naturalized, shall be eligible as a member of the senate or house of representatives of the United States, nor capable of holding any civil office under the authority of the United States.

" *Seventh.* The same person shall not be elected president of the United States a second time; nor shall the president be elected from the same state two terms in succession.

" *Resolved*, That if the application of these states to the government of the United States, recommended in a foregoing resolution, should be unsuccessful, and peace should not be concluded, and the defence of these states should be neglected, as it has been since the commencement of the war, it will, in the opinion of this convention, be expedient for the legislatures of the several states to appoint delegates to another convention, to meet at Boston, in the state of Massachusetts, on the third Thursday of June next, with such powers and instructions as the exigency of a crisis so momentous may require.

" *Resolved*, That the Hon. George Cabot, the Hon. Chauncy Goodrich, and the Hon. Daniel Lyman, or any two of them, be authorized to call another meeting of this convention, to be holden in Boston, at any time before new delegates shall be chosen, as recommended in the above resolution, if in their judgment the situation of the country shall urgently require it.

GEORGE CABOT,	SAMUEL SUMNER WILDE,
NATHAN DANE.	JOSEPH LYMAN,
WILLIAM PRESCOTT,	STEPHEN LONGFELLOW, *Jr.*,
HARRISON GRAY OTIS,	DANIEL WALDO,
TIMOTHY BIGELOW,	HODIJAH BAYLIES,
JOSHUA THOMAS,	GEORGE BLISS,
	Massachusetts.
CHAUNCEY GOODRICH,	NATHANIEL SMITH,
JOHN TREADWELL,	CALVIN GODDARD,
JAMES HILLHOUSE,	ROGER MINOT SHERMAN,
ZEPHANIAH SWIFT,	*Connecticut.*
DANIEL LYMAN,	EDWARD MANTON,
SAMUEL WARD,	BENJAMIN HAZARD,
	Rhode-Island.
BENJAMIN WEST,	MILLS OLCOTT,
	New-Hampshire.
WILLIAM HALL, JR.	
	Vermont.

Election of James Monroe, as President of the United States, to succeed James Madison, which election took place in the fall of 1816.

The war question terminating so happily under the democratic administration of James Madison, while his efforts were combatted by the Federalists, from the commencement to the termination of the agitation of the war question, the people became convinced that the policy had been a judicious one, and they felt disposed to continue in power the adherents to the then administration. Such was the unanimity of sentiment upon the subject, that in 1816 the only competitor of James Monroe, the democratic candidate, was Rufus King, who received only 34 electoral votes while 183 were cast for Mr. Monroe, as follows:

	Monroe.	*King.*
New-Hampshire, - - -	8	
Vermont, - - - - -	8	
Massachusetts, - - -		22
Rhode-Island, - - -	4	
Connecticut, - - - -		9

	Monroe.	King.
New-York,	29	
New-Jersey,	8	
Pennsylvania,	25	
Delaware,		3
Maryland.	8	
Virginia,	25	
North-Carolina,	15	
South-Carolina,	11	
Georgia,	8	
Tennessee,	8	
Kentucky,	12	
Ohio,	8	
Illinois,	3	
Louisiana,	3	
	183	34

The Federalists placed no one in nomination, or rather run no candidate for Vice President, while the democracy supported and elected Daniel D. Tompkins of New York.

Mr. Monroe, immediately after his inauguration, turned his attention to the defence of the frontier, and to acquire a through knowledge of the wants, requirements and necessities of the government and people, he left the city of Washington on the 31st of May, 1817, upon an excursion of personal observation, and passing through the principal towns in the New England states, he extended his journey west, and visited the various important points along the St. Lawrence and Lake Ontario, and thence up the Niagara to Buffalo, where he embarked by sail vessel, visiting the various points upon Lake Erie, and landed at Detroit. From thence he passed through the territory of Michigan, and on his return visited all important points in Ohio, Pennsylvania and Maryland. The effort was productive of much good, and we believe it is the only case on record where a president of the United States has entered into a thorough personal examination of the wants and necessities of the government and the people.

In 1816 the policy was adopted of paying members of Congress $8 a day and $8 for every twenty miles' travel, in lieu of a permanent salary of fifteen hundred dollars. An act was also passed granting pensions to soldiers.

Nothing of any great importance transpired after this until the next Presidential election. Such was the confidence of the masses in Mr. Monroe's administration that in 1820 he was re-elected President, there being but one electoral vote against him. Daniel D. Tompkins was re-elected Vice-President, there being only 14 votes against him.

Mr. John W. Taylor, of New-York, was elected Speaker, upon the declination of Mr. Clay, after a constant succession of ballotings for three days. Mr. Taylor was of that section of Republicans of the state of New-York, who supported De Witt Clinton, then governor of the state. He was decidedly favorable to a tariff for protection to domestic manufactures, and opposed to the extension of slavery in Missouri. The election of a speaker with these views, was of course the cause of some excitement and dissatisfaction, at a time when questions of great interest were to be determined by the action of Congress, which for a time seemed even to threaten a dissolution of the Union. The mild, impartial and conciliatory course of the new speaker, however, tended to allay much of the feeling at first excited, at the same time that the respect of the members was elicited toward himself.

The most important question agitated in Congress at this session, was the admission of Missouri into the Union. The constitution framed by the people of that state was communicated to Congress in the early part of the session, and referred to a committee who through Mr. Lowndes, made an able report on the subject, declaring the constitution of the state republican, and concluding with a resolution that Missouri be admitted into the Union on an equal footing with the original states, in all respects whatever. Mr. Lowdnes in moving to refer the resolution to a committee of the whole, stated that the report was the act of a majority of the committee, and not of every individual of the committee. The debate on the subject cotinued a week, and the discussion was managed with great ability and good temper. It was decided by a majority of fourteen, in the house, that Missouri could not be admitted into the Union with the constitution as presented. Those who voted against the admission, did so on the ground that the constitution of the state permitted slavery, and that there were other objectionable features in that instrument, particularly in relation to free persons of color. The members from the slave states voted unanimously for the admission of Missouri, while those from the northern and middle states, with few exceptions, voted against it.

Matters were in this situation, when the Missouri question again presented itself, on the fourteenth of February, 1821, the day appointed by law for opening and counting the votes for president and vice-president. Missouri having chosen presidential electors, and transmitted her votes for president and vice-president to Congress, a resolution passed the senate directing that in case any objection should be made to counting the votes from Missouri, the president of the senate should declare that, if the votes of Missouri were counted, the number of votes for A. B. for president would be so many, and if the votes of Missouri were not counted, the number would be so many, and that in either case A. B. is elected. The same course to be pursued in relation to vice-president. This resolution was taken up in the house on the morning of the day when the votes were to be counted. Mr. Clay having by this time taken his seat as a member, warmly supported the resolution as the only mode of avoiding the dificulty. It was also generally supported by the members in favor of restricting Missouri as to slavery, but opposed by most of those from the slave states. It was finally agreed to on the part of the house, sometime after the hour appointed for the meeting of the two houses to count the votes. Considerable delay and confusion took place while the votes were being counted, and some of the southern members, particularly John Randolph, of Virginia, made an effort to compel the house to declare that Missouri was a state of the Union. The course recommended by the joint resolution was finally adopted, and the president of the senate declared James Monroe and Daniel D. Tompkins duly elected president and vice-president, for the term of four years from the 4th of March, 1821.

On the 25th of February, Mr. Clay, from a joint committee of the two houses appointed on the Missouri question, reported a resolution for the admission of the state into the Union, on condition that the said state, by their legislature, should assent to a condition that a part of the state constitution should never be construed to authorize the passage of a law by which any citizen of either of the states in the Union should be excluded from the enjoyment of any of the privileges and immunities to which such citizen is entitled under the constitution of the United States. After debate, the final question was taken on this resolution, which was carried in the house by a vote of 87 to 81, and was concurred in by the senate on the 28th of February, and being approved by the president on the 2d of March, 1821, Missouri was admitted into the Union. Thus this exciting question was finally settled, principally through the efforts of Mr. Clay, who had also at the former session proposed and procured the adoption of a resolution, or section of compromise, in the act authorizing Missouri to form a constitution, by which slavery was to be forever prohibited in that part of the territory west of the Mississippi (excepting the state of Missouri,) lying north of thirty-six degrees and thirty minutes north latitude.

At the next session of Congress Mr. John W. Taylor was a candidate for speaker, but was finally defeated by Philip P. Barbour of Virginia, who was regarded as a strong opponent of the principal of a protective tariff.

The subject of a general bankrupt law was again debated, and occupied much of the time of this Congress. It was finally rejected, by a vote of 99 to 72. The question of a further protection to manufactures, particularly cottons and woollens, by additional duties on importations of those articles, was rejected, but the standing committee to whom the subject was referred, having been appointed by a speaker who was opposed to protection, reported that any additional legislation was inexpedient. The tariff question excited great attention and interest throughout the United States. The friends of protection to American manufactures were zealous and active in spreading their views among the people, and in many of the northern and western states the agriculturalists were convinced that their interests were very materially promoted by the system of protection, as well as that of the manufacturers. Members of Congress from the southern, and from some of the eastern states, at that time, were opposed to an increase of the tariff on foreign goods, from an impression that high duties operated unequally on different classes and sections of the community.

At this juncture, great excitement prevailed on the subject of the next presidential campaign. The names of many gentlemen were mentioned as candidates, but the number gradually diminished, until the contest finally seemed to be confined to William H. Crawford, secretary of the treasury; John Quincy Adams, secretary of state; Henry Clay, speaker of the house of representatives; John C. Calhoun, secretary of war; and General Andrew Jackson, at that time a private citizen. Each of these candidates, during the war with Great Britain, were warm and efficient supporters of Mr. Madison's administration, and zealous members of the democratic party.

It soon became evident that a large proportion of the old politicians of the democratic party had decided to support Mr. Crawford for the succession. He had been, it will be recollected, a formidable candidate against Mr. Monroe in the congressional caucus in 1816.

Previous to the meeting of Congress, the annual election took place in the state of New-York, in November, 1823, for members of the legislature, by whom the electors of president were to be chosen. The result was unexpected and very unsatisfactory to the friends of Mr. Crawford, for although they claimed a majority of the members elect, yet the city and county of New-York, and many other counties, had decided against them, and the anti-Crawford men likewise claimed a majority in the legislature. The latter, moreover, rested their hopes of success on the passage of a law by the legislature, giving the choice of electors to the people. This question, which was for many months agitated in New-York, gave rise to what was called the people's party, which comprised in its ranks most of the people opposed to Mr. Crawford for the presidency.

On the 1st day of December, 1823, the eighteenth Congress held their first session, which continued until the 26th of May, 1824. Mr. Clay, who was again elected a member from Kentucky, was chosen speaker of the house, by a large majority, over Mr. Barbour, speaker of the last Congress.

Many were opposed to a congressioanal caucus, but the friends of Mr. Crawford insisted opon it and it was held on the 14th of February 1824. On a ballot for president, Mr. Crawford received 64 votes, Mr. Adams 2, General Jackson 1. Mr. Gallatin was nominated for vice-president, but afterwards declined.

The issue of this attempt to nominate Mr. Crawford proved injurious to his prospects. In the state of New-York the Crawford party became very unpopular, in consequence of some of their leading men having rejected a law proposed by the people's party in the legislature, providing for the choice of presidential electors by the people. The electors in the state of New-York were therefore chosen by the legislature; but owing principally to the efforts of General James Tallmadge, the champion of the people's party in the legislature on that occasion, with the aid of Mr. Henry Wheaton and other zealous members of that body, the friends of Mr. Crawford met with an unexpected defeat, and the electoral vote of the state was given as follows: for Adams 26, for Crawford 5, for Clay 4, for Jackson 1.

The canvass for a successor to James Monroe was singular in many respects. Mr. RITCHIE, now of the Washington Union, but then of the Richmond (Va.) Enquirer, advocated, with great pertinacity, the nomination and election of WILLIAM H. CRAWFORD for the Presidency. Mr. R. went so far as to engage in a system of abuse of the character of General Andrew Jackson. Edwin Croswell, of the Albany Argus, entered into the same strain. This was regarded as unfair and ungenerous by the democrats throughout the country, and was particularly pleasing to the federalists. The management of those two men, with a few others, brought about a majority for Mr. Crawford, in the Congressional caucus, which, however, was but very slimly attended. This determined spirit of obstinacy and dictation manifested by Ritchie and Croswell, had a tendency to weaken the caucus or convention system in those days materially. The democracy felt as though there was an attempt to drive them to do what they were not disposed to do. They did not consider William H. Crawford as a genuine democrat. In 1808 he voted with the federalists upon the embargo question, and in 1811 he voted with the federalists for the United States Bank bill, which all other democrats opposed. It was not easy for the democrats of those days to forget those who betrayed them in trying times. There is no doubt the defeat of General Jackson in 1824, was owing to the obstinacy of the gentlemen referred to.

The contest in the fall of 1824 was a very strong one, and resulted in the election of no one as President of the United States by the people. The candidates voted for were Andrew Jackson, Wm. H. Crawford, John Quincy Adams and

Henry Clay. The question was then to be settled by the House of Representatives.

On the 3d Feb., 1825, the members of the Senate and House of Representatives in joint Convention counted the votes, and declared the same as follows:

	For President.				*For Vice President.*					
	John Q. Adams,	Wm. H. Crawford,	Andrew Jackson,	Henry Clay,	John C. Calhoun,	Nathaniel Macon,	Andrew Jackson,	Nathan Sanford,	Henry Clay,	Martin Van Buren,
Maine, - -	9	0	0	0	9	0	0	0	0	0
New-Hampshire, -	8	0	0	0	7	0	1	0	0	0
Massachusetts, -	15	0	0	0	15	0	0	0	0	0
Rhode-Island, -	4	0	0	0	3	0	0	0	0	0
Connecticut, - -	8	0	0	0	0	0	8	0	0	0
Vermont, - -	7	0	0	0	7	0	0	0	0	0
New-York, - -	26	5	1	4	29	0	0	7	0	0
New-Jersey, -	0	0	8	0	8	0	0	0	0	0
Pennsylvania, -	0	0	28	0	28	0	0	0	0	0
Delaware, - -	1	2	0	0	1	0	0	0	2	0
Maryland, - -	3	1	7	0	10	0	1	0	0	0
Virginia, - -	0	24	0	0	0	24	0	0	0	0
North-Carolina, -	0	0	15	0	15	0	0	0	0	0
South-Carolina, -	0	0	11	0	11	0	0	0	0	0
Georgia, - -	0	9	0	0	0	0	0	0	0	9
Kentucky, -	0	0	0	14	7	0	0	7	0	0
Tennessee, - -	0	0	11	0	11	0	0	0	0	0
Ohio, - -	0	0	0	16	0	0	0	16	0	0
Louisana, - -	2	0	3	0	5	0	0	0	0	0
Mississippi, -	0	0	3	0	3	0	0	0	0	0
Indiana, - -	0	0	5	0	5	0	0	0	0	0
Illinois, - -	1	0	2	0	3	0	0	0	0	0
Alabama, - -	0	0	5	0	5	0	0	0	0	0
Missouri, - -	0	0	0	3	0	0	3	0	0	0
	84	41	99	37	182	24	13	30	2	9

The president of the senate then rose, and declared that no person had received a majority of the votes given for president of the United States; that Andrew Jackson, John Q. Adams and William H. Crawford, were the three persons who had received the highest number of votes, and that the remaining duties in the choice of a president now devolved on the house of representatives. He further declared, that John C. Calhoun, of South Carolina, having received 182 votes, was duly elected vice-president of the United States, to serve for four years from the 4th day of March next.

The members of the senate then retired.

The speaker directed the roll of the house to be called when it was discovered that all of the members were present, when the voting by states was commenced, which resulted as follows, each state being entitled to one vote, it being cast in accordance with the views of the majority of the delegation of such state:

For John Q. Adams, of Mass., 13 votes,

For Andrew Jackson, of Tennessee, 7 votes,

For William H. Crawford, of Georgia, 4 votes.

The speaker then stated this result to the house, and announced that John Quincy Adams, having a majority of the votes of these United States, was duly elected president of the same, for four years, commencing with the 4th of March next.

Gen. Jackson having 99 electoral votes to 81 for Adams, 41 for Crawford, and 37 for Clay, there was of course some considerable excitement when Mr. Adams was elected by the house.

The inauguration of John Quincy Adams as President of the United States, took place on the 4th of March, 1825.

After delivering his address, Mr. Adams descended from the chair, and took the oath of office, at the close of which the house rang with the cheers and plaudits of the immense audience.

The senate being in session, the president immediately nominated the members of his cabinet, namely: Henry Clay, of Kentucky, for secretary of state; Richard Rush, of Pennsylvania, secretary of the treasury; James Barbour, of Virginia, secretary of war. These nominations were all confirmed, and unanimously, except that of Mr. Clay, to which a warm opposition was made on the part of a few senatoıs, and the injunction of secrecy being removed, the votes appeared to have been twenty-seven in favor, and fourteen against it. The remaining member of the cabinet; William Wirt, of Virginia, was continued as attorney-general. John M'Lean, of Ohio, postmaster-general (not then a member of the cabinet,) who had been appointed by Mr. Monroe, was also continued in office.

After disposing of the nominations made by the executive, the senate took into consideration the treaty made with the republic of Columbia, for the suppression of the slave-trade. This treaty was made in conformity with a resolution of the house of representatives, recommending to the executive to make treaties, giving the mutual right of search of vessels in suspected parts of the world, in order more effectually to prevent the trafic in slaves. The amendments proposed by the senate, at the last session, to the treaty with Great Britain, for the same purpose, were introduced into this treaty; but the fate of the treaty with England had probably caused a change in the minds of some of the senators and other views had been taken of the subject by others, and the treaty with Colombia was rejected by 28 votes to 12.

The divisions which had been taken on the foregoing questions, in the senate, left little doubt that the new administration was destined to meet with a systematic and organized opposition; and previous to the next meeting of Congress, the ostensible grounds of opposition were set forth at public dinners and meetings, so as to prepare the community for a warm political contest, until the next election.

Those who placed themselves in opposition to the administration, without reference to its measures, urged as reasons for their hostility, that Mr. Adams' election was the result of a bargain between Mr. Clay and himself; and his selection of Mr. Clay as secretary of state, was relied upon as a conclusive proof of the bargain; that he was elected against the expressed will of the people; and that Congress by not taking General Jackson, the candidate having the highest number of votes, had violated the constitution, and disobeyed their constituents.

The first session of the nineteenth Congress commenced on the 5th of December, 1825, and continued until the 22d of May 1826. Mr. Calhoun, the vice-president, took the chair in the senate, and Nathaniel Macon, of North Carolina, was chosen president *pro tem.* previous to the adjournment in May.

In the house, on the second ballot for speaker, John W. Taylor, of New-York, a friend of the administration, received 99 votes, against 94 for all others, and was elected.— In the senate the administration had a decided majority, but it soon became obvious that in both houses the friends of General Jackson and Mr. Crawford, with few exceptions, were disposed to unite, and embarrass and defeat the measures proposed by the president and his cabinet, or by their friends in Congress.

Many of the most important of the suggestions in the president's message were not acted on during the session; other topics having occupied the attention of Congress, which were introduced apparently for the purpose of agitating the public mind on the subject of the recent election of president. Amendments to the constitution were proposed in the senate by Mr. Benton, of Missouri, to provide for a direct vote by the people, in districts, for president, and dispensing with the colleges of electors; and by Mr. M'Duffie, of South-Carolina, in the house, providing for a choice of electors by districts, and preventing the choice of president from devolving on the house of representatives. Mr. Benton's proposition was accompanied with an able report, but no action was taken on it in the senate. A long and spirited debate took place in the house on the proposed amendments, in the course of which Mr. M'Duffie went into a history of the late election, ceusuring in severe terms the course of Mr. Clay and his friends, to which Mr. Trimble, of Kentucky, and others, replied in severe and pointed language, which caused a scene of great excitement. On the first resolution, which took the election from Congress, the house divided, 123 in the affirmative, and 64 in the negative. The second resolution, in favor of the district system, was rejected, by a vote of 101 to 91.

The recommendation in the president's message, that the United States should take part in a congress of North and South American states, proposed to be held at Panama, was at this time the subject of great political interest, and much agitated in Congress at this session. In certain official conversations had in the spring of 1825, with the ministers of those powers, invitations were given, on the part of Columbia, Mexico, and Central America, to the United States, to send commissioners to Panama. The proposed congress at that place was supposed to have been first suggested by General Bolivar, who was for some time at the head of the republic of Columbia; and that Peru and Chili should also join in it. The views of Bolivar were, to form a close alliance, and to pledge mutual assistance to resist European governments.

Mr. Clay, the secretary of state, in replying to the communications from the ministers of the republics of Spanish America, remarked, that those communications were received with proper feelings of the friendly motives which dictated them; but that the United States could not take any part in the existing war with Spain, nor in concils for deliberating on its further prosecution; though the president believed that such a congress might be highly useful in settling several important disputed questions of public law, and in arranging other matters of deep interest to the American continent, and strengthening the bonds of friendship between the American powers; that it appeared to him, however, expedient, before such a congress met, to adjust, as preliminary matters, the precise objects to which the attention of the congress would be directed, and the substance and form of the power of the ministers representing the several republics. In reply to this suggestion, notes were received from them, stating the objects of the assembly, and formally renewing the invitation. The president determined to accept this invitation, and to send ministers to the congress, should the senate consent to the measure.

This determination he memtioned in his opening message to Congress, and on the 26th of December he sent to the senate a confidential message, setting forth the objects of the Panama congress; his reason for accepting the invitation to send commissioners; and nominating Richard C. Anderson and John Sergeant as ministers on the part of the United States, and William B. Rochester, of New-York, as secretary to the mission.

This message, with the accompanying documents, was referred to the committee on foreign relations, by whom a report was made on the 16th of January, 1826, condemning the mission, and ending with a resolution, declaring it to be inexpedient to send ministers to Panama.

The report of the committee on foreign relations occasioned a long debate in secret session in the senate, and the resolution reported by that committee, condemning the Panama mission, was negatived by a vote of 24 to 19, on the 14th of March. The nominations by the president were then confirmed by the senate; and the injunction of secrecy on the subject removed from the journal. Thus the administration was sustained in this measure by the senate; and in the house of representatives the bill making the appropriation for the mission, was carried, after a debate of many days, on the 21st of April, by a vote of 133 to 61.

The house having thus concurred with the senate in assenting to the policy of the mission, measures were taken to carry it into effect; and orders were transmitted to Mr. Anderson, who was then minister of Columbia, to attend the congress, which was to hold its first meeting in the month of June. In his way to Panama he was unfortunately attacked, at Carthagenia, by a malignant fever, which proved fatal, and deprived the country of an able and useful representative.

The representatives of Peru, Mexico, Centaral America, and Columbia, met there on the 22d of June, 1826. Upper Peru, or Bolivia, had not then organized its government, and was not represented, nor was the republic of Chili. The governments of England and the Netherlands, though uninvited, sent diplomatic agents, who were not permitted to be present during the deliberations of the congress, but communications were made to them of their proceedings.

The first session of the twentieth Congress commenced on the 3d of December, 1827, and closed on the 26th of May, 1828.

The subject of a revision of the tariff on imports, with a view to additional protection to American manufactures, was brought before Congress at an early period of the session. A committe appointed for that purpose, after great deliberation, introduced a new tariff bill, in which an increased rate of duties was proposed on many articles of produce and manufacture.

The discussions on the tariff bill continued from the 12th of February to the 15th of April; various amendments proposed by Mr. Mallary, chairman of the committee which reported the bill, and a friend of the administration, having been rejected, and others, offered by him and others, being adopted; the bill finally passed the house by a vote of 109 to 91. In the senate, after sundry amendments, which were afterwards concurred in by the house, the bill passed, by 26 ayes to 21 nays, and being approved by the president, became a law a few days before the adjournment. This tariff became very unpopular in the southern states, where the policy was denounced on all occasions as unconstitutional and oppressive. The law of 1828, however, continued in operation for about four years after its passage, namely, till 1832, when another revision took place.

Nothing else of particular interest transpired during the session. Congress adjourned on the 26th of May, without much regret on the part of the community, at the termination of its protracted debates.

At this time the subject of a successor to John Quincy Adams for the Presidency was the all-engrossing topic of discussion from one extreme of the Union to the other. Never has there been known, since the formation of our government, so much bitterness of feeling to exhist as during this controversy. The character, moral and political, of all candidates was thoroughly canvassed. General Jackson was represented as being a low-bred, rough, uneducated man, totaly unfit for the station to whlch the democracy seemed bent upon calling him. Such were the violence of the attacks made upon him by the Federalists throughout the country, that, notwithstanding we were but a boy, and could do nothing in the way of elevating General Jackson to the presidential chair, except to peddle tickets at the polls on the day of election in his favor, we did this with as good a cheer as any one living, yet we had imbibed the impression that he was a rough, uncouth *bear* of a man, possessed of a determined spirit of perseverance. Being impressed with such views, we shall never, to the day of our death, forget the interview had with him while on his way to Washington to take his seat as President of the United States. When presented by a friend, and one who had noticed our attachment to the man, although not a voter, we found instead of the rough, unpolished back-woodsman, one of the most gentlemany polished men in his manners we ever met. From the squeeze of the hand, we discovered that there was some little *iron* in the composition. We revert to this matter to correct an error which to this day exists in the minds of many of General Jackson's most ardent admirers. There never was an impression more erroneous.

In the contest of 1828, the democracy brought forward Gen. Andrew Jackson, and the federal party the then president, John Quincy Adams.

The result was as follows;

	Jackson.	*Adams.*
Maine, - - - - -	1	8
New-Hampshire, - - - -		8
Vermont, - - - -		7
Massachusetts, - - - -		15
Rhode-Island, - - - -		4
Connecticut, - - - -		8
New-York, - - - -	20	16
New-Jersey, - - - - - -		8
Pennsylvania, - - - -	28	
Delaware, - - - - -		3
Maryland, - - - - - -	5	6
Virginia, - - - - - -	24	
North-Carolina, - - - -	15	
South-Carolina, - - - -	11	
Georgia, - - - - - -	9	
Alabama, - - - - - -	5	
Mississippi, - - - - - -	3	
Louisiana, - - - - - -	5	
Tennessee, - - - -	11	
Kentucky, - - - - - -	14	
Ohio, - - - - - - -	16	
Indiana, - - - - - -	5	
Illinois, - - - - - - -	3	
Missouri, - - - - - -	3	
	178	83

John C. Calhoun, of South-Carolina, was elected vice-president by 171 electoral votes to 83 for Richard Rush, and 7 for William Smith, of South-Carolina.

On the fourth of March, 1829, General Andrew Jackson entered on his duties as President of the United States. At twelve o'clock of that day, the senate, which had been convened by his predecessor, Mr. Adams, adjourned, after a session of one hour, during which the president entered the senate-chamber, attended by the marshal of the district and the committee of arrangements. He had been escorted to the capitol, from Gadsby's hotel, by a few of the surviving officers and soldiers of the revolution, and made the following reply to an address delivered to him at the hotel:—

RESPECTED FRIENDS: Your affectionate address awakens sentiments and recollections which I feel with sincerity and cherish with pride. To have around my person, at the moment of undertaking the most solemn of all duties to my country the companions of the immortal Washington, will afford me satisfaction and grateful encouragement. That by my best exertions I shall be able to exhibit more than an imitation of his labors, a sense of my own imperfections, and the reverence I entertain for his virtues forbid me to hope.

"To you, respected friends, the survivors of that heroic band who followed him so long and so valiantly in the path of glory, I offer my sincere thanks, and to Heaven my prayers, that your remaining years may be as happy as your toils and your lives have been illustrious."

After the adjournment of the senate, about noon, a procession was formed to the eastern porto of the capitol, where, in the presence of an immense concourse of spectators, the president delivered his inaugural address; and having concluded it, the oath to support the constitution was administered to him by Chief-Justice Marshal.

Salutes were fired by two companies of artillery, stationed in the vicinity of the capitol, which were repeated at the forts, and by detachments of artillery on the plains. When the president retired, the procession was re-formed, and he was conducted to the presidential mansion. He here received the salutations of a vast number of persons, who came to congratulate him upon his induction to the presidency.

The members of Mr. Adams' cabinet having resigned, President Jackson, immediately after his inauguration, nominated to the senate the following gentlemen for the heads of the respective departments, who were promptly confirmed: Martin Van Buren, of New-York, secretary of state; Samuel D. Ingham, of Pennsylvania, secretary of the treasury; John H. Eaton, of Tennessee, secretary of war; John Branch, of North-Carolina, secretary of the navy; John M'Pherson Berrien, of Georgia, attorney-general. It was determined to introduce the postmaster-general into the cabinet; the incumbent of that office John M'Lean, was appointed associate justice of the supreme court, and William T. Barry, of Kentucky, received the appointment of post-master-general. Certain duties in the department of state requiring immediate attention on the accession of a new president, James A. Hamilton, son of the late General Alexander Hamilton, was charged temporarily with the duties of secretary of state, until Mr. Van Buren could close his business as governor of New-York, on the duties of which office he had only entered on the first of January, 1829.

The secretaries of state and the navy, and the attorney-general, had been leading supporters of Mr. Crawford, in the presidential contest of 1824. Mr. Ingham was selected through the influence of the vice-president, Mr. Calhoun, and Messrs. Eaton and Barry were among the original supporters of Gen. Jackson.

The determination of the respective friends of Jackson, Crawford, and Calhoun, to combine in support of the General at the election of 1828, induced much speculation as to the course he could pursue, in order to satisfy the various conflicting views upon different topics. But he was elected without being particularly pledged upon any subject, and having received an overwhelming majority of electoral votes, he was left to adopt such course as he thought proper.

Under these fortunate circumstances, Gen. Jackson had assumed the executive government, with a surplus of more than five millions of dollars in the national treasury, the country respected abroad, at peace with all the world, and in a state of unexampled and progressive domestic prosperity.

Such was the state of affairs when the twenty-first congress assembled on the 7th of December, 1829; and this first session continued until the 31st of May, 1830. The majority in each branch in favor of the new administration was decided. The vice-president being absent at the commencement of the session, Samuel Smith resumed the chair, as president *pro-tempore* of the senate. In the house of representatives, Andrew Stevenson was re-elected speaker by 152 votes against 39.

The message of the president in point of expression was considered equal to those of his predecessors, and gave an elaborate view of the foreign relations and domestic concerns of the United States. Many of its recommendations were considered at this session of Congress, but in several instances the president's views met with an unfavorable reception from many of his friends in both houses. On the subject of a renewal of the charter of the bank of the United States, the standing committees of the senate and the house, to whom it was referred, made reports diametrically apposite to the recommendation of the president. The friends of the administration formed a majority in both committees, and the marked difference in the opinions entertained by them from that expressed in the president's message, afforded a striking proof of the want of harmony between the president and cabinet, and the party which had brought them into power. On the subject of a revision of the tariff, the recommendation of the president met with favor.

The tariff of 1828 became a law during the excitement of the presidential election, and in adjusting its details, more regard had been paid to the political effect of the law, than to the permanent interests of the country, or to the rules of political economy. Hostility to the tariff had been manifested early in the session of 1829-'30, by many of the friends of the administration; but an equally strong feeling of dissatisfaction with the existing law, on the ground of its inadequate protection to the woolen manufactures, had induced the friends of the policy to bring forward the subject, with a view of obtaining a modification of the law more favorable to their interests, and to prevent the frauds which were alleged to be daily practised on the revenue.

A bill was accordingly reported in the house of representatives, by Mr. Mallary, chairman of the committee on manufactures, on the 27th of January, 1830, to regulate the entry of importations of woolens. After much debate in both houses, it was passed, and being sanctioned by the president, became a law in May following.

Several unsuccessful attempts were made to engraft upon the above mentioned bill amendments reducing the duties on various articles. It was finally concluded to attack the tariff in detail, and separate bills were introduced providing for a reduction of duties on salt and molasses; both of which were passed, by considerable majorities. Another bill was passed, reducing the duties on tea and coffee.

The following laws, in addition to the foregoing, were the most important which were passed during this session: For the re-appropriation of thirty thousand dollars for the suppression of the slave-trade, which had been appropriated two years before, but was not expended, and which was founded on an act of congress of 1819; for repealing an act imposing tonnage duties on vessels of which the officers and two-thirds of the seamen were citizens of the United States; for the more effectual collection of impost duties, appointing eight additional appraisers to examine goods imported, but no new regulations to prevent defaults in the officers of the customs; for the appointment of an additional officer to be attached to the treasury department, called the solicitor of the treasury; for allowing a portion of the claims of Massachusetts, for services and expenses of the Militia in 1812–'14, in time of war, and for which that state had not been reimbursed, the amount allowed being four hundred and thirty thousand dollars, about half the sum claimed; for the removal of the Indians from lands occupied by them within any state of the union, to a territory west of the Mississippi, and without the limits of any state or organized territory, and belonging to the United States.

Although the unequivocal testimonies of popular feeling checked the tendency on the part of many leading politicians to nullification, and the doctrines of Mr. Webster's speech were in substance sustained subsequently by president Jackson in his proclamation respecting the difficulties in South Carolina, in 1832; yet the views of Mr. Hayne respecting state-rights and the powers of the general government continued to be entertained and asserted by a large and respectable portion of the people of the southern states.

Besides those of Mr. Hayne and Mr. Webster upon the questoin of the public lands, many of the other speeches in the senate during the great debate referred to, were distinguished for eloquence, ingenuity, and power. No particular law resulted from this protracted and able discussion.

There was early indications of a want of harmony among the different sections of which the administration party was composed. Efforts had been made from the commencement of the presidential term of General Jackson, by the respective partisans of the vice-president and of the secratary of state, to direct the executive patronage to the aggrandizement of their own friends. A division of the party was early seen to be inevitable, but the personal predilections of the president were as yet unknown. In the formation of the cabinet, the first post had been given to Mr. Van Buren himself, but the extensive influence of the treasury department was placed under the control of Mr. Ingham, a devoted friend of the vice-president. The other members of the cabinet were not selected with reference to the views of either of the competitors for the succession to the presidency, but upon grounds of personal preference on the part of the president. The views of the secretary of state and of the secretary of the navy had not harmonized with those of the secretaries of war and of the treasury. The attorney general had belonged to the old federal party, and the postmaster general had not shown that his political principles necessarily inclined him to a narrow construction of the powers of the federal government. Upon the whole, however, the cabinet was formed with an apparent preference of the political creed professed by the friends of the vice-president, rather than that of the radical party. The star of the vice-president was deemed to be in the ascendant, and it was generally believed that the influence of the executive would be exerted to promote his elevation to the presidential chair upon his own retirement. These opinions, however were, not realized.

While the patronage of the executive was so directed publicly to strengthen Mr. Calhoun's political party, by placing many of his friends in important posts, the ground on which he stood was crumbling beneath him, and measures were in train to create a breach between him and the president. To him, as a more early and efficient supporter, the president had given a greater share of confidence, and manifested a warmer feeling than he had originally bestowed upon the secretary of state. In this particular the secretary labored under a disadvantage; but circumstances soon enabled him to obtain a great superiority of influence over the mind of the president.

The secretary of war had been brought into the cabinet on account of the confidential relations and intimate friendship subsisting between him and the president, and of course was entitled to and received his entire confidence. Upon the arrival of the secretary of state at Washington, he found a coolness existing between the secretay of war and the vice-president, and a division in the cabinet itself, in consequence of some disagreement in their private relations. As the president warmly sympathized in the feelings and resentment of the secretary of war on this point, the secretaries of the treasury and navy, as the objects of that resentment, gradually lost his confidence, which was transferred to the secretary of state, whose course both in public and private had so completely harmonized with the wishes of himself and his friends.

The loss of influence on the part of the secretary of the treasury had impaired the indirect power of Mr. Calhoun, and the same cause had injured his own standing with the executive. No open breach had, however, as yet taken place between them, and the vice-president and his friends in congress continued to support the administration, some of whose appointments were carried by the casting vote of the vice-president as president of the senate.

Affairs remained on this uncertain footing until nearly the close of the first session of the twenty-first congress. At that time, and after the greater part of the questionable nominations had been confirmed, a movement was made which ripened the misunderstanding between the president and the vice-president into a complete alienation of feeling, and prepared the way for an open rupture. Before this event occurred, the influence of the coutroversy above alluded to had effected a change in the political relations of some of the members of the cabinet; and upon that question the president, the secretaries of state and of war, and the post-master-general, were opposed to the secretaries of the treasury and navy, and the attorney general; and the division was understood to have no inconsiderable bearing upon other questions of greater importance.

This misunderstanding continued to increase, until finally an open rupture was produced. This quarrel, however, professedly originated in the view taken by Mr. Calhoun of the conduct of General Jackson during the Seminole campaign, in 1818.

General Jackson had commanded the American troops in that war, and acting, as he conceived, in the execution of his orders; had invaded the territory of Florida, then belonging to Spain, and occupied the forts and towns of Pensacola, to which the Indians had fled for protection. The Spanish minister at Washington remonstrated and in the discussion which took place in Mr. Monroe's cabinet respecting this transaction, Mr. Calhoun as secretary of war proposed that a court of inquiry should be held on General Jackson's conduct, inasmuch as he had transcended his orders.

Mr. Crawford, then secretary of the treasury, also advocated a course which would have been deemed a censure on General Jackson; but the secretary of state (Mr. Adams,) conceding that the orders from the war department had been transcended, so forcibly vindicated the course of General Jackson, upon principles of national law, that all proceedings against him were relinquished, and the government determined, in its discussions with Spain, to justify the invasion, while it delivered up the posts. This was done by an able reply from the secretary of state to the complaints of the Spanish minister, in which the course of the American general was successfully vindicated.

The subject was afterwards agitated in Congress, and the friends of Mr. Crawford in that body were particularly distinguished for their efforts to censure the conduct of General Jackson. As might have been expected the General felt greatly aggrieved by this attack, and his resentment was roused both against Mr. Crawford and Mr. Clay, whose opinions on this subject were openly avowed, in the debate on the Seminole war. Toward Mr. Adams, by whom he had been so ably defended, and toward Mr. Calhoun, who had publicly sustained him, notwithstanding his first impressions, he had, until lately, expressed the warmest feelings of gratitude This harmonious footing (with regard to the latter,) which was first disturbed by the controversy above mentioned, was now destined to be totally destroyed.

Toward the close of the first session of the twenty-first congress, a letter from Mr. Crawford to Mr. Forsyth was placed in the hands of General Jackson, by the agency of a particular friend of the secretary of state, then at Washington, accusing Mr. Calhoun of having proposed a censure upon him for his conduct in the Seminole campaign. This letter was transmitted to Mr. Calhoun by the president, with an intimation, that it was so contrary to his impressions of the course he had supposed Mr. Calhoun to have pursued, as to require some explanation. Mr. Calhoun replied, and showed, by referring to the correspondence between General Jackson and the government, in 1818, that he must have known Mr. Calhoun's opinion to be that he had transcended his orders, and that his vindication had then been placed on other and distinct grounds. Mr. Calhoun then proceeded to inquire into the motives which had led, at this late period, to a renewal of this discussion, and avowed his belief that it had originated in a desire to detract from his influence with the president and thus to destroy his political standing with the friends of the administration. A long and protracted correspondence ensued, in which the late secretary of the treasury, Mr. Crawford, and several of his confidential friends took part, and although the secretary of state distinctly disclaimed all knowledge of the preliminary movements, and all motive to detract from the political standing of the vice-president, still, their respective claims upon the succession, his course in public and private, after being appointed secretary of state, and the political relations of the agents who appeared as the prime movers in this affair, produced a general impression that its sole object was to create a breach between the president and vice-president, with the view of destroying the influence of a formidable competitor for public favor.

Having alluded to the subject of nullification, as evinced by the acts of a portion of the people of the southern states, at this period, it is proper that we should notice in this place, the origin and progress of that political doctrine, as connected with controversies and events which occurred during this administration. It may be remarked, as a general proposition, that the southern states have, with the exception of South-Carolina, been uniformly hostile to the exercise of power by the general government. That state, although voting with the adjacent states on all local and most national questions, had on some occasions, as in 1790, '91, and in 1816, been foremost in asserting the right of congress to legislate on certain disputed points. Among those were the subjects of internal improvement, the United States bank, and the tariff. A change of opinion had now taken place there, and it began to go beyond any of the advocates of the state-rights, in its assertion of state sovereignty. A vehement opposition to a protective tariff, both in 1824 and on the subsequent modification in 1828, had been led by the talented delegation in congress, and when they were defeated in the halls of legislation, with characteristic energy they renewed their efforts to overturn the system and to render it unpopular with the people.

At first it was contemplated, on its passage, to resign their seats in congress, and a meeting of the delegation was held at Washington, with the view of deciding upon the steps which should be taken.

The delegation, however, did not concur in adopting violent measures, and it was determined to endeavor, upon their return home, to rouse their constituents to a more effectual opposition to the protective system. No exertions were spared to excite public feeling against the law. It was denounced as a measure local in its character, partial and oppressive in its operation, and unconstitutional in principle.

Having convinced themselves of this, they began to question the right of the federal government to require obedience, and almost simultaneously with the legislature of Georgia, which, December 24, 1827, resolved to submit only to its own construction of the federal compact, the senate of South-Carolina instituted a committee to inquire into the powers of the federal government, in reference to certain subjects then agitated.

The report of this committee, which received the sanction of both branches of the legislature, in December, 1827, asserted that the federal constitution was a compact originally formed, not between the people of the United States at large, but between the people of the different states, as distinct and independent sovereignties; and that when any violation of the letter or spirit of that compact took place, it is not only the right of the people, but of the state legislatures, to remonstrate against it; that the federal government was responsible to the people whenever it abused or injudiciously exercised powers intrusted to it, and that it was responsible to the state legislatures whenever it assumed powers not conferred. Admitting that, under the constitution, a tribunal was appointed to decide controversies, where the United States was a party, the report contended that some questions must occur between the United States and the states, which it would be unsafe to submit to any judicial tribunal. The supreme court has already manifested an undue leaning in favor of the federal government; and when the constitution was violated in its spirit, and not literally, there was peculiar propriety in a state legislature's undertaking to decide for itself, inasmuch as the constitution had not provided any remedy.

The report then proceeded to declare all legislation for the protection of domestic manufactures to be unconstitutional, as being in favor of a local interest, and that congress had no power to legislate, except upon subjects of general interest. The power to construct roads and canals within the limits of a state, or to appropriate money for that purpose, was also denounced as unconstitutional, as was all legislation for the purpose of meliorating the condition of the free colored or the slave population of the United States.

On this last topic, it was intimated that no reasoning could take place between the United States and South-Carolina. It was a question of feeling too intimately connected with their tranquility and safety to be discussed.

In remonstrating against these violations of the constitution, the state should appear as a sovereign, and not as a suppliant, before the national legislature; and resolutions, expressive of the approbation of the state legislature of these principles, having passed both houses, they were transmitted, with the report, to the delegation in congress, to be laid before that body, then engaged in the consideration of the tariff.

That law having passed, the legislature of the state, at the next session, sanctioned a protest against it as unconstitutional, oppressive, and unjust, which was transmitted to their senators, to be entered upon the journal of the senate. This was done on the 10th of February, 1829. The change which took place in the federal government caused a belief that some satisfactory modification would be made of the tariff; and during the summer of 1829 the excitement appeared to be directed less against the administration, and more concentrated against the law itself. The doctrine, however, of the right of a state to nullify an act of Congress was not relinquished, although it seemed to be conceded that it would be best to attempt first to procure the repeal of the obnoxious law. In these opinions the state government of Georgia fully concurred. As a measure of policy the tariff was equally unpopular; and the controversy respecting the Indians had been carried to that length, as to bring the state in collision with a law of congress, and to induce the legislature to declare that it should be disregarded and held void.

The legislature of Virginia also declared its assent to the same principle of nullification, by a vote of 134 to 68; and judging from the opinions expressed by the public functionaries of those states, the time appeared to be near at hand when the Union was about to be dissolved, by the determination of a large section not to submit to the laws of the federal government, nor to any common tribunal appointed to decide upon their constitutionality.

A check was indeed given to this spirit by the state of North-Carolina, which, although not then less averse to the policy of the tariff, declared itself against all violent measures in opposition to it.

The state of Alabama also, assumed nearly the same ground with Virginia, South Carolina, and Georgia; still the qualified opposition first made to the law, proved that the south was not united in the unconstitutional stand taken by some of the states on that subject, and that the injustice and oppression which were so vehemently denounced, were not so plainly and generally felt as to render resistance to the tariff a popular step. Indeed, it was doubted whether the feelings of the people in the three states which had declared in favor of nullification, were not misrepresented by the local legislatures.

The federative principle of the constitution, and the whole authority of congress and of the federal judiciary, were put in issue by the question now started, and however unwilling the leaders might be to destroy the union, still experience had too clearly shown the difficulty of restraining an excited people, not to create apprehension as to the result of these efforts to throw off the general government.

The question of internal improvements by the general government was discussed during the first session of the twenty-first congress, when it appeared that the friends of the system retained a majority in both houses. Among the bills passed at this session was one authorizing subscription to the stock of the Maysville and Lexington road company, in Kentucky. It passed the house by a vote of 102 to 85, and the senate 24 to 18. After retaining the bill eight days, the president returned it to the house on the 27th of May 1830, with his objections, as set forth in his message of that date.

The reading of this message caused much excitement in congress. Many of the friends of the president from Pennsylvania, and from the west, had relied upon his adhering to his former opinions upon this question, and this message first forced upon their minds a conviction as unwelcome as it was unexpected. The question being taken upon the passage of the bill, notwithstanding the objections of the president, after a warm debate on the reconsideration, the vote stood, yeas 96, nays 92. Two-thirds of the house not agreeing to pass the bill, it was rejected although a majority of the house thus refused to sanction the objections of the president.

On the 29th of May, the house of representatives took up several bills relating to internal improvement which originated in the senate, and, notwithstanding the presidential veto of the Maysville road bill, passed by large majorities, three acts, viz: 1st, authorizing a subscription to the Washington turnpike company; 2d, authorizing a subscription to the Louisville and Portland canal company; 3d, appropriating money for lighthouses, improving harbors, directing sur-surveys, &c. The first bill, being similar to the one already rejected by the president, was returned by him to the senate, where it originated, with a reference to the message on the Maysville bill for his reasons.

The other two bills were retained by the president for further consideration, until the next session of Congress.—This determination of the executive against the system of internal improvement, gave great offence to many of his friends, and entirely alienated some from his party. Even in congress such an increasing want of confidence was manifested, that the decided majorities which the administration possessed in both houses at the commencement of the session, had dwindled before its close into feeble and inefficient minorities. Nor was this the only difficulty in which the executive was involved by the course he had taken on internal improvement. He had sanctioned a bill for continuing the Cumberland road, and making other appropriations for roads and surveys ; and another for the improvement of harbors and rivers, both of which were branches in the general system of internal improvement. The former bill he approved of, with a qualification, by referring to a message sent to the house, together with the bill, wherein he declared, that as a section appropriating $8,000 for the road from Detroit to Chicago, might be construed to authorize the application of the appropriation to continue the road beyond the territory of Michigan, he desired to be understood as having approved the bill, with the understanding that the road was not to be extended beyond the limits of the said territory and that it should be regarded strictly as a military thoroughfare.

The approval of the acts authorizing the appropriations above mentioned, left it still doubtful how far the president felt at liberty to assent to internal improvement bills, and of the exact extent and limits of the principles by which he intended to be governed during the residue of his administration.

The most important of the foreign relations of the United States left unsettled by President Adams, were those of the commercial intercourse with Great Britain, and the boundaries between the American colonies of that power and the United States : and the claims of the United States on France for indemnity on account of depredations on our commerce and navigation. Efforts had been making, for more than ten years, to obtain compensation for these losses, but the subject had not been finally and satisfactorily settled. And the restrictions imposed by the British government on the trade between the British colonies and the United States had not been removed.

In 1829, President Jackson appointed Louis M'Lane, of Delaware, envoy to Great Britain, William C. Rives, of Virginia, to France, and Cornelius P. Van Ness to Spain.

By an act of congress of May, 1830, provision was made for reviving and opening the direct trade with the British ports, in the West India islands, which had long been prevented by the measures of the British government.

A negociation, which occupied much time to consummate, was entered into, and upon the conclusion of which the president issued a proclamation, dated October 5th, 1830, opening the ports of the United States to British vessels from all the British colonies on or near the North-American continent, and declaring the acts of congress of 1818, 1820, and 1823, absolutely repealed. The trade in British vessels, accordingly, at once commenced, and on the 5th of November following, the British government, by an order of council, opened the colonial ports to vessels of the United States.

The controversy was thus terminated, and, although the principle of reciprocity was so far given up as to concede to Great Britain the circuitous voyage as well as the right to encourage the indirect importation of American produce, through the northern colonies, by augmenting the duties on the direct importation, the United States, on their part, gained a participation in the direct intercourse, upon terms of reciprocity, and the additional privilege of exporting goods from the British colonies to foreign countries. The controversy resulted, substantially, to the advantage of Ameriban interests, although the principle contended for by Great Britain prevailed.

The subject of internal improvement was again agitated at this session of Congress. The president returned the two bills heretofore mentioned, which he had retained at the last session, and he now gave his reasons for withholding his assent to them. He objected to the power of making internal improvements by the general government, and recommended the distribution of the surplus funds in the national treasury among the states, in proportion to the number of their representatives, to be applied by them to objects of internal improvement.

The proposition was generally regarded as evidence of the hostility of the president to the whole policy; and that part of his message being referred to the committee on internal improvement, a report was brought in by Mr. Hamphill, an administration member of the house from Pennsylvania, strongly and pointedly condemning the views contained in the message, and concluding with a resolution that it is expedient for the general government to continue to prosecute internal improvements by direct appropriations of money, or by subscriptions for stock in companies incorporated in the respective states.

This intimation on the part of the friends of internal improvement, of their determination to act on that question in defiance of the opinions of the president, was followed up by the introduction of several bills for the internal improvement of the country. The first of these bills was one making appropriations for the improvement of harbors, and removing obstructions in rivers. It passed the house by a vote of 136 yeas to 53 nays, and the senate by 28 to 6.

The decisive votes in both houses, on this bill showed the determination of congress to act on the subject of internal improvement, without regard to the veto of the president, and as the friends of the bill now formed more than two-thirds of congress, the executive yields his scruples to the force of public opinion, and signed the bill. The constitutional objection to the power of the federal government, was no longer adhered to by the president, and he also gave his assent to a bill making large appropriations for carrying on certain roads and works of internal improvement, including improvements of rivers, and providing for surveys. The bill for building light-houses passed by large majorities and was also sanctioned by the president.

The executive thus yielded to public opinion, expressed in congress, and by the decisive votes given in both houses, the policy of internal improvement was considered as firmly established, although the action of the federal government in relation to the system had been checked by the previous vetoes of the president.

An act was passed at the second session, for the relief of certain insolvent debtors of the United States, extending to all debtors to the general government, except the principals on official bonds, or such as had received the public moneys and not paid the same over to the treasury.

The alienation of feeling between the president and a large portion of his early and prominent supporters, in consequence of his dispute with the vice-president, had existed some months before it was generally suspected. From the moment when the breach was produced between the president and vice-president, Mr. Van Buren was consulted by the president on all occasions.

It had now become a desirable object to effect the reelection of President Jackson. The difficulty of uniting the dominant party upon a succession, had induced him to relinquish his professed intention of serving but one term, and now he was formally announced as a candidate for re-election. He was nominated by his friends in the legislature of Pennsylvania, and at the caucus of the Jackson members of the legislature of New-York, on the 13th of February, 1830, it was resolved that General Jackson ought again to be nominated for the presidency. This movement, (says Mr. Hammond, in his political history of New-York) was probably made at the suggestion of Mr. Van Buren, or some of his confidential friends. It was well known that Mr. Van Buren expected to be the suceessor of General Jackson. This would afford evidence of the ardent personal attachment of Mr. Van Buren's immediate friends to General Jackson, and aid in securing to that gentleman the continued confidence and support of the president.

General Jackson had, before his election in 1828, expressed an opinion that the president ought to hold his office but one term, and had recommended an amendment of the constitution to render the president ineligible to two successive elections. But in 1831 he yielded to the importunity of his political friends, and consented to be a candidate for re-election.

It is more than probable that the friends of Mr. Calhoun looked to him as the successor of General Jackson, and expected, from the repeated declarations of the president, that he would not allow himself to be again a candidate. They could not, therefore, have learned with much complacency, that the president had changed his determination. Accordingly, it will have been perceived that the solicitations that General Jackson would consent to a re-election, originated, generally with the friends of Mr. Van Buren.

In this posture of affairs the country was astonished by the information promulgated on the 20th of April, 1831, through the official journal, at the seat of government, that the cabinet ministers of the president had resigned, and the most lively curiosity was manifested to learn the causes of this unexpected movement. The letters of the several members of the cabinet were published, but they served to inflame rather than to gratify the public feeling. The secretary of war, Mr. Eaton, first resigned, without assigning any reason, on the 7th of April, and he was followed by the secretary of state, Mr. Van Buren, on the 11th of April, who assigned as a reason, that circumstances beyond his control had presented him before the public as a candidate for the succession to the presidency, and that the injurious effects necessarily resulting from a cabinet minister's holding that relation to the country, had left him only the alternative of retiring from the administration, or of submitting to a self-disfranchisement, hardly reconcilable with propriety or self-respect.

Mr. Ingham, secretary of the treasury, and Mr. Branch, secretary of the navy, soon after resigned. Their resignations were accepted by the president, in formal letters, expressing his satisfaction with their official conduct, and stating his motive for requiring their resignation. This was, to use his own words, that having concluded to accept the resignation of the secretaries of state and of war, he had come to the conviction that he must entirely renew his cabinet. "Its members had been invited by me," he said, "to the stations they occupied. It had come together in great harmony, and as a unit. Under the circumstances in which I found myself, I could not but perceive the propriety of selecting a cabinet composed of entirely new materials, as being calculated, in this respect at least, to command public confidence and satisfy public opinion."

The attorney-general, Mr. Berrien, on his arrival, from Georgia, also resigned on the 15th June.

The consequence of this explosion of the cabinet, and the quarrel between the president and vice-president before mentioned, was to place the latter, and his friends generally in opposition to the administration, and to advance the political fortunes of Mr. Van Buren, in consequence of his close connexion with General Jackson and those devoted to his interest.

The new cabinet, which was not completely organized until late in the summer of 1831, was constituted as follows:

Edward Livingston, of Louisiana, secretary of state: Louis M'Lane, of Delaware, secretary of the treasury; Lewis Cass, of Ohio, secretary of war; Levi Woodbury, o New-Hampshire, secretary of the navy; Roger B. Taney, of Maryland, attorney-general.

This cabinet was not only superior to that which preceded it, but might fairly compare, in point of talent and ability, with most of those of previous administrations; and its character furnished strong testimony of the tribute paid to public opinion in the selection of his advisers, by a chief magistrate of great personal popularity.

Before the organization of this cabinet, an opposition was formed to the re-election of General Jackson on various grounds. This party, in some portions of the Union called "national republicans," manifested a disposition to support Henry Clay, of Kentucky, as its candidate for the presidency. He was accordingly nominated by the legislatures of several states, and a national nominating convention was recommended to be held at Baltimore, on the 12th of December, 1831.

The opposition party which rallied under the name of "national republican," was composed principally of the friends of the late administration, and those who had opposed Mr. Adams, but were now dissatisfied with the course of General Jackson, excepting the friends of the vice-president, who formed a distinct section of the opposition.

Another party; at first merely local, had arisen previous to these events, was fast gathereing strength, and had now so far extended itself as to assume consequence as a national party, and claimed the right of being consulted as to the candidates to be nominated for president and vice-president. This was called the anti-masonic party, and had its origin in the abduction and supposed murder of William Morgan, a citizen of western New-York, which affair took place in 1826, in consequence of an alleged violation of his masonic obligations, and a disclosure, real or pretended, of the secrets of free-masonry. This caused the organization of a political party in the western part of the state of New-York, which gradually extended into some of the adjoining states, upon the simple ground of hostility to masonry.

Having met with partial success in elections in several of the states, the anti-masons held a national convention at Philadelphia, in September, 1830, which was attended by delegates from eleven of the northern and middle states. After adopting various proceedings against masonry, they recommended a national convention to be held at Baltimore, in September, 1831, for the purpose of nominating candidates for president and vice-president of the United States.

The effect of the political organization of the anti-masons was to compel a more strict and intimate union among the adhering members of the fraternity, and to induce them to exercise a more direct influence in the politics of the country, in the hope of crushing a party whose avowed object was the annihilation of their order. In some parts of the country, where the leading national republicans showed a disposition to unite with the anti-masons, many of the most zealous masons forsook their political association with the former party, and to oppose the anti-masonic party, with efficiency, joined the ranks of the administration.

Thus the opposition to General Jackson seemed destined to be as much thwarted by their own divisions as by the discipline and concert prevailing in the party sustaining his administration. It was, indeed, believed that it would be practicable to concentrate the votes of the anti-masons and national republicans on one candidate for the presidency. Mr. Clay being a mason, his nomination by the anti-masons was out of the question. When the anti-masonic convention assembled at Baltimore, in September, 1831, it was expected that John M'Lean, of Ohio, formerly post-master general, and appointed by General Jackson a judge of the supreme court, would receive the nomination of that party for the presidency, but he declined, and William Wirt, of Maryland, formerly attorney-general of the United States was nominated for president, and Amos Ellmaker, of Pennsylvania, for vice-president.

The national republicans, on their part, professed great confidence in the integrity and qualifications of Mr. Wirt, but insisted that they could not with honor, sacrifice Mr. Clay to what they denominated an unreasonable prejudice, nor could they, consistently with their self-respect, give up the candidate of the great majority of the opposition, to quiet the scruples of the minority.

Shortly after his resignation as secretary of state Mr. Van Buren received from the president the appointment of minister to England, and embarked for London in August, during the recess of the senate.

The twenty-second congress commenced its first session on the 5th of December, 1831, and continued the same until the 16th of July, 1832. The elections had evinced a large majority of the members chosen to the house of representatives in favor of the administration, but the vote for speaker exhibited a considerable increase in the strength of the opposition, although divided. The candidate of the administration, Andrew Stevenson, was elected by 98 votes, against 97 for all other persons; thus receiving the exact number necessary to constitute a choice.

The appointments made during the recess were nominated to the senate early in December, and on the 10th of January the committee on foreign relations reported in favor of Martin Van Buren, minister to England, Aaron Vail, secretary of legation, and Louis M'Lane secretary of the treasury. On the 13th of January the other nominations were confirmed, but that of Mr. Van Buren was laid on the table, by the casting vote of the vice-president, John C. Calhoun. When this nomination came before the senate, it was warmly opposed on two distinct grounds. Four of the senators, who were friends of the vice-president, declared themselves opposed to its confirmation, on account of the agency of Mr. Van Buren in breaking up the late cabinet, and in the domestic politics of the country.

After a full discussion on this nomination, with closed doors, the senate, finally, by the casting vote of the vice-president, John C. Calhoun, resolved not to confirm the nomination, yeas 23, nays 23. Mr. Van Buren was accordingly rejected, and, soon after having presented his credentials, was compelled to return to the United States.

This being the first time that a minister of the United States had been compelled to return from his post, on account of the refusal of the senate to concur in his appointment, great cxcitement was produced by this decision, which resulted finally in placing Mr. Van Buren in the presidential chair.

Among the most urgent subjects of consideration at the present session of congress, was the apportionment of representation according to the census of 1830. By that census, the southern and eastern states had lost a portion of their relative weight, and the western states had acquired a greater preponderance than before. With the view of giving each state the power intended by the constitution, at the next presidential election, steps were taken to bring this subject at an early day before the consideration of the house, and on the fourth of January, Mr. Polk, from a select committee, reported a bill fixing the ratio of representation under the fifth census of the United States. By that report the ratio was fixed at one representative for forty-eight thousand inhabitants, according to the federal enumeration, which would increase the number of members to 237. This ratio was at first adopted by the house, after a long debate, but afterward stricken out, and the number fixed at forty-seven thousand seven hundred, in which form the bill finally passed, and became a law in May, 1832. The senate amended the bill, and sent it back to the house but the house disagreed to the amendment, and the senate receded therefrom. By the census of 1790, the ratio fixed on was thirty-three thousand ; by that of 1800 the same ratio was continued ; in 1810 it was fixed at thirty-five thousand ; in 1820, forty thousand ; and by the census of 1830, forty-seven thousand seven hundred.

Many subjects of great interest came under the consideration of congress at this session ; and among them none excited more of the public attention than that of the renewal of the charter of the bank of the United States. That institution was incorporated, as we have stated, in 1816, during Mr. Madison's administration, by a democratic congress, for the term of twenty years; of course, the charter would expire in 1836. In the first message of General Jackson to congress, namely, in 1329, he expressed an opinion against the constitutionality and expediency of the bank, and an assertion that it had failed in the great end of establishing a uniform and sound currency.

The attack was renewed in the next annual message, in 1830; and congress was recommended to inquire into the expediency of renewing the charter of the existing bank, with the view of substituting in its place a bank based on the public deposites, but without the power of making loans, or purchasing property. This recommendation met with no better reception than that contained in the previous message. No steps were taken by either house upon the subject, at that session. The bank made no application to congress, and when Mr. Benton asked for leave to introduce a resolution in the senate adverse to the renewal of the charter, that body refused permission by a vote of 23 nays to 20 ayes. The stock maintained its price in market, and in the message of the president at the opening of the twenty-second congress, in December, 1831, his objections to the bank were expressed for the third time.

The directors and stockholders of the bank, now deemed it proper to submit the claims of the institution for an extension of its charter to congress. A memorial to this effect was therefore presented, on the part of the bank of the United States, and no sooner was this determined upon, than the friends of the president began to express their dissatisfaction at being forced to act upon the subject at this time. It was too early, they said, notwithstanding the president had not deemed it too early for congress to act upon the matter two years before. A memorial having been presented in the senate, on the 9th of January, by Mr. Dallas, an administration senator from Pennsylvania, it was referred to a select committee for consideration. On the 13th of March this committee reported in favor of renewing the charter for fifteen years, with certain modifications. A bill accompanied this report, which was ordered to a second reading, and then laid upon the table of the senate, until after the report of the committee appointed by the house of representatives to inquire into the affairs of the bank.

It was in that body that the main battle concerning the bank was to be fought. The memorial of the bank was presented by Mr. M'Duffie, of South Carolina, and referred to the committee of ways and means, by whom, on the 10th of February, a report was made in favor of the renewal of the charter. A motion was then made by the opponents of the bank for a committee of inquiry into the affairs of the bank. Two reports were made by this committee: one from the majority, adverse to the bank, and another from the minority, favorable to the institution.

On the 22d of May, the bill for a renewal of the charter was taken up in the senate, and after a long discussion and undergoing various amendments, the bill finally passed the senate, on the 11th of June, by a vote of yeas 28, noes 20. When it came into the house, strenuous exertions were made to postpone its consideration, but it was made the special order of the day for the 18th of June. The house being then engaged on the tariff, it was not taken up until the 30th of June, and it finally passed that body on the 3d of July, by 107 yeas, to 85 nays; and an amendment proposed by Mr. M'Duffie, being concurred in by the senate, the bill was sent to the president for his decision. It was by many apprehended that he would resort to the mode previously adopted by him, and that he would retain it until after the adjournment of congress. To prevent this, the senate declined acting on the resolution of adjournment until the bill had been sent to him for concurrence, and then the 16th of July was inserted, so as to leave him full ten days, exclusive of Sundays, by which he was compelled to return the bill to congress, or permit it to become a law.

On the 10th of July, the next day after the senate had fixed the time of adjournment, the president sent a message to that body, stating his reasons for refusing his signature to the bill.

This veto-message having been read, Mr. Webster moved that the senate should proceed to reconsider the bill the next day. At the appointed hour, the bill being again brought under the consideration of the senate, Mr. Webster reviewed the reason and arguments of the executive at length, to which Mr. White of Tennessee, replied; and the discussion was contiuued until the 13th of July, when the question being taken on the passage of the bill, notwithstanding the objections of the president, the senate divided—yeas 22, nays 19; and the bill, not having received two thirds of the votes, was of course rejected.

The president's bank-veto message was circulated extensively throughout the Union, and proved a popular document in his favor in its effects on the public mind, wherever the bank was but little known, or in ill favor. Many of the political friends of the president, however, as well among the people, as in congress, differed in opinion from him on the subject of the bank. In the state of Pennsylvania, where the bank was located, and where the institution was popular, the president's course was severely censured, and the strength of the administration so much diminished, as at one period to make its success doubtful. At a very large meeting of citizens of Philadelphia, composed of his former political friends, in July 1832, soon after the veto of the president, resolutions were adopted disapproving of his course with regard to the bank and other public measures, and deprecating his re-election to the presidency as a national calamity, which they pledged themselves "to use all lawful and honorable means to avert, by opposing the re-election of Andrew Jackson."

The subject of internal improvement was discussed at length during the session. The members from the south, and the supporters of the administration from the eastern states and New-York, were decidedly opposed to appropriations of this character ; and a systematic effort was generally made by them to defeat the bill introduced making appropriations for that object, including the improvement of certain rivers and harbors, the Cumberland and other roads, surveys, &c. The bill finally passed both houses, and having received the sanction of the president, became a law. By the act, as amended in its passage, various appropriations were made for works not enumerated : it having been extended by these amendments to an amount exceeding one million two hundred thousand dollars, and altogether beyond its original scope—adding thus an additional sanction to the policy of internal improvement.

The other appropriations for internal improvement were contained in a bill for the improvement of certain harbors and rivers, which was not taken up in the house until the 25th of May. Certain amendments were then made ; and on the first of June, a motion by Mr. Polk of Tennessee, to strike out the enacting clause, was lost—yeas 72, nays 101—and the bill finally passed, 95 to 67. In the senate, it was taken up on the 3d of July, and in the course of the discussion which ensued, Mr. Clay, " expressed his extreme surprise that the president, after putting his veto on the appropriations for works of such public utility as the Maysville and Rockville roads, should have sanctioned the internal improvement bill in which appropriations were made to a very large amount, and which differed in principle not one particle from the one he had rejected ? They first held appropriations for certain objects of internal improvement to be unconstitutional, and then sanctioned appropriations for other objects depending entirely on the same principles with those held to be unconstitutional ; and the result has been to open an entire new field of internal improvement.

Favorite objects had been considered constitutional, while objects in states not so much cherished, had been held to be local." Mr. Miller, of South-Carolina, said: "We have just heard that the president has signed the internal improvement bill, containing appropriations for the most limited and local purposes. I hope we shall never again be referred to the veto of the Maysville and Rockville roads, as a security against this system. The senate and house of representatives, and the president, all concur in this power."

The harbor bill, as it was called, passed the senate, and was sent to the president for his approbation, on the 13th of July, three days before the close of the session. This bill which did not differ in principle from the internal improvement bill which he had signed, the president resolved not to sanction, but retained the bill until after the adjournment of congress, and thus prevented it from becoming a law.

The same course was adopted by the president, in relation to a bill providing for the repayment to the respective states of all interest actually paid, for moneys borrowed by them on account of the federal government, and expended in the service of the United States. This bill was passed by both houses at this session, but when it came into the hands of the president, it was doomed to the fate of the harbor bill.

The president having in his annual message, recommended a modification of the tariff of duties on imports the subject was referred to the committee on manufactures, which as well as the committee of ways and means, who had been selected by the speaker (who was hostile to the protective system) with a view to a reduction of the tariff. Mr. John Quincy Adams was placed at the head of the committee on manufactures, which, on the 23d of May, reported a new tariff bill. Mr. M'Duffie, chairman of the committee of ways and means, had, at an earlier period of the session, namely, on the 8th of February, reported a bill intended to meet the ultra opponents of the protective system, and the report which accompanied it denounced the tariff system as imposing a tax upon the south for the benefit of the north. The secretary of the treasury, Mr. M'Lane, on the 27th of April also transmitted to congress, in compliance with a resolution of the house, a bill for the reduction of the tariff, with a report giving his views on this topic.

Before the report of the secretary was printed, Mr. M'Duffiy brought on a discussion of the bill reported by him. On the first of June a motion was made to strike out the first section, which was carried—81 yeas to 41 nays.

Mr. Adams' bill was then taken up, and after a long and animated discussion, it passed the house, with few amendments, by 132 yeas to 66 nays, many of the opponents of protection voting in the affirmative. The bill finally passed the senate on the 9th of July, yeas 32, nays 16, and receiving the sanction of the president became a law.

This act provided for a great reduction of the revenue, and for no small diminution of the duties on the protected articles of domestic manufacture, but it was a direct admission of the principle of protection, and it was so regarded by all parties. It was, however, a great concession on the part of the friends of the protective system, to the advocates of "free trade," and as such, a general expectation prevailed that it would be received by the dominant party in South-Carolina, and that a temporary calm at least would succeed the agitation upon this exciting topic.

Different views, it appeared, were entertained by the leaders of that party, and the very day after the passage of this act, the representatives of South-Carolina, who thought nullification the right remedy, met at Washington, and published an address to the people of South-Carolina on the subject of the tariff. In that address they assert, that in the act just passed the duties upon the protected articles were augmented, while the diminution was made only in the duties upon the unprotected articles; that in this manner the burden of supporting the government was thrown exclusively on the southern states, and the other states gained more than they lost by the operations of the revenue system.

The address concludes thus: "They will not pretend to suggest the appropriate remedy, but after expressing their solemn and deliberate conviction that the protecting system must now be regarded as the settled policy of the country, and that all hope of relief from congress is irrevocably gone, they leave it with you, the sovereign power of the state, to determine whether the rights and liberties which you received as a precious inheritance from an illustrious ancestry, shall be tamely surrendered without a struggle, or transmitted undiminished to your posterity."

Meetings were accordingly held in South-Carolina, denouncing the tariff, which had just received the sanction of congress, and pledging the persons attending to support the state government in any measures it might adopt to resist it. Strong efforts were made to excite the people of the state against the general government, and notwithstanding the exertions of a respectable portion of the community, who remained faithful to the union, they succeeded in obtaining a majority in both houses of the legislature.

As soon as this was ascertained, Governor Hamilton convened the legislature, which met at Columbia, on the 22d of October, 1832. Immediately upon its assembling, the tariff question was taken up, and a bill was reported authorizing a convention to meet at Columbia on the 19th of next month. This bill finally passed on the 25th of October, in the senate 31 to 13, and in the house 96 to 25.

The state convention met at the time appointed, and the governor was elected president of that body. The annual meeting of congress was at hand, and if any impression was to be made upon that body, it could only be done by prompt and decisive movements. Upon the people of the United States generally no impression could be made. A general sentiment pervaded the union, that it was better to appeal to the power of the government to enforce the laws, than longer to encourage a spirit of insubordination by yielding to demands which, originating in a feeling of arrogance, were rendered more unreasonable by concession. Still, however, all hasty movements were deprecated, and so long as the nullifiers confined themselves to discussions and resolves, any interference on the part of the general government would have been deemed improper. Nothing but actual resistance to the laws of the United States could justify such interposition. The time of forbearance, however, was now rapidly passing away.

The committee of the convention, to whom was intrusted the duty of reporting what steps should be taken, recommended the passage of an ordinance, which declared all the acts of congress imposing duties on imported goods, and more especially the laws of May 19th, 1828, and July 14th, 1832, to be null and void within the state of South-Carolina. It further provided, that no appeal should be permitted to the supreme court of the United States in any question concerning the validity of the ordinance, or of the laws passed to give effect thereto. It also prohibited the authorities of the state, or of the United States, from enforcing the payment of duties within the state, from and after the 1st of February, 1833. There were various other provisions in this ordinance, which concluded with a declaration that any attempt on the part of the general government to reduce the state to obedience, or to enforce the revenue laws, otherwise than through the civil tribunals, would be deemed inconsistent with the longer continuance of South-Carolina in the union, and that the people of the state would forthwith proceed to organize a corporate and independent government. By this ordinance, the rubicon was passed, and the state government forthwith proceeded to take the necessary steps to carry it into effect.

The legislature, which met directly after the adjournment of the convention, on the 27th of November, 1832, passed the laws required by the ordinance. Thees related principally to the nullification of the revenue laws of the United States, by prohibiting their enforcement within the state. An additional act was passed authorizing the governor to call the militia into service to resist any attempt on the part of the government of the United States to enforce the revenue laws; and to render the resistance of the state effectual, he was empowered to call out the whole military force of the state, and to accept of the services of volunteers for the same purpose. Ten thousand stand of small arms, and the requisite quantity of military munitions, were ordered to be purchased, and any acts done in pursuance of that law, were to be held lawful in the state courts.

These proceedings by the party that had obtained possession of the state government, brought on an issue between the state and the federal governments, that could no longer be neglected. The very existence of the government depended upon its decision. South-Carolina had set at defiance the authority of the general government, and declared that no umpire should be admitted to decide between the contending parties.

It had, in its capacity as a sovereign state, decided the question for itself, and its decision could be reversed only by superior force. In taking this stand, the nullifiers apparently had not perceived, that, although their principles were precisely those which Georgia had carried into effect into her affairs with the Indians, the subject-matters more directly affected the existence of the government. Five sixths of the revenue were derived from the customs, and the abolition of the duties in one state, would necessarily destroy the revenue system, and of course suspend the operations of the federal government. While the nullification of Georgia only tended to bring the federal government into contempt, and weakened the bonds of the union, that of South-Carolina at once severed those bonds, and arrested the action of the government.

At such a crisis, the president felt that there was no room for hesitation. The difficulty must be met, not only to save the union from being broken up, but to protect those citizens of South-Carolina who still adhered to its standard, from the horrors of civil discord. The president determined to come at once to an issue with the nullifiers: to place the powers of the government upon the broad ground, that the federal judiciary was the only proper tribunal to decide upon the constitutionality of its laws; and to enforce the revenue acts with an entire disregard to the pretended rights of sovereignity which were assumed by the state of South-Carolina.

With that view, all the disposable military force was ordered to assemble at Charleston, and a sloop-of-war was sent to that port to protect the federal officers, in case of necessity, in the execution of their duty. On the 10th of December, the eloquent and energetic proclamation of the president was issued, plainly and forcibly stating the nature of the American government and the supremacy of the federal authorities in all matters entrusted to their care, and exhorting the citizens of South-Carolina not to persist in a course which must bring upon their state the force of the confederacy, and expose the union to the hazard of dissolution.

A difficulty occured in 1832 with the Sack and Fox tribe of Indians, who, with Black Hawk at their head, commenced an attack upon the settlers of the upper Mississippi. The war lasted but a few months.

About this same time arose the difficulty on the north-eastern border of the United States, in relation to the Maine boundary line, which however, was soon brought to a close in a satisfactory manner to all parties.

Generally the foreign relations of the country were conducted with ability as well as energy, by the administration of General Jackson. In the course of the year 1831, treaties were concluded and ratified with the republic of Mexico—one relating to boundaries between the two countries, and the other to commerce and navigation. Mr. Rives, our minister to France, also concluded a treaty between the United States and the king of the French, which was signed at Paris in July, 1831, on the subject of claims for depredations committed on American commerce, under the government of the directory, the first consul, and the emperor. Negotiations for this purpose had been long continued, by various ministers from the United States, but no satisfactory terms had been definitely settled. The French government had set up an opposing claim, on account of the non-fulfillment of a treaty made in 1778 between the United States and the king of France for the assistance of the former to defend the West India islands of the latter, if attacked by the British. The American government contended that they were exonerated of all such demands by the government of France, by subsequent events. The change in the French government, by the revolution of 1830, enabled Mr. Rives to bring the long-pending negotiations to a close. By this treaty the French government agreed to pay to the United States, in complete satisfaction of all claims of American citizens for depradations on their commerce, twenty-five millions of francs, or nearly five millions of dollars, in six annual instalments. One and a half million of francs were to be allowed by the American government to France or French citizens, for ancient supplies, accounts or other claims. An additional article was inserted, by which the United States engaged to reduce the duties on French wines for ten years in consideration of which stipulation France agreed to reduce the duties on the long staple cotton of the United States to the same rates as on short staple cotton, and to abandon all claims for indemnity under the Louisiana treaty. The sum thus stipulated to be paid by France, did not amount to more than one third of the just claims of the citizens of the United States, but their liquidation, even upon terms comparatively unfavorable, was so desirable, that the conclusion of this treaty was hailed with universal satisfaction by all parties. After deliberate consideration, it was sanctioned by the senate; but the French chamber of deputies refused to make the appropriation to carry the treaty into effect, and the delay furnished occasion for an unpleasant dispute between the two countries, which was not terminated until the final settlement of the affair in 1836.

Many amusing incidents occurred during the existence of the excitement upon this question, one of which will be related, as nearly as memory serves us. The French Minister, stationed at Washington, about to return to France, called upon the president and asked him what he should say to the king, in relation to the difficulties existing between the United States and France, to which the president promptly replied: "Tell the king, your master, that Andrew Jackson says, *he must pay or fight!*"

The administration of General Jackson had been eminently successful in the management of our foreign affairs, and the negotiation of numerous treaties contributed largely to sustain the popularity of the president, tending also to insure his re-election.

The tone of the government toward foreign nations during General Jackson's administration was moderate but firm, and the honor and interest of the country were maintained in a manner indicative both of spirit and ability

The first presidential term of General Jackson was now drawing to a close, and parties arrayed themselves for the approaching election. We have already mentioned the meeting of the anti-masonic convention, in September 1831, which nominated as a candidate for president, William Wirt, and for vice-president, Amos Ellmaker. The national republican convention met at Baltimore in December 1831, and nominated Henry Clay of Kentucky, for president, and John Sergeant, of Pennsylvania, for vice-president. In May, 1832, a numerous convention of delegates of the administration party met also at Baltimore for the purpose of nominating a candidate for vice-president to be placed on the ticket with General Jackson, to whose nomination for re-election no dissent was manifested in the administration ranks. Martin Van Buren, of New-York was, with great unanimity, nominated for vice-president. The friends of the president insisted that he was personally dishonored by the rejection of Mr. Van Buren as minister to England; and that it was incumbent on his supporters to convince the world that he had not lost the confidence of his countrymen, by electing Mr. Van Buren to preside over the body which had declared that he was unworthy to represent the country at the British court.

This mode of reasoning prevailed, and, notwithstanding the objections of a few delegates from the states where Mr. Van Buren was unpopular, he received the vote of the administration party, for vice-president.

The friends of Mr. Calhoun were entirely alienated from the administration by this nomination, and, although the ultra state-rights and nullifying doctrines espoused by his adherents prevented them from joining the opposition in their support of Mr. Clay, it was soon understood that the president had lost their confidence, and would not receive their suffrages. The character of the contest, however, effectually precluded them from openly lending their aid to overthrow the administration. It was a contest in relation to the powers of the federal government, although from the cautious and ambiguous manner in which the opinions of the executive were promulgated, the true nature of the question at issue was not fully understood by the people in certain portions of the union. Even where it was so understood, no deep universal conviction prevailed that the result of this election would be decisive as to the power of the federal government. Many hoped, from the strong personal enmity manifested toward Mr. Calhoun, that the president would finally be brought to oppose doctrines, of which that gentleman was now considered the chief advocate; and the experience of a few years had furnished ample proof, that he would not be deterred from taking that step by any apprehension of a charge of inconsistency. The further development of the views of the dominant party, in South-Carolina too, now began to excite great fears of a premeditated design to dissolve the union; and it was supposed, that while on one hand the inclination to anti-federal doctrines previously shown by the president, would prevent the dissaffection from extending itself to the other southern states; on the other, that the energitic manner in which he executed his decisions would completely put down the dangerous heresy of nullification, and in the end strengthen the general government.

The apprehension that the re-election of General Jackson would tend to unsettle the government, consequently did not operate upon the mass of the voters to the same extent as upon the leaders of the opposition.

They were governed by the more obvious consideration growing out of the pressing question of nullification on the part of South-Carolna, and as he had declared himself opposed to the pretensions of that state, the distant dangers to be apprehended from the effect of the principles advocated by the president in the Georgia controversy were by many disregarded. Even among the mass of those who professed to be governed by a desire to preserve the constitution from destruction there was a want of that untiring energy and self-devotion which flow from a deep conviction of the importance of a cause. An unwillingness to postpone plans of personal advancement, or to sacrifice individual prejudices and private views to the good of the cause, too much characterized the opposition to the administration. Its members, professing great independence of character, were too apt to forget, that when combined effort is required, individual will must give way, and the plans of the party were constantly thwarted by the refusal of its members to unite upon a single candidate.

The anti-masons professed an equal dislike with the national republicans to the principles and policy of the administration, and declared themselves ready to combine to defeat the election of General Jackson. Neither, however, were willing to yield to what they called the dictation of the other.

Anti-masonic electoral tickets were formed in the states of Massachusetts, Rhode-Island, Connecticut, New-York, New-Jersey, and Pennsylvania. The national republicans adopted the anti-masonic tickets in New-York and Pennsylvania, but in the other states named, and the remaining states of the union, with thh exception of three or four southern states, tickets were nominated favorable to Mr. Clay for the presidency. In Ohio the anti-masonic ticket for electors first nominated was withdrawn, and the contest in that state was between Jackson and Clay.

While the two divisions of the opposition were prevented from coalescing, by what they considered insuperable obstacles, excepting the imperfect union in the three states named, the friends of the administration united in its support with a zeal and earnestness which both deserved and insured success. Local divisions were done away; personal difficulties adjusted, and private quarrels forgotten in the general desire to promote the triumph of the party. The people at large, witnessing on one side so much party devotion, and on the other so much of the opposite quality, were led to regard the cause of the administration with more favor than it would have obtained upon a mere view of its principles and policy.

Although the elections for state officers in some of the states, in the autumn of 1832, were either favorable to the opposition, or, from the small majorities given in favor of the administration, they indicated a close contest at the approaching presidential election; the result of the latter was a complete triumph of the electoral licket pledged to Jackson and Van Buren.

The great military services of General Jackson had gained for him general popularity, and many who did not altogether approve of his measures, attributed his errors to mistaken views. His honesty of purpose was questioned by comparatively few, and all admired the boldness and firmness with which he pursued those measures that had been adopted and avowed as the policy of his administration.

He was styled, too, the representative of the democratic party, and the people were constantly assured that his sole object was to deprive the federal government only of those powers which it had usurped, and to bring it within the limits prescribed by the constitution.

In the electoral colleges the votes for president and vice-president stood as follows: Andrew Jackson 219, Henry Clay 49, John Floyd 11, William Wirt, 7. For vice-president—Martin Van Buren 189, John Sergeant 49, William Wilkins 30, Henry Lee 11, Amos Ellmaker 7. The votes for John Floyd and Henry Lee were given by the state of South-Carolina. Pennsylvania refused to vote for Mr. Van Buren; therefore Mr. Wilkins, one of the U. S. senators from that state, received the vote for vice-president.

Considering this election with that of 1828, it will be observed, that General Jackson gained the votes of Maine (except one vote.) New-Hampshire, New-Jersey, and part of New-York, which were then given to Mr. Adams, while he now lost the vote of Kentucky and South-Carolina, which he received in 1828. The majority in the electoral colleges was not, however, a fair test of the measure of approbation bestowed upon his administration.

The large majority received by General Jackson in the electoral colleges, however, was by him, and his supporters generally, construed into an unqualified approval by his countrymen of all his measures. Upon all points where his course had been questioned by his opponents, his re-election was urged as a final decision of the people, from which there was no appeal.

The second session of the twenty-second congress commenced on the 4th of December, 1832, and continued until the expiration of their term, on the 3d of March, 1833. The president *pro tem.* of the senate, Mr. Tazewell, having resigned, the Hon. Hugh L. White, of Tennessee, was elected in his place. On the 28th of December, the vice-president of the United States, Hon. John C. Calhoun, resigned that office, and was elected a senator from South-Carolina, in place of Mr. Hayne who had been chosen governor of the state.

The secretary of the treasury, Mr. M'Lane, in his report to congress, urged upon that body a reduction of duty to the revenue standard, and declared that "there was not the same necessity for high protecting duties as that which was consulted in our past legislation."

It was now distinctly foreseen that the final contest relating to a protective tariff was about to be decided. Upon distributing the various subjects recommended to the consideration of congress, this was referred in the house to the committee of ways and means, of which Mr. Verplanck, of New-York, was chairman.

Notwithstanding a new tariff had been adopted at the last session, after a lengthened discussion, and by large majorities, it was now determined to remodel the whole, to conciliate its opponents at the south, and on the 27th of December, a bill was reported by the committee of ways and means, which was understood to embody the views of the administration.

In the senate, also, the subject was taken up at an early period, and on the 13th of December, the chairman of the committee of finance presented a resolution calling on the secretary of the treasury for the plan and details of a bill in conformity with his suggestions. After some debate as to the propriety of calling on a branch of the executive department for an opinion, instead of facts of information, the resolution was adopted.

The bill reported in the house by Mr. Verplanck, proposed a dimunition on all the protected articles, to take effect immediately, and a second diminution on the 2d of March, 1834. By this bill, a great and immediate reduction was contemplated upon the chief manufactures of the country, and a further reduction to the revenue standard in 1834. This would afford to the domestic manufacturer a protecting duty from 15 to 20 per cent., and with this advantage, the opponents of high duties argued that he should be content. On the other side, it was contended that the dimunition was too great, and that by suddenly bringing the duties down to the minimum point, the government would violate its faith with those who had been induced to embark in manufacturing, by the adoption of what was declared to be the settled policy of the country, and who would be ruined by a sudden and unexpected withdrawal of the protection they enjoyed.

The bill of last session which was framed with the view of settling the question, had not been fairly tested, and it was insisted that such a vacillating course on the part of the government, was positive injustice to those who had vested their capital under the existing laws.

While the discussion on the bill was going on new interest was imparted to the subject by a message from the president to congress, on the 16th of January, communicating the South-Carolina ordinance and nullifying laws, together with his own views as to what should be done under the existing state of affairs. Upon the message being read in the senate, Mr. Calhoun repelled in the most earnest manner, the imputation of any hostile feelings or intentions against the union on the part of South-Carolina. The state authorities, he asserted, had looked only to a judicial decision upon the question, until the concentration of the United States troops at Charleston and Augusta had compelled them to make provisions to defend themselves.

The judiciary committee, to whom the message was referred, reported a bill to enforce the collection of the revenue where any obstructions were offered to the officers employed in that duty. It vested full power in the land and naval forces of the United States, if necessary to carry the revenue laws into effect.

After the bill was reported to the senate, Mr. Calhoun offered a series of resolutions embodying his views and those who sustained the doctrines of nullification, with regard to the powers of the general government and the rights of the states. Mr. Grundy, of Tennessee, offered other resolutions as substitutes for Mr. Calhoun's and which set forth the views of the administration. The latter were not deemed, by a portion of the senate, fully to set forth the character of the government, inasmuch as while they declare the several acts of congress laying duties on imports to be constitutional, and deny the power of a single state to annul them *or any other constitutional law*, tacitly yield the whole doctrine of nullification, by the implied admission that any unconstitutional law may be judged of by the state in the last resort, and annulled by the same authority. With the view of having placed upon record his opinions upon that point, Mr. Clayton, of Delaware, an opposition senator proposed a resolution, setting them forth, and declaring that "the senate will not fail, in the faithful discharge of its most solemn duty, to support the executive in the just administration of the government, and clothe it with all constitutional power necessary to the faithful execution of the laws and the preservation of the Union."

The whole subject was now before congress; and the state legislatures, being generally in session, passed resolutions expressing their opinions as to the course which that body ought to adopt.

In the legislatures of Massachusetts, Connecticut, New-York, Delaware, Tennessee, Indiana, and Missouri, the doctrines of nullification were entirely disclaimed, as destructive to the constitution. Those of North-Carolina and Alabama were no less explicit in condemning nullification, but they also expressed an opinion that the tariff was unconstitutional and inexpedient.

The state of Georgia also reprobated the doctrine of nullification, as unconstitutional by a vote of 102 to 51 in her legislature; but it denounced the tariff in decided terms and proposed a convention of the states of Virginia, North-Carolina, South-Carolina, Georgia, Alabama, Tennessee, and Mississippi, to devise measures to obtain relief from that system.

The legislature of Virginia assumed a more extraordinary ground. The subject was referred to a committee on federal relations, and a general discussion was had on the powers of the government: and finally resolutions were passed, earnestly requesting South-Carolina not to proceed further under the ordinance of their convention to reduce the import duties to a revenue standard, and declaring that the people of Virginia expect that the general government and the government of South-Carolina will carefully abstain from all acts calculated to disturb the tranquility of the country.

After further resolving that they adhere to the principles of the Virginia resolutions of 1798, but that they do not consider them as sanctioning the proceedings of South-Carolina, or the president's proclamation, they proceeded to appoint Benjamin W. Leigh, as a commissioner on the part of the state, to proceed to South-Carolina, to communicate the resolutions of Virginia, and to express their good will to the people of that state, and their anxious solicitude for an accommodation between them and the general government.

The state of New-Hampshire expressed no opinion as to the doctrines of South-Carolina, but the legislature passed resolutions in favor of reducing the tariff to the revenue standard.

On the other hand, the legislatures of Massachusetts, Vermont, Rhode-Island, New-Jersey, and Pennsylvania, declared themselves to be opposed to any modification of the tariff.

While the states were sutsaining their respective views and interests, congress was slowly proceeding in the discussion of the questions belonging to the subject. In the house the bill for reducing the tariff was subjected to an ordeal that threatened to prove fatal to its passage through that body. The discussion upon its general principles occupied the house for two weeks after its introduction, and was resumed from time to time, during the examination of its details, for the purpose of amendment; and but little prospect appeared of bringing about any satisfactory termination of this long disputed question.

The authorities of South-Carolina, in the meantime, exerted themselves to increase the military force of the state. Munitions were provided, depots formed, and the militia in the nullifying districts were called upon to volunteer in her defence. On the other hand, the minorty of the people, who called themselves the union party, were equally determined not to submit to the nullifying ordinance and laws, and prepared themselves with equal firmness and zeal to sustain the federal authorities. A spark was sufficient to kindle the flame of civil war, but fortunately no accident occurred to bring about a collision. The revenue laws, under the protection of the forces of the general government, were carried into effect without any opposition by violence. No attempt was made to enforce the laws under the ordinance of the state convention, and on the 31st of January, at a meeting of the leading nullifiers at Charleston, after reiterating their determination to maintain their principles, and expressing their opposition to modify the tariff, it was resolved that during the session of congress, all collision be avoided between the state and federal authorities, in the hope that the controversy might be satisfactorily adjusted.

During these proceedings in South-Carolina, the enforcing bill, providing for the collection of duties was pressed forward to a vote. It was, however, delayed in the senate, by a lengthened discussion, until the 20th of February, when it passed that body by a vote of 32 ayes; Mr. Tyler, only, voting in the negative, the opponents of the bill generally having withdrawn. It also passed the house on the 28th of February, 150 to 35, and became a law.

The tariff bill reported by Mr. Verplanck, and supported by the friends of the administration, in the house of representatives, was delayed in that body until the 12th February; when Mr. Clay, of the senate, apprehending either the passage of that bill, which he considered would be destructive to the manufacturing interests, or that congress would adjourn, leaving the matter unsettled, and the country in danger of civil war, introduced, pursuant to notice, a measure of compromise in the senate. This was a bill which had been prepared, after much consultation, for the permanent adjustment of the tariff. It provided, that where the duties exceeded 20 per cent, there should be one tenth part of the excess deducted after December 30, 1833, and one tenth each alternate year, until the 31st of December 1841, when one half of the residue was to be deducted, and after the 30th of June, 1842, the duties on all goods were to be reduced to 20 per cent, on a home valuation, and were to be paid in cash.

After Mr. Clay had stated that his views for introducing the bill were to preserve the protective tariff for a length of time, and to restore good feelings and tranquility among the people, he explained the proposed measure and its probable operation. Mr. Calhoun expressed his approbation of the bill; and it was discussed by various senators until the 23d of February, when it was ordered to a third reading. On the 25th Mr. Clay stated that a bill identical in its provisions to the one before the senate, had just passed the house, and would probably be presented to the senate for approval. The senate, on his motion, therefore ad journed.

In the house of representatives, Mr. Verplanck's bill was taken up for discussion, when, on motionof Mr. Letcher, of Kentucky, it was recommitted, with instructions to report Mr. Clay's bill. The bill being referred to the committee, the substitute was agreed to, forthwith reported to the house, and the following day passed, by a vote of 119 to 85. In the senate, after some further discussion it passed, yeas 29, nays 16, and received the signature of the president on the 2d of March, 1833.

The passage of this bill was regarded by all as a concession to South-Carolina, and many considered it as sanctioning the ultimate triumph of principles advanced by that state.

The supporters of the bill who were friendly to the system of protection insisted, on the contrary, that this was the only mode of preventing an entire and immediate destruction of the manufacturing interests. That the administration had a decided majority in the next congres; and if the question was not settled now, the manufacturers would be entirely at the mercy of their enemies.

Those who looked to the ultimate results of this compromise, preferred to test rather than to surrender the powers of the government, and they strongly reprobated the idea of abandoning the policy of the government upon the demand of a single state.

The leaders of the nullifying party, on their part, affected to to regard the compromise as an unqualified triumph. The convention of South-Carolina assembled at Columbia, at the call of the governor, on the 11th of March, and deeming it expedient to consider the compromise tariff as satisfactory, they repealed the ordinance nullifying the revenue laws, and nullified the enforcing law. After this the tariff controversy in South-Carolina ended.

The bill providing for the distribution of the proceeds of the sales of the public lands among the states was again introduced by Mr. Clay, at an early period of this session. After much discussion, it passed that body on the 25th of January, yeas 24, nays 20. It was not taken up in the house until the 1st of March, when, after being amended, it was passed, yeas 96, nays 40, and sent back to the senate. The amendment of the house was concurred in by the senate, 23 to 5. These votes indicated that two-thirds of both houses were in favor of the policy proposed to be established by Mr. Clay's bill, and if the president had returned the bill with his objections, it was understood that it would have become a law, notwithstanding the veto.

This opportunity, however, was not given to them, as the president retained the bill until after the adjournment, which took place at the termination of their constitutional term on the 3d of March, and thus prevented congress from expressing its opinion upon his objections. The bill was thus defeated by the executive, who in this manner assumed an absolute instead of a qualified veto upon the acts of congress, which was confided to him by the constitution. The reason of the president for his course in this matter, as given to the next congress, was want of time for a due consideration of this important measure.

Among the subjects recommended by the president in his annual message in December, 1832, was the propriety of removing the public moneys from the United States bank. The secretary of the treasury, who had hitherto advocated the re-charter of the bank, followed up the president's recommendation by the expression of his doubts as to their safety, if continued in its custody. An agent appointed by the treasury to investigate the actual condition of the bank, shortly after made his report, and it appeared that this intitution had an excess of funds of more than seven millions of dollars over its liabilities, besides its capital of $35,000,000.

The president also recommended a sale of the stock of the bank belonging to the United States. A proposition to that effect, reported by Mr. Polk from the committee on ways and means in the house, was rejected on the first reading, 102 to 91.

The subject of the public deposites was referred to the same committee, who, through Mr. Verplanck, made a report stating the situation of the bank. They consequently recommended a resolution that the government deposites may, in the opinion of the house, be safely continued in the bank of the United States. This resolution was adopted by the house—ayes 109, noes 46.

Appropriations were made at this session of congress, for carrying on certain works before commenced, and the improvement of harbors and rivers, also for the Cumberland road, and certain territorial roads. Acts were also passed for improving the navigation of certain rivers in Florida and Michigan; making provision for publishing the documental history of the American revolution; and sundry other laws of less general interest.

At the close of the first term of president Jackson, the foreign relations of the United States, with the exception of France, were in a favorable position. The first instalment of the indemnity to be paid by the treaty with France, was drawn for, in a bill of exchange by the American government, but the French Chambers had not made any appropriation to meet it, and the bill was not expected. This neglect was warmly resented by the president. Instructions were given to the American minister to urge upon the French government a prompt compliance with the treaty

With Russia a treaty of commerce was concluded in December, 1832, upon the principles of reciprocity. A similar treaty was made with Belgium. Some claims of American merchants against Portugal, for illegal captures, were prosecuted to a successful result, and an effort was made by the administration to procure satisfaction from Spain, for illegal detentions and captures of American property subsequent to the treaty of 1819, and an acknowledgement of their justice was finally extorted from that government. A treaty of commerce was concluded with Chili.

The second presidential term of General Jackson commenced on the 4th of March, 1833. At twelve o'clock on that day, the president and vice-president elect, attended by the heads of department, foreign ministers and their suites, judges of supreme court, senators, and members of the house of representatives, the mayor and citizens of Washington, and strangers, entered the hall of representatives. The president took the seat of the speaker of the house, with the vice-president, Mr. Van Buren on his left, and his private secretary, Mr. Donelson, on his right. After a pause of a few minutes, the president rose, and was greeted by the cheers of the large assembly present. He then proceeded, in an aubible and firm voice, to pronounce his inaugural address, at the close of which he was again greeted with cheers and applause. The chief justice then administered the usual oath to the president. The oath was also administered to Mr. Van Buren, after which, the president and vice-president retired, amid the plaudits of the assembly.

The excitement of the political contest was at an end; nullification was virtually relinquished by South-Carolina; and the modification of the tariff had tranquilized the public mind. The angry feelings engendered by the election had subsided; and in a tour which the president made through the middle and eastern states, in the summer of 1833, both parties united to do honor to the chief magistrate of the republic; his opponents heartily approving of his course toward South-Carolina, and of the principles avowed by him in his proclamation and message, and his supporters giving vent to those feelings which had originally enlisted them, as a party, in his favor.

A political calm had succeeded the tempest, and it seemed as if the second term of General Jackson's administration was about to prove as quiet and tranquil, as the first had been stormy and turbulent. This expectation was not destined to be realized. A new subject of excitement was at this time introduced into our politics, which continued to agitate the public mind for a large portion of the remaining period of General Jackson's administration, affecting, as it did, the interests of the community generally. We allude to the removal of the government deposites from the bank of the United States, by order of the president.

By the law of 1816, creating the bank of the United States, the public moneys were deposited in the vaults of the bank and its branches, and, as an equivalent for that deposite, the bank assumed the responsibitity of acting as the fiscal agent of the government.

In the same act, however, it was provided that the public deposites might be removed by the secretary of the treasury; but requiring him to lay his reasons for removing them immediately before Congress.

After the veto of the bill to recharter the bank, the president soon determined that that institution should be deprived of the public deposites, although the charter did not expire until 1836. We have already seen that congress, in 1833, refused, by a decisive vote, to authorize the removal of the deposites, as recommended by the president, and new means were adopted to effect the contemplated end.

The secretary of State, Edward Livingston, being appointed minister to France, on account of the state of our relations with that power, Louis M'Lane, secretary of the treasury, who had declined to sanction the removal of the deposites from the United States bank, was transferred to the state department, and William J. Duane, of Pennsylvania, was appointed his successor. It was soon, however, found, that Mr. Duane was not willing to act in the matter without sufficient reasons to sustain him before the world.

The president had urged Mr. Duane during his northern tour in the summer of 1833, to remove the public moneys from the obnoxious institution, without convincing him of the propriety of the step. He finally obtained from him his consent to appoint Amos Kendall, as an agent, to inquire into the terms upon which the local banks, incorporated by the several states, would take the public deposites, upon the basis of mutual guarantee. This basis, however, was found to be inadmissable. The banks refused to guaranty for each other, and the secretary was soon made to understand that it was the president's determination to remove the deposites at all hazards.

To this he explicitly refused to lend himself. He even refused to fix a day after the adjournment of congress, for their removal, in case that body did not act upon the subject. The most he would agree to was, to remove them in case congress ordered him to do so.

In this dilemma, the president convoked the cabinet on the 10th of September, 1833 and laid before its members an exposition of his views upon this important question. The doctrines advanced in this document were, that the power of the secretary to remove the deposites was unqualified, and not limited to particular contingencies; that the speedy termination of the charter of the bank rendered it incumbent on the secretary to introduce a plan for keeping and disbursing the public revenue, before its dissolution, to avoid any derangement consequent upon such a change at that moment; that the conduct of the bank in relation to the redemption of the three per cent stocks, and the bill on the French government; and its interference with politics, deserved punishment; and under those circumstances, the president assumed the responsibility himself, of removing the public deposites from the United States bank, and fixed upon the 1st of October, 1833, as the day for their removal.

The secretary of the treasury deliberated upon the question thus authoritatively pressed upon him, and on the 21st of September he announced to the president his determination not to carry his directions into effect. He also resolved not to resign, and as he was the only officer who could give a legal order for the removal of the public moneys, the president was compelled, in order to carry his designs into effect, to remove the secretary. This was done on the 23d of September, and Roger B. Taney, (then attorney-general) appointed in his place. Benjamin F. Butler, of N. Y. was appointed attorney-general in place of Mr. Taney.

The new secretary was known to entertain similar opinions to those of the president, both as to the right and expediency of removing the deposites, and he immediately issued the necessary orders for their removal to the loca banks selected by him as agents of the government.

Almost simultaneously with this step an attempt was mad to destroy the credit of the bank, by suddenly presenting for payment, at one of the distant branches, a large amount of their circulating notes, which had been secretly accumulated. This demand was promptly met; but, connected with the withdrawal of the public deposites, it evinced a settled hostility against the bank, and compelled the directors to adopt a general system of retrenchment, with a view to its own safety.

Gre commercial distres immediately ensued. The amount of the loans of the bank, on the 1st of October, 1833, was over sixty millions of dollars; and the amount of deposites of the U. S. government at that time in the bank, was $9,868,435, all of which amount was removed during a period of about nine months, and the greater part of the same during the first four months. At the moment of taking this step, the business of the country was unusually active. The capitalist and the merchant, mechanics and manufacturers, had unlimited confidence in each other, and all the moneyed institutions of the country, had extended their loans to the utmost bounds of their ability.

At such a juncture, great and rigid retrenchment, attended with want of confidence, was necessarily productive of ruinous consequences. Private credit was deeply affected, and the business of the country was interrupted to a degree that could be attributable only to the panic which followed this violent attack upon the pecuniary concerns of the community.

The twenty-third congress held its first session from December 2, 1833, to June 30, 1834. There was a decided administration majority in the house of representatives. Andrew Stevenson was again elected speaker, receiving 142 votes, against 66 for all others, and 9 blanks. In the senate the new vice-president, Mr. Van Buren, took his seat, as presiding officer, but in that body the administration were in the minority, in consequence of Mr. Calhoun and other state-rights senators acting with the opposition.

The principal topic of discussion at this session of congress was the removal of the deposites, by order of the president, from the bank of the U. States. The subject was brought before the two houses by the president's message and the report from the secretary of the treasury. On the 26th of December, 1833, Mr. Clay offered a resolution, in the senate, which it will be recollected, was afterwards expunged, by drawing black lines around it. The resolution which follows, gave rise to long and animated debates, and was finally adopted on the 28th March, 1834, ayes 26, noes 20:

"*Resolved, That the president, in the late executive proceedings in relation to the public revenue, has assumed upon himself authority and power not conferred by the constitution and laws, but in derogation of both.*"

Against this resolution the president sent in his protest to the senate, containing an elaborate argument on the subject, in which he denied the right of the senate to censure him in this way, and demanded that this remonstrance should be placed on their records. This the senate refused.

The senate, on the 4th of June, also adopted two joint resolutions offered by Mr. Clay, declaring, 1st, that the reasons of the secretary of the treasury were unsatisfactory and insufficient; 2d, requiring the deposite of the public moneys to be made in the bank of the United States. The first of these resolutions was adopted, 29 to 16; the second 28 to 16. In the house of representatives they were laid on the table, ayes 114, noes 101.

The removal of the deposites or the action of the bank, in connection with the withdrawal of the deposites from its vaults, caused intense excitement and much commercial distress throughout the union. Numerous committees, appointed by merchants, mechanics, tradesmen, and others, in the principal cities and towns, waited on the president, asking that he would recommend some measure of relief. To these he replied, in substance, "that the government could give no relief, and provide no remedy; that the banks were the occasion of all the evils which existed, and that those who suffered by their great enterprise, had none to blame but themselves; that those who borrowed capital ought to break." Petitions for the restoration of the deposites, or some other measure of relief, were poured into congress during the whole session; they were favorably received in the senate, but as the house of representatives sustained the president, petitions to conteract his views met with but little favor in that body.

Resolutions reported by the committee of ways and means in the house, were adopted on the 4th of April; 1st, that the bank of the United States ought not to be rechartered, ayes 132, noes 82; 2d, that the public deposites ought not to be restored to the bank of the United States, ayes 118, noes 103.

On the 2d of June, the speaker of the house, Mr. Stevenson, having been nominated by the president, minister to Great Britain, resigned his situation as speaker; and the house proceeded to ballot for a speaker in his place. John Bell, of Tennessee, was elected, on the tenth ballot receiving 114 votes, to 78 for James K. Polk and 26 scattering and blanks. Mr. Polk was the administration candidate, and Mr. Bell was elected by the votes of the opposition and a portion of the administration party who were opposed to Mr. Van Buren as successor to Gen. Jackson.

On the 23d of June the senate rejected the nomination of Mr. Taney as secretary of the treasury, 28 to 18; and on the 24th Andrew Stevenson was rejected as minister to England, 23 to 22. The ground taken on the rejection of Mr. Stevenson was, that he had received the offer of the mission to Great Britain in a letter from the secretary of state, by order of the president, in March 1833, after which he had been elected to congress and made speaker of the house, the committees of which he had appointed in conformity with the views of the president. Being called on by the senate for a copy of the letter to Mr. Stevenson offering him the mission, the president communicated the same; although denying their right to ask for it, he informed the senate that the contingency on which Mr. Stevenson was to be appointed did not arise, but the nagotiation expected was commenced at Washington instead of London. The mission to England continued vacant for several years after the rejection of Mr. Van Buren in 1832, and the affairs of the United States, with that kingdom were, during that period, intrusted to Aaron Vail, who had been secretary of legation under Mr. Van Buren. The president declined nominating any other person as minister, until Mr. Stevenson was named, and after he was rejected the place still continued vacant until March 1836, when Mr. Stevenson was again nominated, and then confirmed by the senate. Strong objections were raised in the senate in 1834, against the frequent appointment of members of congress to office by General Jackson. During the first five years of his administration he had appointed to office thirteen senators and twenty-five representatives. In June, 1834, Mr. M'Lane having resigned, John Forsyth, of Georgia, was appointed secretary of State, Mahlon Dickerson, of New-Jersey, secretary of the navy, in place of Levi Woodbury, appointed secretary of the treasury.

An important act respecting the coinage of the United States was passed at this session. By this law the weight of the gold eagle of the United States was reduced twelve grains, being equal to 66½ cents less in value than the old coin of that denomination. Two other acts were passed, regulating the value of certain foreign gold and silver coins. The objects of these several acts was to infuse a larger proportion of gold and silver into the currency of the United States than had been used; and this became a favorite project of the president and his supporters in the cabinet and in congress. Increased activity was given to the mint, and the display of the new gold coin among the people had an important bearing on the elections in the different states, and operated favorably to the administration.

Among the other acts passed at this long and arduous session, those of most general interest were as follows; making appropriations for certain harbors and rivers; for completing a road from Memphis to Little Rock, in Arkansas; authorizing certain roads in Arkansas; aiding roads in Michigan; continuing the Cumberland road; appropriations for light-houses; for improvement of the Hudson river; authorizing the purchase of the papers and books of General Washington.

The course of the president with regard to the bank of the United States, although it was popular with the mass of the people in some sections of the country, caused a considerable diminution of the strength of the administration in the commercial states, as evinced by the elections in 1834. Many of those who had supported General Jackson, now joined the opposition, the combined forces of the party opposing the administration now assuming the name of "WHIG." This title of *Whig*, as a substitute for Federalism, Anti-masonry, National Republicanism, &c., originated in the city of New-York; and it has always been understood that James Watson Webb, of the Courier & Enquirer, first advanced the idea. Mr. Webb in 1828, was a strong advocate and supporter of General Jackson, but left him and the democratic party upon the United States bank question. Upon this question, Hammond's Political History of New-York, says: "The opposition party in the city of New-York, assumed the name of "whig" in the winter of 1834, and this designation was soon after applied to their political friends, as a body, throughout the state. The institution of Masonry, had almost ceased to exist, and the Anti-masons generally united with the National Republicans, under this new cognomen." It soon became the party title throughout the United States. The friends of the administration adhered to the old party name of "DEMOCRATS."

In the summer of 1835 a party, which claimed to be opposed to all monopolies, to bank notes and paper money as a circulating medium, and to legislative prerogatives, was formed in the city of New-York, comprising some of the prominent men, who called themselves the "*Equal Rights Party.*" A majority of the equal rights men were democrats, and in consequence of their dissatisfaction at the nomination of Gideon Lee for congress and others, of the same stamp for assembly, they rallied in great force, at the meeting held in Tammany Hall, to receive the report of the nominating committee. The old Tammany men supported Isaac L. Varian, for chairman, and the Equal Rights men presesented Joel Curtis. Each faction claimed that its candidate was elected, and a scene of complete disorder and confusion ensued, in the midst of which the *gas lights in the room were extinguished.* The Equal Rights men had provided themselves, in anticipation of this result, with *locofoco* matches and candles, and the room was almost instantly re-lighted. Soon after this disturbance, the Equal Rights men, or anti-monopolists received the name of "LOCOFOCO," and this appellation was subsequently bestowed by the whig presses and politicians, upon the whole democratic party.

The twenty-third congress held its second session from December 1, 1834, to March 3, 1835. George Poindexter, of Mississippi, had been chosen president *pro. tem.* of the senate, at the close of the last session, but as the vice-president, Mr. Van Buren, was constantly in his seat as presiding officer, president Jackson was saved from the mortification of seing at the head of the senate, one to whom he was personnally inimical; a quarrel having occurred between the president, and the senator from Mississippi.

But few acts of general interest were passed at this short session. Appropriations were made for roads and surveys, also for certain harbors and rivers; and, as usual, for the Cumberland road. Branches of the mint were established at the gold mines in North-Carolina and Georgia; also at New-Orleans. In conformity with the recommendation of the president, an act was passed regulating the government deposites in the state banks. At the close of the session, John Tyler, of Virginia, was elected president *pro. tem.* of the senate. He had generally acted with the opposition after the removal of the deposites from the United States bank, by president Jackson.

There was an impression at this time, that General Jackson contemplated retiring from the presidency, leaving the reins of government in the hands of Mr. Van Buren for the remainder of his term; but if he had such an intention it was abandoned. He was, however, anxious that Mr. Van Buren should be his successor in the presidency, and in February, 1835, he came out with a letter to a friend, in which he expresses himself in favor of a national democratic convention, to nominate a president and vice-president. The convention was a favorite project ot Mr. Van Buren, and it soon appeared that all the supporters of the administration who were in favor of Mr. Van Buren as successor to General Jackson, advocated a nomination by a convention, while the opponents of Mr. Van Buren, in the same ranks, denounced that mode of nomination. A large section of the Jackson party gave early indications of an intention to support Hugh L. White, one of the Tennessee senators, for president, and in January, 1835, he was nominated by the legislature of Alabama, and, about the same time, by the people of Tennessee; and by the Tennessee delegation in the house of representatives, all of whom signed a letter in his favor, except James K. Polk and

Cave Johnson. Mr. Van Buren was already nominated for the presidency by a state convention in Mississippi. Three candidates had been named by the whig opposition, namely, Gen. William H. Harrison, of Ohio, by a meeting at Harrisburg; John M'Lean, of Ohio, by a legislative caucus in that state; and Daniel Webster, by the whigs in the legislature of Massachusetts.

The national democratic convention for the nomination of president and vice-president of the United States, met at Baltimore on the 20th of May, 1835. More than six hundred delegates were in attendance, and twenty-two states were represented. Upon the first ballot, Martin Van Buren received the unanimous vote of the convention for president. This was expected, as none but the friends of Mr. Van Buren took part in the convention. Colonel Richard M. Johnson, of Kentucky, received the nomination for vice-president, by 178 votes to 87 for William C. Rives, of Virginia. The delegates from Virginia protested against the nomination of Colonel Johnson, declaring that he could not receive the vote of that state.

William T. Barry being appointed minister to Spain, Amos Kendall was appointed postmaster-general in his place in May 1835.

The payment of the first instalment of the French indemnity being still refused by the French chambers, the president instructed Mr. Livingston, minister to that court, to return to the United States. He accordingly asked for his passports, and arrived home in June, 1835. The affairs between the United States and France now wore a threatening aspect, but the matter in dispute was finally settled, through the intervention of the British government in 1836.

The twenty-fourth congress assembled on the 7th of December, 1835, and the first session continued until the 4th of July, 1836. James K. Polk, of Tennessee, was elected speaker of the house of representives, having received 132 votes, against 84 for John Bell, the late speaker, and 9 scattering votes. Mr. Polk was the administration candidate, and Mr. Bell was supported by the opposition, including the friends of Judge White for the presidency.

The message of the president at the opening of this session indicated a high state of public prosperity, so far as the national treasury was concerned. The public debt had then been extinguished and there was a large surplus remaining in the treasury. The country had at this time somewhat recovered from the panic and shock affecting public and private credit, occasioned by the removal of the deposites, and concominant circumstances.

Mr. Clay again introduced a bill to provide for the distribution of the proceeds of the public lands among the states, which passed the senate by a vote of 25 to 20, but was not acted upon by the house of representatives.

The most important act of the session was the distribution act or a bill to regulate the deposites of the public money, which was passed in June, 1836; it provided that the money which should be in the treasury on the 1st day of January, 1737, reserving the sum of five million of dollars, should be deposited with the several states, in proportion to their respective representation in congress, which should by law authorize their treasurer or other competent authorities to receive the same. The deposites to be made with the states in quarterly amounts commencing on the 1st of January, 1837.

The bill to distribute the proceeds of the public lands, as proposed by Mr. Clay having failed, and there being a large surplus in the treasury, the bill just mentioned, for the distribution of the surplus revenue, was devised, to effect temporarily the same purpose; and to obviate the scruples of the president, the law provided for a deposite, with the states without interest, instead of a positive transfer or quitclaim from the general government to the states. The law, however, received the support of more than two-thirds of each house. The amount thus divided among the states with no expectation of being recalled (and that can not be done till directed by congress,) was over twenty-eight millions of dollars. The balance of the public debt was paid off in 1835, and the amount of revenue, from customs and sales of the public lands, in that and the succeeding year, had swollen the surplus in the treasury, in 1836, to more than forty millions of dollars. Owing to the subsequent pecuniary difficulties of the government, in 1837, congress suspended the fourth instalment to be deposited with the states.

A new law respecting patents was also enacted at this session, and all former general laws on that subject were repealed. The State of Michigan was admitted into the union, on certain conditions; but those conditions were not complied with until the following year, when the state was formally admitted. The state of Aarkansas was also admitted into the union. Among other important acts of the session those of most general interest were those making appropriations for the improvement of certain harbors and rivers, and for continuing the Cumberland road. At the close of the session, William R. King, of Alabama, an administration senator, was elected president *pro tem.* of the senate. At the commencement of the session there was an opposition majority in the senate; but several changes had taken place, and the administration now claimed a majority in both branches of congress.

A bill was passed by congress fixing the day of meeting and adjournment, which was vetoed by the president.

After the adjournment of congress, the public mind was much agitated by the promulgation of an executive order from the treasury department, called "the specie circular." During the session, Mr. Benton, of Missouri, had offered a resolution in the senate, on the 22d of April, declaring that nothing ought to be received but gold and silver in payment 'or the public lands, and that the committee on the public nds be instructed to report a bill accordingly. This reution was not acted upon in the senate; but soon after congress had adjourned, a circular was issued by Mr. Woodbury, secretary of the treasury, dated the 11th of July, 1835, (by order of the president) directing the receivers of the public moneys to receive in payment of the public lands, nothing but gold and silver (and Virginia land scrip in certain cases.) As the sales of the public lands had been very large for two or three years, and many of the purchases had been made on speculation, through the facilities afforded by the state banks, the operation of this specie circular from the treasury department, proved very disastrous in its effects upon the business community.

When it was ascertained that the bank of the United States would not be re-chartered as a national institution, numerous banks were incorporated by the several state legislatures, to supply the supposed want of banking capital. The bank of the United States was chartered by the legislature of Pennsylvania, in 1836, with the same amount of capital as the national institution (the charter of which expired the same year,) viz., thirty-five millions of dollars. The panic occasioned by the removal of the deposites having subsided, and the state banks being without the check of a national regulator to prevent excessive issues of paper circulation, the facilities of bank accomodations occasioned a scene of speculation which extended far and wide, over the whole union, and all classes of citizens were more or less entangled in the operations which ensued. Extensive purchases of public lands, by individuals and companies, were among the schemes of the day, for the employment of the abundance of bank paper.

The immediate effect of the treasury circular, requiring specie to be paid for purchases of the public lands, was to divert the flow of specie from the legitimate channels of commerce, and otherwise to derange the currency, thus embarrassing the operations of the business community. So far as the circular tended to check the tide of speculation, particularly in the public lands, its operation was deemed salutary.

In March, 1836, the senate confirmed the nomination of Roger B. Taney as chief justice of the supreme court, in place of John Marshall, deceased; Phillip P. Barbour, to fill a vacancy on the same bench; Amos Kendall, postmaster-general; and John H. Eaton, minister to Spain. Mr. Kendall succeeded William T. Barry, in May, 1835, but was not confirmed until 1836. In June, 1834, the senate passed a vote of censure unanimously (yeas 41,) on Mr. Barry, for borrowing money illegally of banks, on account of the post-office department. When he resigned the office of postmaster-general, president Jackson appointed him minister to Spain, 1835; his health at the time was precarious, and he died at Liverpool, in England, on the 30th of August, the same year. Mr. Eaton formerly secretary of war, was appointed to succeed him.

The presidential election, which took place in the fall of 1836, was warmly contested. The different sections of the opposition, although they were unable to concentrate their forces upon a single candidate for president, had strong hopes of defeating the election of Mr. Van Buren by throwing the final choice into the house of representatives, and it was not believed that Mr. Van Buren could obtain a majority of the electoral votes, over all his opponents. The result was contrary to all reasonable calculations, and proved the potency of party discipline, even in electing the chief magistrate of the American republic. The great portion of the opposition supported William H. Harrison, of Ohio, for president, but Judge White, of Tennessee, was preferred in some of the southern and south-western states, and in several states the friends of Harrison and White united on the same electoral tickets, in no instance did they run in opposition to each other, in the same state. The friends of General Harrison, generally nominated for vice-president, Francis Granger, of New-York, while the supporters of Judge White nominated John Tyler, of Virginia, who also received the votes of the Harrison men in Maryland, and the states-rights men in South-Carolina. Massachusetts supported Daniel Webster for president, and the vote of South-Carolina was given to Willie P. Mangum, of North-Carolina.

Upon the meeting of the electoral college Mr. Van Buren was declared president as will be hereafter stated.

The second session of the twenty-fourth congress commenced on the 5th of December, 1836, and terminated on the 3d of March, 1837. But few acts of general interest were passed; among them were an act to admit the state of Michigan into the union; and acts making appropriations for harbors, rivers, roads, and lighthouses. Mr. King was continued as president of the senate *pro tem.* The most exciting subject of the session was the passage, by the senate, after a warm debate, of a resolution, on the 16th of January, offered by Mr. Benton, to expunge from the records (by drawing black lines around it) the resolution offered by Mr. Clay, and adopted on the 28th of March, 1834, viz:

> *"Resolved, That the president, in the late executive proceedings in relation to the public revenue, has assumed upon himself authority and power not conferred by the constitution and laws, but in derogation of both."*

The expunging resolution which was now adopted by a vote of 24 to 19, and immediately carried into effect, by the secretary of the senate, was offered by Mr. Benton at a previous session, but was not pressed to a decision until an administration majority was secured in the senate.

In consequence of the dissatisfaction felt in the country with the operation of the specie circular of the treasury department, before mentioned, a bill passed both houses at this session, designating and limiting the funds receivable for the revenues of the United States. This bill, which provided for the reception of the notes of specie-paying banks, in certain cases, was warmly debated, and particularly opposed by Mr. Benton. The president prevented it from becoming a law, by retaining it in his hands after the adjournment of congress, and this informal veto formed the last act of his administration. His reasons for so doing were set forth in a letter published in the Globe, after he retired from the executive chair.

Having issued to his countrymen the farewell address which is to be considered as imbodying his political views and principles, General Jackson remained at Washington, to witness the inauguration of his chosen friend and successor, into whose hands he cheerfully committed the reins of government, and immediately went into retirement, at the hermitage, in Tennessee.

Thus terminated the administration of Andrew Jackson; of which it may be remarked, that the space it occupies in our history is one which must always be considered an eventful era, characterized by scenes of continued agitation and excitement of the public mind. At no period since the formation of our government, have the principles of free institutions and particularly our constitution, as well as important measures bearing on the interests of the people, been discussed with more ardor and ability.

The seven presidents of the United States whose lives and administrations we have noticed in the preceding pages, it will have been observed, were all descended from emigrants from the Brittish Isles; their official terms occupy a space of forty-eight years, or nearly half a century from the adoption of the constitution; and each of them had witnessed the period when the nation acpuired her independence.

The ancestors of Mr. Van Buren, both paternal and maternal, were among the early emigrants from Holland to the colony of New Netherlands, now the state of New-York. The family have always resided in the ancient town of Kinderhook, Columbia county, on the east bank of the Hudson river. The father of the president, Abraham Van Buren, was a farmer of moderate circumstances, who is represented to have been an upright and intelligent man, of strong common sense, and pacific disposition. The maiden name of the mother of the president was Hoes, also of Dutch descent. The name was originally Goes, and was one of some distinction in the history of the Netherlands. She was twice married; first Mr. Van Alen, by whom she had two sons and a daughter, all of whom have been many years deceased. James I. Van Alen was a respectable lawyer of Columbia county, who was honored with several important offices, and with whom his younger half-brother, was connected in business at his entrance to the bar.

Martin Van Buren is the eldest son of these parents. He was born at Kinderhook, December 5, 1782. At an early age, he exhibited indications of a superior understanding. His opportunities of instruction were limited, probably on account of the moderate property of his father, who had two other sons, and two daughters.

After acquiring the rudiments of an English education, he became a student in his native village. He there made considerable progress in the various branches of English literature, and gained some knowledge of Latin. It may be inferred, however, that all these acquisitions were not great in amount, as he left the academy when about 14 years of age, to begin the study of his profession.

At that age he evinced a strong passion for extempore speaking, and literary composition. Even at that early age, too, he is represented, by those who knew him, to have had a spirit of observation, with regard to public events, and the personal disposition and characters of those around him, which gave an earnest of his future proficiency in the science of politics and of the human heart.

In the years 1796, at the age of fourteen, Mr. Van Buren commenced the study of the law, in the office of Francis Sylvester, Esq., a respectable lawyer of Kinderhook. His father was a firm whig in the revolution, and a democrat in the days of John Adams; and the son was educated in the same principles, and of course formed his most intimate connection with persons of the same political faith. The democratic party was then a small minority in the town and county of his nativity. His political opinions, as well as his talents, led to his employment by the members of his own party, in their controversies with regard to personal rights and rights of property.

In 1836 Martin Van Buren was nominated as the Democratic candidate for president, and William Henry Harrison as the whig candidate.

The result of the vote of the electoral college in 1837, was as follows :

	Martin Van Buren,	William H. Harrison,	Daniel Webster,	Hugh L. White,	Willie P. Mangum,
Maine, - - - - - -	10				
New-Hampshire, - - -	7				
Vermont, - - - - -		7			
Massachusetts, - - -			14		
Rhode-Island, - - - -	4				
Connecticut, - - -	8				
New-York, - - -	42				
New-Jersey, - - - -		8			
Pennsylvania, - - - -	30				
Delaware, - - - -		3			
Maryland, - - - - -		10			
Virginia, - - - -	23				
North-Carolina, - - - -	15				
South-Carolina, - - -					11
Georgia, - - - - -				11	
Alabama, - - - -	7				
Mississippi, - - - -	4				
Louisiana, - - - -	5				
Tennessee, - - - -				15	
Kentucky, - - - -		15			
Ohio, - - - - - -		21			
Indiana, - - - -		9			
Illinois, - - - - -	5				
Missouri, - - - -	4				
Arkansas, - - - -	3				
Michigan, - - - - - -	3				
	170	73	14	26	11

The inauguration of Mr. Van Buren, the eighth president of the United States, took place at the capitol, in the city of Washington, on Saturday, the fourth of March, 1837. At twelve o'clock on that day, the weather being remarkably pleasant, the president elect took his seat with his venerable predecessor, General Jackson, in a beautiful phæton made from the wood of the frigate Constitution, and presented to General Jackson by the democracy of the city of New-York. They were escorted from the president's house to the capitol, through Pennsylvania avenue, by a body of cavalry and infantry, and were also accompanied by an immense concourse of citizens. After reaching the senate chamber the procession was formed, and Mr. Van Buren, attended by the ex-president, the members of the senate, of the cabinet, and the diplomatic corps, led the way to the rostrum erected on the ascent to the eastern portico. He then delivered his inaugural address, in clear and impressive tones, and in an easy and eloquent manner. At the close of the address, the oath of office was administered by Chief-Justice Taney.

The language of the inaugural address, the assurances of the government official journal, published at the seat of government, and other declarations, satisfied the people that the measures of Mr. Van Buren's administration would be a continuation of those adopted by General Jackson, and consequently no change might be expected. The new president selected for his cabinet, John Forsyth, of Georgia, for secretary of state; Levi Woodbury, of New-Hampshire, secretary of the treasury; Joel R. Poinsett, of South-Carolina, Secretary of war; Mahlon Dickerson, of New-Jersey, secrctary of the navy; Amos Kendall, of Kentucky, post-master-general; and Benjamin F. Butler, of New-York, attorney-general. All of these gentlemen, except Mr. Poinsett, had been appointed by General Jackson to the respective offices named, and they were continued by Mr. Van Buren. Mr. Poinsett succeeded General Cass, who, in 1836, was appointed by General Jackson minister to France.

Early in the year 1837, indications were perceived of a money pressure of unexampled severity, not produced as that of 1834 had been, by the contest with the bank of the United States (for that institution was not only a state bank, and so much embarrassed as to be powerless,) but other and more formidable causes. It was some time before those unacquainted with banking operations could be induced to believe the alarm of the bankers in New-York and othe cities to be so well founded as experience proved it really was. It was not until the failure of several great commercial and banking houses in New-York, New-Orleans, and other Atlantic cities, that the panic became general among the people,

The specie circular issued by General Jackson in the summer of 1836, which we have noticed in our account of his administration, had been powerful in its operation on the banks and currency. This circular or order, requiring all payments for the public lands to be made in gold or silver, produced frequent and sometimes large drafts for specie on the banks. This course not only prevented the banks from extending their line of discount but compelled them to commence calling in their circulating notes.

The distribution of the surplus funds among the several states also seriously embarrassed the operations of the banks, and for the mode in which it was managed, contributed to derange the currency. The banks with whom the accumulated surplus had been deposited, were not prepared for the distribution, inasmuch as they had presumed these funds would generally remain in deposite with them until the exigencies of the government should require its expenditure, and had, therefore, treated the funds of the United States as so much capital on which they could make loans to their customers. They had, therefore, undoubtedly, made large loans, relying on these government funds as an addition to their ordinary means, not likely soon to be called for.

The order issued from the treasury department in pursuance of the law for the distribution of these funds among the several states, were to the banks extremely embarrassing, and compelled them to call in their loans. They complain-d that the mode of distribution adopted by the secretary, Mr. Woodbury, was unwise and unnecessarily oppressive.

Another cause of pecuniary embarrassment and pressure was the excessive importation of merchandise from Europe, beyond the abilities and wants of the country, payments for which falling due, and American credit being impaired in London, occasioned a demand on the banks for specie to be shipped to Europe.

The reaction in speculation had now commenced, and this accumulation of difficulties could not be withstood by the banks. On the 10th of May, 1837, all the banks in the city of New-York, without exception, by common consent, suspended payments in specie. The banks of Boston, Providence, Hartford, Albany, Philadelphia and Baltimore, and others in every quarter, on learning that the banks in New-York had suspended specie payments did the same. On the 16th of May, the legislature of New-York passed an act authorizing the suspension of specie payments by the banks of that state for one year.

During the preceding two months, unprecedented embarrassments and difficulties were experienced among the mercantile classes, and were felt in all commercial towns in the United States; especially in New-York and New-Orleans. The number of large failures which took place in New-York in a short time, was about three hundred, their liabilities amounting to many millions. In two days, houses in New-Orleans stopped payment, owing an aggregate of twenty-seven millions of dollars. In Boston one hundred and sixty-eight failures took place in six months.

A committee was appointed by a numerous meeting of the citizens of New-York, to proceed to Washington and request the president of the United States to rescind the specie circular, to defer commencing suits upon unpaid bonds, and to call an extra meeting of Congress. In their interview with the president they presented an address stating, that "under a deep impression of the propriety of confining their declarations within moderate limits, they affirmed, that the value of their real estate had, within the last six months, depreciated more than forty millions of dollars; that within the preceding two months there had been more than two hundred and fifty failures of houses engaged in extensive business; that within the same period a decline of twenty millions had occurred in their local stocks, including those railroad and canal incorporations which, though chartered in other states, depended chiefly upon New-York, for their sale; that the immense amount of merchandise in their warehouses had, within the same period, fallen in value, at least thirty per cent.; that within a few weeks not less than twenty thousand individuals, depending upon their daily labor for their daily bread, had been discharged by their employers, because the means of retaining them were exhausted; and that a complete blight had fallen upon a community heretofore so active, enterprising and prosperous: "the errors of our rulers," they declared, "had produced a wider desolation than the pestilence which depopulated our streets, or the conflagration which had laid them in ashes."

Several petitions from other commercial cities and towns, had been presented to the president, requesting that he would summon a meeting of Congress at an early day. The president for some time declined to act on the petitions, but the suspension of specie payments by the banks, and the consequent exigency in which the financial affairs of the government was placed, finally induced him to issue his proclamation, on the 15th of May, for the convening of Congress on the first Monday in September, on account of "great and weighty matters, claiming their consideration."

Previous to the suspension of specie payments by the banks, some of the friends of the president entertained a hope that he would afford some relief to the business community, by revoking the "specie circular" of the treasury department, which had been issued by order of General Jackson in 1836, requiring gold and silver in payment for the public lands; but in this hope they were disappointed, and it was soon evident that it was the intention of president Van Buren to carry out the designs of his predecessor in establishing a specie currency, especially in all concerns relating to the finances of the general government. According to the report of the secretary of the treasury, in December 1836, the condition of the currency of the United States was estimated as follows at that period; bank paper in active circulation, one hundred and twenty millions of dollars; specie in active circulation, twenty-eight millions; specie in banks, forty-five millions.

The extra session, being the first, of the twenty-fifth Congress, commenced on the 4th of September, 1837, and continued forty-three days, namely, until the 16th of October. The state of parties in the house of representatives was exhibited in the choice of speaker. James K. Polk, the administration candidate, was for the third time elected to that station, receiving 116 votes, against 103 for John Bell, (whig,) and 5 scattering. It became evident, however, that there was in the administration ranks a small section, whose views respecting the currency did not coincide with those of the president, but were favorable to banking institutions and the preservation of the credit system, as applied to the transactions of the business community. Hence arose a third party, which exercised considerable influence in many parts of the union, and adopting the name of "conservatives," eventually became an ally of the whigs, in their opposition to the administration. In consequence of the course of these conservatives, some of the measures recommended by the president were defeated in the house of representatives at this and the following session.

The recommendations of the president in his message to congress at the extra session, promised no relief to the people. Indeed, the opinion that document distinctly expressed was, that the national legislature could do nothing to mitigate the evils which existed, and which, it stated, were occasioned by the unwise conduct of the business community; that it was not the duty or design of the general government to interfere in such cases. The doctrine was advanced in the message, that all the government could do or was designed to do, was to take care of itself, and could not be expected to legislate with reference to the monetary concerns of the people. The actual condition of the government, in relation to its financial concerns, was stated with great clearness and precision, and the reasons were given which rendered the call of the extra session absolutely necessary.

The most important recommendation of the message, was the measure which received from its opponents the name of the sub-treasury scheme. By the friends of the administration it was called the independent treasury. As the funds of the government were in the possession of banks, all of which refused to pay specie, and the use of their circulating notes was a violation of the act, or resolution of congress, passed in 1816 ; and the president having been elected under a pledge against a national bank, he recommended that the treasury of the United States, should be kept by public officers, and that there should be an entire and total separation of the business and funds of the government from those of the banks.

The announcement of this scheme by the administration, caused great excitement in congress and among the people. It was very unfavorably received by the political friends of the president, in the different states, who were interested in banks. It was represented by the opposition as a direct attack upon the banks and what was called the credit system. They insisted, that if the president's views were carried out, the prostration and destruction of all banks would be inevitable, and that finally a metalic currency would alone constitute the circulating medium, which would be wholly inadequate to the exigencies of the commercial community. Another consequence which they predicted, assuming that the banks were to be destroyed, was a reduction of prices, fatal and ruinous to the debtor.

The official paper at the seat of government, the Globe, having been zealous and active in support of the new treasury scheme and in opposition to the banking system, the conservatives in the house of representatives opposed the election of the publishers of that paper (Messrs. Blair and Rives) as printers to the house. After several ballotings, the whigs joined the conservatives, and elected Thomas Allen, editor of the Madisonian, a conservative newspaper, printer to the house.

A bill to establish the proposed independent treasury was reported by Mr. Wright, chairman of the committee on finance, in the senate, and, after considerable discussion, passed that body by a vote of 26 ayes, to 20 noes. In opposing the measure, Mr. Clay, said that, "the project was neither desirable nor practicable, nor within the constitutional power of the general government, nor just; and that it was contrary to the habits of the people of the United States and dangerous to their liberties. He declared, that after the most deliberate and anxious consideration of which he was capable, he could conceive of no adequate remedy for the disorders which unhappily prevailed, which did not comprehend a national bank as an essential part. The great want of the country was a general and uniform currency, and a point of union, a sentinel, a regulator of the issues of the local banks; and that would be supplied by such an institution." No effort, however, was made at this time to introduce the question of a national bank, in congress, in consequence of the well known feelings of the president and his party against it.

The sub-treasury bill from the senate was teken up in the house of representatives but after an excited debate it was laid on the table, by the combined vote of whigs and conservatives, ayes 120, noes 107. It was thus evident that the administration were in the minority on their favorite measure, in the popular branch of congress. Having passed a bill postponing until January 1, 1839, the deposite with the states, of the fourth instalment of the surplus funds directed to be made with them; acts authorizing the issue of ten millions of dollars in treasury notes, for the immediate wants of government: appropriating $1,600,000 for the suppression of Indian hostilities in Florida; extending the time of bonds for duties on imports; and providing for adjusting claims upon the late deposite banks, with a few acts of minor importance.

The second session of the twenty-fifth congress commencnd on the 4th of December, 1837, and continued until the 9th of July, 1838.

The independent, or sub-treasury scheme was again pressed upon the consideration of congress, by the president, and a bill for that purpose, similar to that proposed at the extra session, being reported in the senate, the subject underwent an elaborate discussion in that body. The bill was ably sustained by senators Wright and Benton, and opposed also with ability by Mr. Clay, Mr. Webster, and other whig senators. Mr. Clay's speech was of great length, and he endeavored to establish the following proposition: "First, that it was the deliberate purpose and fixed design of the administration of General Jackson to establish a government bank—a treasury bank—to be administered and controlled by the executive department. Secondly, that, with that view, and to that end, it was its aims and intention to overthrow the whole banking system, as existing in the United States when that administration came into power, beginning with the bank of the United States, and ending with the state banks. Thirdly, that the attack was first confined, from considerations of policy, to the bank of the United States; but that after its overthrow was accomplished, it was then directed, and has since been continued, against the state banks. Fourthly, that the present administration, by its acknowledgment, emanating from the highest and most authentic source, has succeeded to the principles, plans, and policy of the preceeding administration, and stands solemnly pledged to complete and perfect them. And fifthly, that the bill under consideration (the sub-treasury plan) was intended to execute the pledge, by establishing, upon the ruins of the late bank of the United States, and the state banks, a government bank, to be managed and controlled by the treasury department, acting under the commands of the president of the U. S."

Among those who supported the sub-treasury bill in the senate, was Mr. Calhoun, of South-Carolina, who, with the South-Carolina members in the house of representatives, now sustained the administration. Mr. Preston, the senatorial colleague of Mr. Calhoun, acted with the opposition.

The sub-treasury bill passed the senate, but was rejected in the house of representatives on the 25th of June, 1838, by 125 to 111 votes. This plan of finance was proposed originally in congress in 1834, by Mr. Gordon, of Virginia, but was then opposed by the friends of the administration and rejected. A bill was passed at this session granting pre-emption rights to settlers on the public lands. Other important acts passed, were the following: to establish the territory of Iowa; granting land for opening a canal in the territory of Wisconsin; to encourage the introduction and promote the cultivation of tropical fruits in the United States; making appropriations for lightboats and beacons, and making surveys; authorizing the printing of the Madison papers; to provide for certain harbors, and the improvement of navigation of certain rivers in Florida; making an appropriation for the Cumberland road; appropriating money also for suppressing Indian hostilities and for fortifications.

Mr. Preston, whig senator from South-Carolina, introduced, in the senate, resolutions in favor of the annexation of Texas to the United States, but they did not receive favorable action at this time. The independence of that republic had been recognised by the United States in the last year of General Jackson's administration.

In June, 1838, Mr. Dickerson resigned the office of secretary of the navy, and James K. Paulding, of New-York., was appointed in his place.

During this year serious disturbances against the colonial government occurred in Canada, and many of the citizens of the United States, on the northern frontiers prepared to join them. President Van Buren, therefore, issued a proclamation, calling upon all the persons engaged in the scheme of invasion of Canada, to abandon the design, and warning all those who had engaged in these criminal enterprises, if persisted in, "to whatever condition they may be reduced, they must not expect the interference of the United States government, in any form, on their behalf, but would be left, reproached by every virtuous fellow-citizen, to be dealt with according to the policy and justice of that government whose dominions they have, in defiance of the known wishes and efforts of their own government, and without the shadow of justification, or excuse, nefariously invaded."

Although there were many individuals largely interested in banks, who continued in good faith to support the democratic party, and the administration of Mr. Van Buren, yet it was generally believed that the great mass of the banking interest was brought to bear against the administration. The state banks, in many instances, had sustained, with all their influence, General Jackson, in his veto of the United States bank bill, and in the transfer which he made of the deposites from the national to the state banks; but when president Van Buren recommended the removal of the deposites from the state banks, and the establishment of the independent treasury, it was quite another matter.

The agitation of the currency question, and a combination of causes adverse to the administration, resulted in a great political change at the elections in the important state of New-York, in 1837 and 1838. The influence of these elections in the native state of the president, which had previously sustained him by large majorities, could not fail to act upon other states; and it was soon evident, nothwithstanding partial successes of the democratic party in some of the states, that the administration was gradually declining in popularity.

The twenty-fifth congress held its third session from December 1838, to the expiration of its term, on the 3d of March, 1839. But few acts of general interest were passed. Among them may be named an act for preventing and suppressing Indian hostilities; this law related particularly to the difficulties with the Seminole tribe in Florida. The war with these Indians was continued during several years, and large sums were expended in maintaining it. In 1836, one million and a half of dollars were appropriated to prosecute that unfortunate contest. In January, 1837, two millions more were voted by congress for the same purpose. These appropriations were made before the retirement of General Jackson. At the extra session, in October, in 1837, and in the two succeeding sessions, large amounts were again appropriated. When the difficulty arose with the Seminoles, president Jackson supposed that it would soon be terminated; and no oue, at that time, had any reason to suppose that it would continue for years and have cost the government eight millions.

Another act was passed at this session, locating and providing for the Seminole Indians, who had been removed from Florida; another abolishing imprisonment for debt in certain cases. The aspect of our relations with Great Britain was at this time threatening, in consequence of the difficulty respecting the northeast boundary. Congress, therefore, passed an act giving to the president additional powers for the defence of the United States.

During the summer of 1839, president Van Buren visited

the state of New-York, for the first time since his election. He traveled through the state, stopping at the principal cities and villages. He was received with public honors, and followed by processions of citizens, civil and military. In an address made to him by Mr. Edmonds, formerly a state senator, upon his arrival at New-York, he made some remarks which rendered it necessary for Mr. Van Buren to speak of political parties and his political friends, and of course to express his strong attachment to those friends. This gave occasion to the opposition to represent, that instead of coming on a visit to the whole people, as a president of the United States ought to do, he was on an electioneering tour, for the sole purpose of stimulating his friends to more active exertions, and of recruiting their dilapidated ranks by proselytes whom he was to gain from his political opponents. Hence everything he did, and every word he uttered, was the subject of the most critical and jealous scrutiny.

In the election of members of the twenty-sixth congress, there had been a considerable gain for the whigs and conservatives, and, until the fall of 1839, it appeared probable that there would be an opposition majority in the house of representatives. But the friends of the administration made a desperate rally in a few of the last states which chose representatives to the twenty-sixth congress, and succeeded in returning a small majority of the members elect, leaving out of view five of the six representatives from the state of New-Jersey, whose seats were contested. The full returns of members elected to the house of representatives were reported to stand thus: administration 119, opposition 118, and five members from New-Jersey claimed by both parties, the certificates of election being given to the whig candidates and their seats contested by the administration candidates. In this situation of affairs, intense interest was felt throughout the country, with regard to the meeting of congress.

The twenty-sixth congress met on the 2d of December, 1839. Every member elect of the house of representatives was present except Mr. Kempshall (whig) from Monroe county, New-York, who was detained by sickness in his family. On the assembling of the house, the clerk of the last house, Mr. Garland, a friend of the administration, agreeably to the usual custom, commenced calling the roll; and having called the members from the several New-England states and the state of New-York, and one of the six members from New-Jersey, who all brought the regular certificates, proposed to pass by the other five (whose rights to seats would be contested) till the members from the rest of the states should be called. This brought on a long, animated and disorderly debate. Scenes of excitement and confusion continued until the 5th, when Mr. John Quincy Adams, of Massachusetts, addressed the members, and called upon them to organize, by choosing a chairman *pro tem.* Thereupon Mr. Rhett, of South-Carolina, nominated Lewis Williams, of North-Carolina, as chairman: he declined; when Mr. Rhett nominated John Quincy Adams, who was immediately chosen chairman *pro tem.*, and entered upon the duties of the same. The debate respecting the contested seats from New-Jersey was continued from day to day, till, on the 6th of December, Robert M. T. Hunter, of Virginia, an opposition member (but in favor of the sub-treasury,) was elected speaker on the 11th ballot. He received 119 votes, to 113 for all others. On the 17th, the members of the house of representatives were sworn, with the exception of the five disputed members from New-Jersey. The whigs having the certificates of election, under the broad seal of the governor, now came forward and demanded, as their right, to be sworn, which gave rise to a new and animated debate, and on the 20th the following resolution was decided in the negative, by a vote of 112 to 116: "*Resolved,* That the representatives of the twenty-sixth congress, now present, do advise and request the speaker to administer the oath required by the law, to the five gentlemen from the state of New-Jersey who have presented credentials to the speaker and demand to be sworn." On the 21st the house completed its organization, by the election of a clerk; and on the 24th the president's message was delivered, just three weeks after the regular time.

A national convention of the whig party was held at Harrisburg, Pennsylvania, on the 4th of December, 1839, for the purpose of nominating candidates for president and vice-president of the United States. Great difference of opinion prevailed among the whigs, with respect to a suitable candidate for president, regard being especially had to the importance of nominating one upon whom the different elements of which the opposition to the administration was composed, could unite with the cordiality and zeal required to be effectual.

It was the expectation of a large proportion of the whig party, especially of those who had been originally opposed to the administration of General Jackson, that Henry Clay of Kentucky, would receive the nomination of the national convention at Harrisburg, as the oppostion candidate for president. Some time before the assembling of that convention, it had been proclaimed that a clear majority of the whole number of delegates had been chosen as friendly to the nomination of Mr. Clay. Yet during the autumn of the year 1839, notwithstanding the unpopularity of the administration, the whig party met with defeats in the elections in Tennessee, Georgia, Maryland, Ohio, Indiana, Massachusetts, Pennsylvania and Maine. In New-Jersey they held the legislature, with a strong majority against them in the popular vote. In New-York the whig majority in the state was obout 4,000 on the vote for senators, against 10,000 in 1838, and 15,000 in 1837. In North-Carolina the whig triumph was not of a decisive character. These results showed that the opposition were losing in 1839 the advantages they had gained in 1837 and 1828, and this cast a shadow over the spirits of the reflecting friends of Mr. Clay.

Under these circumstances, many of those friends began to doubt the expediency of placing him in nomination in opposition to Mr. Van Buren, porticulariy when it was known that the friends of the administration were desirous that Mr. Clay should be the opposition candidate. In that case, inasmuch as they believed that gentleman could not concentrate the opposition vote in his favor, they anticipated an easy victory for the democratic party at the approaching election.

Mr. Clay himself seemed to acquiesce in the doubts expressed by some of his friends, as to his own comparative strength with the whig party. In the summer of 1839, he made a visit for health and recreation, to the country on the lakes, Canada and the state of New-York. At the city of Buffalo, he yielded to the request of his friends, to address the people on the state of public affairs. Alluding to the approaching nomination and election of president, he said: "To correct past evils and avert impending dangers, we see no effectual remedy, but in a change of our rulers. The opposition constitutes the majority—unquestionably the majority—of the nation. A great responsibility, therefore, attaches to it. If defeated, it will be by its own divisions, and not by the merits of the principles of its opponents. These divisions are at the same time our weakness and their strength.

"Are we not, then, called upon, by the highest duties to our country, to its free institutions, to posterity, and to the world, to rise above all local prejudices, and personal partialities, to discard all collateral questions, to disregard every subordinate point, and in a genuine spirit of compromise and concession, uniting heart and hand, to preserve for ourselves the blessings of a free government, wisely, honestly, and faithfully administered, and as we received them from our fathers, to transmit to our children? Should we not justly subject ourselves to eternal reproach if we permit our differences about mere men to bring defeat and disaster upon our cause? Our principles are imperishable, but men have but a fleeting existence, and are themselves liable to change and corruption during its brief continuance.

"If my name creates any obstacle to union and harmony, away with it, and concentrate upon some individual more acceptable to all branches of the opposition. What is a public man worth, who is not ready to sacrifice himself for the good of his country? I have unaffectedly desired retirement, I yet desire it, when, consistently with the duties and obligations which I owe, I can honorably retire."

In the ranks of the opposition to the administration were many who had formerly supported the election of General Jackson, and still retained a prejudice against Mr. Clay; there were also in the same ranks, large numbers of anti-masons who were unwilling to support a mason for the presidency, and Mr. Clay had been a member of the lodge, then came the anti-tariff whigs in the southern states, and the squatters on the public lands, at the west; with both of which classes Mr. Clay was unpopular, from the measures advocated by him in congress, being adverse to their views and feelings. In view of these circumstances and believing that to command success the whig candidate for the presidency must receive the united support of the different branches of the opposition, many of the leading whigs exerted themselves to prevent the nomination of Mr. Clay. It was even charged by those friends who were anxious for his nomination, that intriguers were busy, before the meeting of the convention, by correspondence and otherwise, in circulating false reports with regard to Mr. Clay's unpopularity, and thus influencing the election of delegates and their action in convention.

On the meeting of the convention at Harrisburg, three names were presented as candidates for the nomination of a president of the United States, namely, Henry Clay, of Kentucky, Gen. William Henry Harrison, of Ohio, and General Winfield Scott of the United States Army; all three of whom were natives of Virginia. Twenty-two states were represented in the convention, and on an informal ballot *per capita*, it was found that Mr. Clay had a decided plurality, but neither of the candidates had a clear majority of the delegates. It was then determined to vote by states, each state to be entitled to as many votes as it had electoral votes. On the first ballot, 103 votes were given to Clay, 94 to Harrison, and 57 to Scott; after which each delegation compared views, and endeavored to ascertain which of the three candidates had the best prospects of success, if nominated. The result of their inquiries was a decided preponderance of chances in favor of General Harrison, and after being in session three days, the convention took a final ballot, when, Harrison received 148 votes, Clay 90, and Scott 16. William Henry Harrison was therefore declared duly nominated as the whig candidate for president. John Tyler of Virginia, was unanimously nominated for vice-president. Mr. Tyler had been a candidate for the same office in 1836; was now a member of the convention, and had been anxious for the nomination of Mr. Clay.

Those friends of Mr. Clay in the convention who adhered to him as the best candidate, expressed their cordial concurrence in the decision in favor of General Harrison. A letter from Mr. Clay to one of the delegates was read, in which he remarked, that "if the deliberation of the convention should lead them to the choice of another, as the candidate of the opposition, far from feeling any discontent, the nomination would have his best wishes and receive his cordial support."

The example of Mr. Clay was followed throughout the Union, notwithstanding the first feelings of disappointment, with which the decision of the convention was received by many. The nomination of Harrison and Tyler was everywhere popular, and united in its support the entire force of the opposition.

The national democratic convention, consisting of about

250 members, from twenty-one states, met at Baltimore on the 5th of May, 1840. Mr. Van Buren was unanimously nominated for president, and the convention resolved to make no nomination for vice-president, leaving each state to make its own nomination of a candidate for that office. The principal candidates nominated in the different states for vice-president, were the present incumbent, R. M. Johnson, of Kentncky, and James K. Polk of Tennessee.

The early part of the first session of congress was taken up, in the house, in discussiona respecting the contested seats of the New-Jersey members. That matter being settled, by admitting the democratic claimants to the seats, the house proceeded to the consideration of subjects submitted to them by the president. Long and able debates took place on the bill for establishing an "independent treasury," which had been twice rejected by the last congress. It was now passed, toward the close of the session, and was signed by the president on the 4th of July, 1840, when it became a law. A bankrupt law being much called for by the trading community, a bill was introduced at this session, and passed the senate, but was laid on the table in the house of representatives, 101 to 89.

But few laws of general interest were passed at this session. Appropriations for fortifications, and for the usua expenditures of government were made. An act was passed to refund to Matthew Lyon the amount with interest, paid by him as a fine for violating the sedition law.

Some changes took place in the cabinet, in addition to those already mentioned. In 1838, Benjamin F. Butler resigned as attorney-general, and Felix Grundy of Tennessee, was appointed in his place, in 1839, Mr. Grundy resigned, and Henry D. Gilpin, of Pennsylvania received the appointment in his place; Amos Kendall resigned the office of postmaster-general, and John M. Niles, of Connecticut, was appointed in his place, on the 25th of May, 1840.

The elections for state officers in the several states, during the summer and autumn of 1840, indicated the success of the whigs at the approaching presidential election. The contest of the two great parties at the latter was the most exciting and arduous ever witnessed in the United States. Electoral tickets in favor of the re-election of Mr. Van Buren were formed in every state in the Union, and the whigs also nominated electors in every state except South-Carolina.

A third party, in favor of the abolition of slavery, had also been for some time organized, and now nominated as a candidate for president, James G. Birney of Michigan.

The result of the election was the success of the whig candidates, Harrison and Tyler, by a large majority in the electoral colleges, and on the popular vote.

The second session of the 26th congress was held from the 7th of December, 1840, to the 3d of March, 1841, when their term expired. Very few acts of public interest or importance passed at this session. Appropriations were made for certain fortifications, and for Indian affairs; and an act was passed authorizing another issue of treasury notes. A bankrupt law was again discussed, but was not definitely acted upon.

The public expenditures during this administration greatly exceeded those of any preceding four years, since the war with Great Britain, exclusive of the public debt and the Florida Indian war. Public agents were multiplied, and increased compensation, in many coses, allowed them for their services. Large sums were lost to the national treasury by the defalcation of public officers, and the failure of the deposite banks.

In the fall of 1840, General William Henry Harrison was elected president of the United States, upon the whig ticket, over Martin Van Buren, who had been re-nominated by the democrats.

The following is the electoral vote upon the election of General Harrison, in 1840:

	Harrison.	*Van Buren.*
Maine, - - - -	10	
New-Hampshire, - -		7
Vermont, - - - -	7	
Massachusetts, - - -	14	
Rhode-Island, - - -	4	
Connecticut, - - -	8	
New-York, - - - -	42	
New-Jersey, - - -	8	
Pennsylvania, - - -	30	
Delaware, - - -	3	
Maryland, - - - -	10	
Virginia, - - - -		23
North-Carolina, - - -	15	
South-Carolina, - - -		11
Georgia, - - - -	11	
Alabama, - - -		7
Mississippi, - - - -	4	
Louisiana, - - -	5	
Tennessee, - - - -	15	
Kentucky, - - -	15	
Ohio, - - - -	21	
Indiana, - - - -	9	
Illinois, - - - -		5
Missouri, - - - -		4
Arkansas, - - - -		3
Michigan, - - - -	3	
	234	60

The manner in which this contest was carried on, was entirely new, and somewhat singular in many respects. The candidate of the whigs having never been placed before the people of the nation for an elective office, and therefore uncommitted upon the prominent measures then agitated by the people, he avowed no distinct principles by which he would be governed, in the event of his election, which fact annoyed the democracy of the country sorely.

The views of Mr. Van Buren were familiar to the people of all the states, in consequence, particularly, of his having been so long in political life, and then an occupant of the presidential chair. His opponents always accused Mr. Van Buren of non-committalism, which was doubtless true to some extent, but his position rendered it impossible that his views should be concealed from public view. There were those in the democratic ranks, who differed with him on the subject of a tariff—there were others who differed with him upon the subject of internal improvement—and there were still others who differed with him upon the currency question; upon the line of policy pursued by him in carrying out the sub-treasury scheme. The latter subject turned the state banking interest against him. Upon all those questions Mr Van Buren stood committed before the country, while General Harrison's were not made public, but those engaged in carrying on this singular warfare were careful to commit General Harrison, in their speeches in favor of this or that measure, according to the beatings of the public pulse in the latitude of their labors. The contest was one probably more exciting than any one which has ever bebefore or since transpired. The feeling of enmity between neighbors, even found its way to the social circles. In fact, it was an excitement which, we believe, all would deprecate to see re-enacted in this country.

Mr. Van Buren had rather leaned in favor of southern measures and southern institutions, which created a vast feeling against him at the north. He was denominated by the opposition in the northern and western states, as being the "*northern man with southern principles.*" This position before the public operated very materially against him, as upon other subjects, the views of his opponent were not laid before the public. Mr. Van Buren received but twelve electoral votes from northern states, (New-Hampshire 7, and Illinois 5,) while he received forty-eight electoral votes from southern slaveholding states, (Virginia 23—

South-Carolina 11—Alabama 7—Missouri 4—and Arkansas 3,) such was the feeling at that time upon the subject of southern institutions.

The inauguration of General Harrison as president of the United States, took place on the 4th of March, 1841. The city of Washington was thronged with people, many of whom were from the most distant part of the Union. A procession was formed, civic and military, from the quarters of the president elect to the capitol. General Harrison was mounted on a white charger, accompanied by several personal friends, and his immediate escórt were the officers and soldiers who had fought under him. The scene, as described in the National Intelligencer, was highly imposing. The ladies everywhere, from the windows on each side of the avenue waved their handherchiefs in token of their kind feelings, and General Harrison returned their smiles and greetings with repeated bows. The enthusiastic cheers of the citizens who moved in the procession were, with equal enthusiasm, responded to by thousands of citizen spectators who lined Pennsylvania avenue or appeared at the side windows, in the numerous balconies, on the tops of houses, or on other elevated stands.

At the capitol, the senate having been convened, by the late president, in extra session, assembled at the appointed hour, and was organized by the appointment of Mr. King, of Alabama, president *pro tem.;* after which Mr. Tyler, the vice-president elect, took the oath of office, and on taking his seat as presiding officer, delivered a brief and appropriate address to the senate. The judges of the supreme court, the diplomatic corps, and several distinguished officers of the army and navy, were present in the senate chamber.

At twenty minutes past twelve o'clock, General Harrison entered and took the seat prepared for him, in front of the secretary's table. He looked cheerful but composed; his bodily health was manifestly good; there was an alertness in his movement which was quite astonishing, considering his advanced age, the multiplied hardships through which his frame had passed, and the fatigues he had lately undergone. After he had retained his seat for a few minutes, preparations were made for forming the line of procession to the platform prepared for the ceremony of the inauguration, erected over the front steps of the portico of the east front of the capitol.

On the platform, seats had been provided for the president elect and the chief-justice, who were placed immediately in front. On their right, seats were assigned to the diplomatic corps. Behind sat members of both houses of congress, officers of the army and navy, and many distinguished characters from different parts of the union, intermingled with a great company of ladies who occupied, not only the steps in the rear of the platform, but both the broad abutments of stone which support the steps on either side.

But the sight which attracted and arrested and filled the eye of the observer, was the people. They stood for hours in a solid dense mass, variously estimated to contain in the space before the capitol from thirty to sixty thousand.

While patiently waiting for the arrival of the president, the mass of heads resembled some placid lake; but the instant he was seen advancing from the capitol, it suddenly resembled the same lake when a blast from the mountains has descended upon it, thrown it into tumultuous agitation, and "lifted up its hands on high." A deafening shout went up from the hearts and voices of the people. It sung welcome to the man whom the people delighted to honor, and must have met with overwhelming power, the throbbings of his own bosom.

When the uproar had subsided, it was succeeded by the deep stillness of expectation, and the new president forthwith proceeded to read, in accents loud and clear, his address to the nation. In its delivery, the voice of General Harrison never flagged, but to the end retained its full and commanding tone. As he touched on successive topics lying near the hearts of the people, their sympathy with his sentiments was manifested by shouts which broke forth involuntarily from time to time; and when the reading of the address was concluded, they were renewed and prolonged without restraint.

Previous to delivering the closing sentences of the address, the oath of office, tendered by chief-justice Taney, was taken by the president, in tones loud, distinct, and solemn, manifesting a due and deep impression of the act; after which the president pronounced the remaining passage of his address.

The cannon then announced to the country that it had a new chief magistrate. The procession was again formed; and setting out from the capitol, proceeded along Pennsylvania avenue, to the mansion of the president, cheered throughout the whole route as General Harrison passed, by the immense crowds on foot, which lined the avenue and filled the doors and windows of the buildings.

Nearly the whole throng of visitors accompanied the president to his new abode, and as many as possible entered, and paid their personal respects to him. The close of the day was marked by the repetition of salutes from the artillery, the whole city being yet alive with a population of strangers and residents, whom the mildness of the season invited into the open air.

In the evening, the several ball-rooms and places of amusement were crowded with gentlemen and ladies attracted to Washington city by the novelty and interest of the occasion. In the course of the evening the president paid a short visit to each of the assemblies held in honor of the inauguration, and was received with the warmest demonstrations of attachment and respect.

The president immediately nominated to the senate the members of his cabinet, as follows: Daniel Webster, of Massachusetts, secretary of state; Thomas Ewing, of Ohio, secretary of the treasury; John Bell, of Tennessee, secretary of war; George E. Badger, of North-Carolina, secretary of the navy; Francis Granger, of New-York, postmaster-general; John J. Crittenden, of Kentucky, attorney-general. These nominations were all confirmed by the senate. That body also confirmed a number of other nominations by the president, chiefly to fill vacancies; and after electing a sergeant-at-arms, and dismissing Messrs. Blair and Rives as printers to the senate, also having elected Samuel L. Southard, of New-Jersey, president *pro tem.*, the senate adjourned on the 15th of March.

The members of the diplomatic body, or foreign ministers in Washington accredited to the government of the United States, waited on the president on the 9th of March, and through Mr. Fox, the British minister, being presented by the secretary of state, made to him an appropriate address, congratulating him upon his accession to the presidency. To this address the president of the United States, made the following reply:—

"Sir: I receive with great pleasure the congratulations you have been pleased to offer me, in the name of the distinguished diplomatic body now present, the representatives of the most powerful and polished nations with whom the republic which has honored me with the office of its chief magistrate, has the most intimate relations—relations which I trust no sinister event, will, for ages, interrupt.

"The sentiments contained in my late address to my fellow-citizens, and to which you have been pleased to advert, are those which will continue to govern my conduct through the whole of my administration. Lately one of the people, the undisputed sovereign of the country, and coming immediately from among them, I am enabled, with confidence to say, that in thus acting, I shall be sustained by their undivided approbation.

"I beg leave to add, sir, that both from duty and inclination, I shall omit nothing in my power to contribute to your own personal happiness and that of the friends, whom, on this occasion, you represent, as long as you may continue among us."

The other ministers, with their secretaries, and the persons attached to their respective missions, were then successively presented to the president. The Russian minister was prevented from being present by indisposition; but on the 12th of March he was presented to the president, by the secretary of state, and to his address on the occasion, the president replied as follows:

"I receive, sir, the congratulations which you offer me in your capacity of envoy extraordinary and minister plenipotentiary of the emperor of all the Russias, upon my election to the presidency of the United States with great pleasure.

"From the epoch which introduced the United States to the world as an independent nation, the most amicable relations have existed between them and the powerful and distinguished monarchs who have successively swayed the sceptre of Russia. The presidents, my predecessors, acting in behalf and under the authority of the people, their constituents, have never failed to use every proper occasion to confirm and strengthen the friendship so auspiciously commenced, and which a mutuality of interests, render so desirable to be continued. I assure you, sir, that none of them felt the obligations of this duty more powerfully than I do; and you cannot in language too strong communicate to your august monarch my sentiments on this subject. And permit me to add, that no more acceptable medium of communicating them could have been offered than that of a personage who has rendered himself so acceptable, as well to the people as to the government of the United States."

From the moment General Harrison was elected president, his heart was filled with gratitude to the people, to whom indeed he had always been devoted. Anxious to fulfil the wishes of his political friends, he received with kindness and attention the numerous applicants for office who thronged the seat of government; and although he would doubtless have been better pleased to have deferred many appointments for a time, yet a considerable number of removals were made by him; and appointments made, in compliance with the views of the cabinet, during the month of March. In the generosity of his heart, he invariably opened the doors of the president's mansion wide to the reception of his friends, and that house was the abode of hospitality and kindness. He indulged his friends to his own destruction. From sunrise till midnight, he indulgently devoted himself to his fellow-citizens who visited him, with the exception of an hour each day spent in cabinet council. It was his habit, after rising, first to peruse his bible, and then to take a walk before breakfast. And afterward, the whole day would be spent in receiving company and transacting business.

On Saturday, March 27, president Harrison, after several day's previous indisposition from the effects of a cold, was seized with a chill and other symptoms of fever. These were followed by pneumonia, or bilious pleurisy, which ultimately baffled all medical skill, and terminated his virtuous, useful, and illustrious life, on Sunday morning, the 4th of April, after an illness of eight days, being a little over 68 years of age.

The last time the president spoke, was at nine o'clock on Saturday night, a little more than three hours before he expired. While Doctor Worthington and one or two other attendants were standing over him, having just administered something to his comfort, he cleared his throat, as if desiring to speak audibly, and, as though he fancied himself addressing his successor, or some official associate in the government, said:—"SIR, I WISH YOU TO UNDERSTAND THE PRINCIPLES OF THE GOVERNMENT. I WISH THEM CARRIED OUT. I ASK NOTHING MORE."

He expired a little after midnight, surrounded by those members of his family who were in the city, the members of his cabinet and many personal friends, among whom were Colonels Chambers and Todd, who were the aids of General Harrison at the battle of the Thames, in 1813. The connexions of the president who were present in the executive mansion at the time of his decease, were the following:—Mrs. William Harrison (son's widow); Mrs. Taylor, of Richmond (niece); Mr. D. O. Coupeland (nephew); Henry Harrison, of Virginia (grand nephew), and Findlay Harrison, of Ohio (grandson).

General Harrison left one son and three daughters, all living at or near North-Bend, Ohio. Four sons and a daughter died before their father. All of the sons left children.

In person, General Harrison was tall and slender. Although he never had the appearance of possessing a robust constitution, yet such had been the effects of habitual activity and temperance, that few men at his age enjoyed so much bodily vigor. He had a fine dark eye, remarkable for its keenness, fire, and intelligence, and his face was strongly expressive of the vivacity of his mind, and the benevolence of his character.

The most remarkable traits of General Harrison's character, and those by which he was distinguished throughout his whole career, were his disinterestedness, his regard for the rights and comforts of others, his generous disposition, his mild and forbearing temper, and his plain, easy, and unostentatious manner.

After the death of General Harrison, the cabinet, consisting of Daniel Webster, Thomas Ewing, John Bell, John J. Crittenden, and Francis Granger addressed a letter to John Tyler, informing him of the fact, when the latter left immediately for Washington, where he arrived on the morning of the 6th April, on which day he took the usual oath of office as the acting president, and on the next day attended the funeral of the deceased president elect.

The cabinet appointed by General Harrison was retained by John Tyler.

In entering upon the duties of the office of president, Mr. Tyler did not feel (to use his own words, in his message to congress) that it would be becoming in him to disturb what had been ordered by his lamented predecessor. He therefore concurred in the measure which had been adopted by president Harrison, of convening congress in extra session on the 31st of May. "His own first wish," he stated, "in the circumstances in which he was so unexpectedly placed, would have been, to have called to his aid, in the administration of public affairs, the combined wisdom of the two houses of congress, in order to take their counsel and advise as to the best mode of extricating the government and the country from the embarrassments weighing heavily on both."

After the call of the extra session, and previous to the meeting, members of congress were elected in the states of Connecticut, Rhode-Island, Maryland, Virginia, North-Carolina, Alabama, Kentucky, Tennessee, Indiana, Illinois and Missouri. The state of Mississippi was not represented at the extra session, as no special election was ordered, and the annual election in that state took place in the month of November following. The members from Illinois were elected at the annual election in August, and took their seats in the house during the session.

The result of the elections at this time were equally favorable to the whig party with those which took place in 1840, immediately preceding the presidential election. The majority in favor of the new administration in the 27th congress, according to the returns of members elect, was seven in the senate, and one vacancy; and about fifty in the house of representatives.

The hopes of the democratic incumbents in office which were awakened on the accession of Mr. Tyler to the presidency, were soon dissipated by the course he felt bound to pursue with regard to removals and appointments. The applications and importunities of office-seekers, which had commenced immediately after the inauguration of president Harrison, and which were temporarily suspended by his death, were renewed with increased vigor after his successor was invested with the power and patronage of the executive. A few days only had transpired after his accession, when the removal of the friends of the late administration from office was commenced by the new president; and their places were filled by whigs and conservatives. The removals and appointments continued to follow each other in rapid succession, and a similar course was pursued by the postmaster-general, with the sanction of the president, with respect to the numerous postmasters throughout the Union. President Tyler thus showed a disposition to gratify the desires and expectations of his political friends, with regard to office, even before the senate had an opportunity to act on the subject.

A brief review and notice of political parties in the United States, at this period, is deemed appropriate in this place, for the purpose of showing the position of the president and the new administration, with regard to measures of public policy and the course of events.

We have seen, in the sketches already given of various administrations, that the federal party which was thrown into the minority on the accession of Jefferson, and continued in opposition to the administration of that president, and that of his successor, Mr. Madison, became extinct, as a national party, soon after the termination of the war with Great Britain in 1815. In some of the states the name was kept up for a short period, but after a few feeble struggles the name of federalist became so unpopular that it was abandoned during the administration of president Monroe, whose management of the affairs of the nation was so satisfactory to all parties, that opposition for a time ceased. The parties which were subsequently formed for the support of Adams, Jackson, Crawford, and Clay, for the presidency, were more of a personal character than marked by distinct political principles; those who had been called federalists as well as democrats being found among the adherents of each of those candidates for the presidency. When General Jackson was elected president, his supporters claimed the name of democrats, and his opponents at first called themselves national republicans, but when joined by seceders from the administration ranks, in 1833 and 1834, they took the name of whigs. Thus the two great national parties which divided the country at the accession of Mr. Van Buren to the presidency, in 1837, were respectively known by the name of democrats and whigs. With the latter, several minor parties of more limited extent, or local in character, generally acted, and the greater portion of these parties gradually became amalgamated with, and formed part of the whig party. Such were the antimasons of the middle and eastern states; the state-rights men of the south who disapproved of the removal of the public deposites from the United States bank, and other acts of General Jackson; and those supporters of General Jackson in Tennessee, Georgia, and other states, who were opposed to Mr. Van Buren as his successor.

The party called democratic, which supported the administration of General Jackson, and Mr. Van Buren as his successor, became themselves divided, particularly in the northern and middle states, even previous to the election of the latter to the presidency. In 1835, there arose in the city of New-York, in the ranks of the democratic party, a combination in opposition to banks and other moneyed institutions, which afterward took the name of locofocos, or equal-rights party. The working-men's party, which arose in the cities of New-York and Philadelphia, in 1829, and dissolved in about two years afterwards, was the progenitor, to some extent, of the locofoco or equal-rights party. Certain it is, that most of the measures advocated by the former, some of which were introduced into the United States from Great Britain, by Mr. Robert Dale Owen and Miss Francess Wright, who for some time published a newspaper in New-York, called "The Free Enquirer," were decidedly popular with the latter, and both were equally hostile to banks, and other moneyed institutions, which they considered monopolies. Nevertheless, it was Andrew Jackson, in his contest with the bank of the United States, who enkindled the highest opposition in that direction, and the enthusiasm which he excited against the national bank soon extended itself to the state banks. The New-York election of 1834, with the strong pledge against monopolies which the candidates for members of congress and the legislature, of the democratic party in that city, were required to sign, together with speeches and resolutions of the same character, at political meetings, as well as the circumstances previously mentioned, all combined to plant deeply in the minds of that party the seeds of hostility to monopolies. Consequently, the democratic party became divided within itself. On the one side (in favor of banks and other corporations) were the great majority of the leading men of the party, and nearly all the office-holders under the general state, and city administrations; on the other, comprising then but a small section, composed principally of mechanics and other working-men, were those calling themselves free-trade, anti-monopoly, hard-money men.

The equal-rights party at first deemed it advisable to exercise great caution and secrecy in their movements. It required both moral and physical courage to attack the usages and organization of the democratic party, which were then controlled by those favorable to banking institutions. But at the election in the city of New-York, for a member of congress and members of the legislature, in the autumn of 1835, it was determined to oppose the nomination of certain persons who were brought forward by the friends of banks, which meeting we have previously described, at which originated the title of "locofoco."

The recommendation of a separation of the financial concerns of the United States government from the state banks, brought forward by president Van Buren, in his message to the extra session of congres in 1837, created a division in the ranks of the supporters of his administration, which was first exhibited in congress, but soon extended among the people. Those democrats who were opposed to an exclusive specie currency, and the sub-treasury scheme recommended by Mr. Van Buren, and those in favor of banks as depositories of the public moneys, became a distinct section of the party were called "conservatives!" Those who adhered to these views eventually joined the whigs in opposition to Mr. Van Buren's administration, and in 1840, aided in the election of Harrison and Tyler.

With regard to the state rights men, or those originally attached to the democratic party, who had disapproved of the removal of the deposites from the United States bank, and some other acts of General Jackson; most of them opposed to the election of Mr. Van Buren, and eventually amalgamated with the whig party. A considerable portion of the state-rights men, however, among whom was Mr. John C. Calhoun, and a majority of the people of South-Carolina, left the whigs soon after the accession of Mr. Van Buren to the presidency, and became supporters of his administration, particularly sustaining his views respecting the sub-treasury and other currency measures. Consequently, the vote of South-Carolina was given to Mr. Van Buren, when he was a candidate for the re-election to the presidency in 1840.

The election of 1840, which elevated Gen. Harrison and Mr. Tyler, was effected by the joint efforts of the whigs and conservatives, the latter for all political purposes, becoming merged in the whig party. The party which supported the election of Mr. Van Buren in 1840, calling themselves democrats, while their opponents gave them the name of locofocos, were then united throughout the country in advocating the measures of Mr. Van Buren's administration, particularly his recommendation of a sub-treasury, or the separation of the national funds from the state banks and the collection of the public revenues in gold and silver.

After his nomination for vice-president in 1840, and previous to the election, Mr. Tyler avowed himself a firm and decided whig, stating that on the subject of Mr. Clay's compromise tariff law then in operation, which he considered a protective tariff, and the distribution of the proceeds of the public lands among the states, he concurred with Mr. Clay and Gen. Harrison, on the subject of a national bank, he said, in a letter replying to one from the democratic citizens of Steubenville, in Oct. 1840: "My opinion of the power of congress to charter a bank of the United States, remains unchanged. There is not in the constitution any express grant of a power for such a purpose, and it never could be constitutional to exercise that power, save in the event that the powers granted to congress could not be carried out without resorting to such an institution."

In another letter to several citizens of Henrico county, Va., dated in October, 1840, he remarked: "My votes are repeatedly recorded on the journals of congress, against the power of congress over the subject of internal improvement, in all its phases and aspects, as well in regard to roads and canals, as to harbors and rivers. The first, viz: appropriations to roads and canals, have well nigh entirely ceased, while annual appropriations, to a large amount, have been made to harbors and rivers, with the sanction and approval of the president of the United States."

The 27th congress met in extra session, on the 31st day of May, 1841. The session closed on the 13th of September following. John White, a whig member from Kentucky, elected speaker of the house of representatives, having received on the first vote, viva voce, 121 votes against 84 for John W. Jones, of Virginia, (democrat,) and 16 scattering. In the senate, as already stated, there was also a decided majority in favor of the administration.

A committee of the house being proposed to join one from the senate, as usual, to wait on the president of the United States, and inform him that a quorum of the two houses had assembled, and that congress was ready to proceed to business, &c. Mr. McKeon of New-York, moved to amend the resolution appointing a committee, by striking out the words "president," and inserting the words "vice-president, now occupying the office of president of the United States." This motion, Mr. McKeon supported in a constitutional argument, which was replied to by Mr. Wise of Virginia, and the amendment was rejected, and the original adopted, by which the house recognised John Tyler as president of the United States.

The message of the president, was generally well received by the friends of the administration. Though cautiously worded on the subject of a national bank, and somewhat ambiguous as to his own views with regard to such an institution, it was believed he would sanction any bill that might receive the support of a majority of both houses of congress for the incorporation of a bank or fiscal agent for the regulation of the currency, and for managing the funds of the government.

At the opening of the session, the president's message was accompanied by the report of the secretary of the treasury. This paper earnestly recommended the establishment of a bank. It added: "If such an institution can be so conceived in principle, and guarded in its details as to remove all scruples touching the question of constitutional power, and thus avoid the objections which have been urged against those heretofore created by congress, it will, in the opinion of the undersigned, produce the happiest results, and confer lasting and important benefits on the country."

The bank was thus brought distinctly to the consideration of congress, both by the president and the secretary.

The president was desirous that congress should call on the secretary to report a plan for a bank. He expressed this wish to more than one member, immediately on the opening of the session; in fact, invited the call. Mr. Wise, his confidential friend, introduced a resolution to this end, into the house on the third of June. Mr. Clay did the same thing in the senate on the seventh of June.

On the 12th of June the secretary, Mr. Ewing, made his report, and with it a bill for the incorporation of "the Fiscal Bank of the United States."

The bill was represented by the secretary as creating an institution, in the general plan and frame of which, he had endeavored to free it from the constitutional objections which have been urged against those heretofore created by congress.

The plan accordingly differed from the former bank of the United States, in two essential characteristics—both of which, it was understood, were introduced upon Mr. Tyler's suggestion, and in deference to his peculiar views of the constitution.

First—It proposed a bank to be incorporated in the District of Columbia.

Second—It was to have power to establish branches, only with the assent of the States.

Many provisions were made to guard against the abuses which were known, or alleged to have crept into the old bank.

The amount of capital named was thirty millions of dollars; in other respects—in privileges of discount and exchange, &c., the institution proposed, was similar to the two former banks incorporated by congress.

The plan of a national bank proposed by the secretary of the Treasury, received the approbation of every member of the cabinet as the only plan which would be likely to succeed, considering the opinion of the acting President. Mr. Webster afterwards remarked that "it was the part of wisdom, not to see how much of a case they could make out against the president; but how they could get on as well as they might with the president." Mr. Wise, a confidential friend of the president, in a letter written after the extra session, observed, that "the secretary of the treasury, Mr. Ewing himself, proposed a plan which he recommended to congress as one which would conduct our finances and commerce, equalize exchanges, regulate currency, and avoid all constitutional difficulties. This was the very desideratum, if it was what he desired it to be, and this was emphatically, by a whig administration, recommended from the proper department, said to be acquiesced in by the president, and it was called for by both houses of congress. It was justly regarded as the whig measure of the first moment, and would, as such, have been met and treated doubtless, by the opposition, or Van Buren party."

Mr. Ewing's report and bill were referred in the senate, to the select committee on the currency, of which Mr. Clay was chairman. The committee reported on the 21st of June, a bill, in all essential features, the same as that proposed by the secretary of the treasury, and supposed to have been approved by the president, with one exception. That exception regarded the establishment of branches.

The bank, on this plan, as well as in the other, was to be situated in the district of Columbia, (Washington city;) it was to have the same capital of thirty millions—with a provision for future increase, if congress shall think advisable, to fifty millions.

It provided for a government subscription of ten millions, instead of the secretary's six, and it dispensed with the fourth instalment of surplus revenue, amounting to over nine millions. It allowed dividends as high as seven per cent. It forbade the appointment of members of congress, as directors. It contained other provisions varying in many instances from the bill recommended by the secretary of state. The two propositions were not very materially different.

The president maintained in vindication of the principle inserted in his bill, that although he could find power in the constitution to establish a bank, he could find none to establish a branch without the consent of the different states.

Mr. Clay, on the other hand, held that if the constitution did not give the power to establish a branch, no assent of a state could give it, and therefore that it was unconstitutional to attempt to derive power from the assent of a state.

Upon this question much discussion was elicited, but most generally the whigs in congress sided with Mr. Clay, the democratic members all taking strong ground against such an institution in whatever shape or form it might be brought forward.

The difficulty was at last thought to be settled by a compromise, to which it was reported the president had assented. The compromise proposed to allow the directors to establish branches with the assent of the states. When agreed upon, the whigs hastened to pass the bill embracing this provision. The bill was finally passed on the 6th August. In the senate, the bill passed, 26 to 23. In the house, 128 to 97. When presented to the president, great excitement prevailed; delegation after delegation waited upon him to express to him the disastrous effect it would have upon the whig party, and upon the finances of the country, if the bill should not become a law.

President Tyler finally returned the bill to the senate, with a veto message.

The veto message completely bewildered the whig members of congress, and was received with dismay and anxiety by the friends of the administration throughout the country.

On the receipt of the veto message accompanying the bank bill, immediate efforts were made by the leading whigs in congress, and by the members of the cabinet, to repair, if possible, the evil effects which threatened the party with distraction and dissolution.

The president had shadowed forth in his veto message that which the whigs construed into a plan for a fiscal agent. Upon this they dared to hope for something in the shape of a bank, and Senator Berrien and Mr. Sargeant of the house were deputed by the whigs to ascertain from the president what kind of a bill he would feel himself authorized to ap-approve. They had an interview and understood from the president that he was in favor of a fiscal agent, divested of discounting power, and limited to dealing in bills of exchange, other than those drawn by a citizen of one state upon another citizen of the same state. A bill was proposed in conformity with these suggestions. It was submitted to Mr. Webster, secretary of state, and by him to the president. It was understood that the president assented to their bill. It was submitted to the president on the 19th of August, and on the 20th it was introduced by Mr. Sargeant as an amendment to the bill then pending in committee of the whole.

On the 23d of August it was taken out of the committee of the whole, and passed without the alteration of a word from the original report, by a vote of 125 to 94. It was passed in the senate, 27 to 22, without amendment, on the 3d of September. In the mean time, several important measures proposed by the whigs in congress, had been adopted in both branches, and received the approbation of the president, among the rest a bill to repeal the independent treasury, as also the bankrupt law. The votes of the democratic members in both branches of congress, with very few exceptions, were recorded against the former and in favor of the latter.

While the bill to establish the "fiscal corporation" was pending, the Hon. John M. Botts committed a great mistake in the superscription of a letter, which found its way to a coffee house in Richmond, and from thence into the public papers, in which he said, under date of August 16:

"DEAR SIR:—The president has finally resolved to veto the bank bill. He has turned, and twisted, and changed his ground so often in his conversations, that it is difficult to tell which of the absurdities he will rest his veto upon.

* * * * * *

"Our Captain Tyler is making a desperate effort to set himself up with the locofocos, but he will be headed yet." * * * "The veto will be received without a word, laid on the table, and ordered printed? To-night we meet and will settle matters as quietly as possible, but they must be settled.

Yours, &c.,

JOHN M. BOTTS."

"You'll get a bank bill, but one that will serve only to fasten him, and to which no stock will be subscribed; and when he finds out that he is not wiser than all the rest of the world, in banking, we may get a better. The excitement here is tremendous, but it will be smothered for the present."

On the 9th of September, the president returned the fiscal corporation to the house of representatives, where it originated, with his objections.

The secretary of the treasury, Mr. Ewing, in his letter of resignation, says, he is satisfied that the president's veto of the last bill was brought about by the ufortunate mistake of Mr. Botts. Mr. Webster, the secretary of state, in letters to the two senators from Massachusetts, under date of the 16th August, intimated the same thing.

Mr. Clay, in his speech in the senate on the first veto, said: "It is incontestible that it (the bank) was the great, absorbing, and controlling question, in all our recent divisions and exertions."

Mr. Botts, in the house, in a speech upon the second veto, said:

"It is certain that when we came here no doubt was entertained by either party that he (the president) would sign a bank bill; our friends thought so, or it would not have been discussed, as it was, for ten or twelve weeks; the other party (democratic) thought so, or they would not have gotten up the cry of repeal! repeal! which resounded not only through the walls of this capitol, but became the watchword of the party throughout the country."

The last veto message was sent to the house on the 9th September, and on the 11th all of the members of the cabinet resigned with the exception of Mr. Webster.

On the closing of the session, a manifesto was drawn up and signed by sixty or seventy whig members, declaring that "from that day forth all political connexion between them and John Tyler was at end; that from that day, those who brought the president into power could no longer, in any manner or degree, be justly held responsible or blamed for the administration of the executive branch of the government."

It was expected, by many, that the president would select the members of his new cabinet from the ranks of the democratic party, but he promptly made his appointments of the following distinguished whigs and conservatives, viz: Walter Forward, secretary of the navy; John McLean, secretary of war; Abel P. Upshur, secretary of the navy; Charles A. Wickliffe, postmaster-general; and Hugh S. Legare, attorney-general. Subsequently, John C. Spencer was appointed secretary of war, in consequence of the non-acceptance of Judge McLean.

Among the important acts passed at the session of 1841–2, was an act for the apportionment of representatives, according to the census of 1840, by which the ratio was fixed at 70,680 for each representative, with one additional member for each state having a fraction greater than one moiety of said ratio. By the same act, representatives were directed to be chosen by single districts.

In July, 1843, president Tyler re-organized his cabinet as follows; Abel P. Upshur, secretary of state; John C. Spencer, secretary of the treasury; James M. Porter, secretary of war; David Henshaw, secretary of the navy; Charles

A. Wickliffe, postmaster-general; and John Nelson, attorney-general.

Messrs. Porter and Henshaw were democrats, but the others had been known as whigs or conservatives. At the next session Porter and Henshaw were rejected in the senate. The president then nominated William Wilkins as secretary of war, and Thomas W. Gilman as secretary of the navy, which nominations were confirmed.

By the bursting of a gun on board the steamship-of-war Princeton, on the Potomac, Messrs. Upshur and Gilman were killed. Subsequently the president nominated John C. Calhoun secretary of state, and John Y. Mason as secretary of the navy, which nominations were confirmed. Mr. Spencer resigned, and George M. Bibb was appointed secretary of the treasury, in May 1844.

A treaty of annexation was concluded between the United States and the republic of Texas, at Washington, April 12th, 1844, by Mr. Calhoun, secretary of state on the part of the United States, and Messrs. Van Zandt and Henderson, on the part of Texas. On being submitted to the senate by the president it was rejected, on the 8th of June, by a vote of ayes 16, noes. 35. Of those who voted in the negative, seven were democrats, viz: Messrs. Fairfield, of Maine, Atherton, of New-Hampshire, Niles, of Connecticut, Silas Wright, of New-York, Allen and Tappan, of Ohio, and Thomas H. Benton, of Missouri. Immediately after the rejection of the treaty, Mr. Benton introduced a bill for the annexation of Texas, the consent of Mexico to be first obtained.

The president sent a message to the house of representatives, announcing the rejection of the treaty with Texas, vith a view of inducing that body to originate some measure y which to accomplish the object which the treaty conemplated. The House referred the message to their comittee on foreign relations, but the subject was not definitely cted upon until the next session. In the senate on the

10th of June, Mr. Benton, in a speech of two hours, characterized the Texas project as a fraud upon the people of the country—a base, wicked, presidential intrigue, originating in the most vicious purpose, and so far, prosecuted for the most knavish conclusions, regardless alike of the character of the country, its treaty obligations, or its place. He moved to suspend all previous orders for the purpose of taking up the bill which he had submitted for the annexation of Texas, when Mexico should sanction the measure. The message of president Tyler, appealing from the decision of the senate, in a case in which the constitution makes that body expressly his advisers, and the controllers of his course, Mr. Benton, considered an insult to that body, which merited impeachment. He alluded to his own far back prophecies and writings, concerning Texas, and made some allusions to Messrs. Walker and Woodbury, "Texas Neophites," who had been so anxious to make great demonstrations of love for Texas. For himself he entertained no such anxiety, because his sentiments had always been known. It was not with him a question of "now or never," but Texas then, now and always.

An effort was made by the most zealous office-holders under the general government, and other persons interested in the success of Mr. Tyler, to create a popularity for the president out of the question of the annexation of Texas; but the attempt to enlist the feelings of the advocates of that measure in favor of the re-election of Mr. Tyler to the presidency, proved a total failure.

It was evident, however, that the Texas question was becoming one of great importance, and that the annexation of that territory to the United States was daily growing in favor with the people of the southern and western states. The democratic party, therefore, in the southern sections of the union, resolved to present the Texas question to the people at the then approaching presidential election. As a large proportion of the party in the northern states were opposed to the annexation of Texas, there was a prospect of disunion in the democratic ranks.

The national conventions of both whig and democratic parties were to be held in May, 1844, for the purpose of nominating candidates for president and vice-president. Mr. Clay, of Kentucky, was the whig candidate named for the presidency, by a general consent of that party. Mr. Van Buren appeared to be preferred to any other candidate, by the largest proportion of the democratic party.

In answer to letters and inquiries addressed to them on the Texas question, both Mr. Clay and Van Buren came out, in the month of April, 1844, with their views on the subject. They were both understood to be unfavorable to the immediate annexation of Texas, particularly without the consent of Mexico. Mr. Clay's letter was satisfactory to his political friends; but the course of Mr. Van Buren determined the democrats of the south to prevent his nomination for the presidency, by the convention of that party, if possible, and to seek some other candidate who was favorable to southern views and feelings on the Texas question.

The whig national convention, for the nomination of president and vice-president, met at Baltimore, on the 1st of May, 1844. Every state in the union was represented by delegates; and the Hon. Ambrose Spencer, of New-York, was chosen president of the convention, assisted by a number of vice-presidents and secretaries. Henry Clay, of Kentucky, was nominated by acclamation, as the candidate to be supported by the whigs for president of the United States, at the ensuing election; and on the third vote, Theodore Frelinghuysen, formerly of New-Jersey, but then a resident of New-York, was nominated as the candidate for vice-president. Great unanimity prevailed in the convention after the nominations were announced, and an enthusiastic demonstration to support the candidates named.

The democratic national convention of delegates for the

nomination of candidates for president and vice-president, met at Baltimore, on the 27th of May, 1844. The states were all represented, except South-Carolina. The Hon. Hendrick B. Wright, of Pennsylvania, was chosen president of the convention, assisted by numerous vice-presidents and secretaries. Most of the delegations from the different states had been instructed to vote for Mr. Van Buren for president, but the Texas question had been taken up by the party since those instructions were given, and Mr. Van Buren's letter on the subject had rendered the policy of his nomination doubtful with many who had been anxious for his re-election to the presidency.

On the first ballot by the convention for a candidate for president, Mr. Van Buren received 146 votes, General Cass 83, Colonel Johnson, of Kentucky, 24, Mr. Calhoun 6, and there were 7 for other persons; thus showing a decided majority in favor of Mr. Van Buren. But the convention having adopted the rule which had governed on former similar occasions, requiring two-thirds of the votes for a nomination, no choice was made. Seven subsequent ballots took place, on the last of which Mr. Van Buren received 104 votes, General Cass 114, and 44 for James K. Polk of Tennessee. The Virginia and New-York delegations then each separately retired for consultation, and on their return to the convention it was announced by Mr. Roane, of Virginia, that the delegation from that state would give their vote for James K. Polk. Mr. Butler, of New-York, responded to Mr. Roane, and having the authority of Mr. Van Buren withdrew his name, and stated that the delegation from New-York would cast thirty-five votes in favor of Mr. Polk, the remaining member voting blank. The call of the states being made for a ninth ballot, a unanimous vote from all the delegation was given for James K. Polk, as the democratic candidate for president of the United States. Silas Wright, of New-York, was nominated for vice-president, being then in the United States senate at Washington. The nomination was declined by Mr. Wright, and on the following morning the convention nominated George M. Dallas, of Pennsylvania, for that station.

The candidates nominated, both for president and vice-president, were understood to be in favor of the annexation of Texas to the United States. Resolutions were adopted by the convention, one of which declared, "that our title to the whole of the territory in Oregon is clear and unquestionable; that no portion of the same ought to be ceded to England or any other power; and that the re-occupation of Oregon and the annexation of Texas, at the earliest practicable period, are great American measures, which this convention recommends to the cordial support of the democracy of the Union." Another resolution declared, "that the convention hold in the highest estimation and regard their illustrious fellow-citizen, Martin Van Buren, of New-York, &c.," and that they "tender to him, in his honorable retirement, the assurance of the deeply-seated confidence, affection, and respect of the American democracy."

The nomination of Messrs. Polk and Dallas had the effect of completely uniting the democratic party throughout the country, and the Texas and Oregon questions had a tendency to infuse renewed vigor among the masses attached to the party, enabling them to enter into the election with excited hopes and prospects of success.

At the same time when the democratic convention met at Baltimore, a convention of the friends of president Tyler, composed of delegates from various parts of the Union, principally office-holders and political adventurers, assembled at that city, and placed the name of Mr. Tyler in nomination as a candidate for election to the presidency. The president accepted the nomination, but his case as candidate being hopeless, he yielded, in August, to the solicitations of the friends of Polk and Dallas, who were desirous to have the aid and patronage of the general government in favor of the democratic candidates, and withdrew his name from the presidential canvass. On that occasion Mr. Tyler published an address in the Madisonian, the official paper at Washington, to his friends throughout the union, announcing his intention and desire to withdraw from the position in which his friends had placed him. He concluded his address by saying: "I appeal from the vituperation of the present day to the pen of impartial history, in the full confidence that neither my motives nor my acts will bear the interpretation which has, for *sinister purposes,* been placed upon them."

After a most animated and exciting canvass the presidential election took place, in the fall of 1844, and resulted in the election of the democratic candidates, James K. Polk as president, and George M. Dallas as vice-president of the United States, over the whig candidates, Clay and Frelinghuysen. The votes of the electoral colleges were, for Polk and Dallas 170; for Clay and Frelinghuysen 105. The popular vote was, for Polk 1,335,834; for Clay 1,297,033; for Birney, the abolition candidate, 64,653; exclusive of South-Carolina, which state gave its electoral vote through the legislature, that body choosing the presidential electors. In the states of New-York and Michigan, the democratic electoral ticket received a plurality over the whig vote, less than the amount of abolition votes in those states. In addition to the states which voted for Mr. Van Buren in 1840, giving 60 electoral votes, Mr. Polk received the votes of Maine 9, New-York 36, Pennsylvania 26, Georgia 10, Mississippi 6, Louisiana 6, Indiana 12, and Michigan 5; which states gave their electoral votes to General Harrison in 1840.

The second session of the twenty-eighth congress commenced on the 2d of December, 1844, and closed on the expiration of their term, the third of March, 1845. The most important and exciting subject of the session was that of the annexation of Texas. Joint resolutions for annexing that republic to the United States, as one of the states of the Union, passed the house of representatives, on the 25th of January, 1845, by a vote of 120 to 98; and on the 1st of March the same passed the senate by a vote of 27 to 25; and the same day the resolutions were approved by the president.

Among the public acts of interest passed at this session were the following: to establish a uniform time for holding elections for electors of president and vice-president, in all the states of the Union; to provide for the establishment of the mail between the United States and foreign countries; granting lands to the state of Indiana, to enable the state to extend and complete the Wabash and Erie canal; to reduce the rates of postage, and to limit the use, and correct the abuse of the franking privilege; allowing drawback upon foreign merchandize exported by the interior to Mexico, and the British North American provinces; for the construction and improvement of roads in Wisconsin; making appropriations for fortifications; and an act for the admission of the states of Iowa and Florida into the Union. Florida complied with the terms of the last act, and was consequently admitted into the Union; but the people of Iowa rejected the terms, principally on account of the boundary defined by congress, and therefore Iowa remained a territory.

A bill forbidding the president to build revenue cutters at his own discretion, which had been vetoed by president Tyler, was again passed by the senate and house by more than a two-third vote, (in the latter by 126 to 31,) and thus became a law nothwithstanding the veto. A bill making appropriations for certain harbors and rivers, passed both houses, near the close of the session, but was retained by the president, and thus failed to become a law, in consequence of what was called a "pocket veto," which was the last act of Mr. Tyler's administration.

Mr. Tyler retired without any particular regret on the part of either of the two political parties. He had lost the confidence of the party by which he was elected, and had gained but little confidence with those of the democratic party.

There is no question but the democracy are indebted to John Tyler for thwarting the deep seated plan of Henry Clay and others to fasten upon us a National Bank; but we have been always under the impression that the last bill, the "fiscal corporation," which was presented to Mr. Tyler for his signature would have been signed had it not been for the letter of John M. Botts, in which the president was threatened with being "headed."

We deem it not inappropriate, in this connection, to allude to the early history of Mr. Polk, as when he was nominated for the presidency he was comparatively a new man for such a position, or was so regarded to be by many of his own political party throughout the country.

JAMES KNOX POLK was the eleventh president of the United States, and was the eldest of ten children, and was born on the second of November, 1795, in Mecklenburg Co., North-Carolina. His ancestors, whose original name, Pollock, has, by obvious transition, assumed its present form, emigrated in the early part of the eighteenth century from Ireland. The family trace their descent from Robert Polk, who was born and married in Ireland; his wife, Magadalen Tusker, was the heiress of Mowning hill. They had six sons and two daughters; Robert Polk, the progenitor of James Knox Polk, was the fifth son; he married a Miss Gallett and removed to America. Ezekiel Polk, the grandfather of James K. Polk, was one of his sons.

In August, 1826, being then in his thirtieth year, Mr. Polk was elected to congress. From his early youth he was a democrat, and ever regarded the constitution of the United States as an instrument of specific and limited powers; and he was found in opposition to every measure that aimed to consolidate federal power, or to detract from the dignity and legitimate functions of the state governments. He signalized his hostility to the doctrines of those who held to a more liberal construction of the constitution, in all their modes. He always refused his assent to the appropriation of money by the federal government for what he deemed the unconstitutional purpose of constructing works of internal improvements within the states. He took ground early against the constitutionality as well as expediency of a national bank; and, in August, 1820, consequently several months before the appearance of Gen. Jackson's first message, announced then his opinions in a published letter to his constituents. He has ever been opposed to a tariff of protection, and was at all times the strenuous advocate of a reduction of the revenue to the economical wants of the government. Entertaining these opinions, and entering congress as he did, at the first session after the election of John Quincy Adams to the presidency, he promptly took his station against the doctrines developed in the message of that chief magistrate, and was, during the continuance of his administration, resolutely opposed to its leading measures.

When Mr. Polk entered congress, he was, with one or two exceptions, the junior member of that body. His first speech was in favor of a proposition to amend the constitution in such manner as to prevent the choice of president from devolving upon congress in any event. This speech at once attracted public attention by the force of its reasoning, the copiousness of its research, and the spirit of indignation with reference to the then recent election by congress of John Quincy Adams, by which it was animated. From this time, Mr. Polk's history became inseparably interwoven with that of the house. He was prominently connected with every important question, and upon each took the boldest democratic ground. During General Jackson's terms he was one of the leading supporters of the administration, and at times, and on certain questions of paramount importance, its chief reliance. In December, 1827, Mr. Polk was placed on the committee of foreign affairs, and some time after, as chairman of a select committee, he made a report on the surplus revenue, denying the constitutional power of congress to collect from the people, for distribution, a surplus beyond the wants of the government, and maintaining that the revenue should be reduced to the exigencies of the public service. In 1830, he defended the act of General Jackson in placing his veto on the Maysville road bill, and thus checking the system of internal improvement by the general government, which had been entered upon by congress.

In December, 1832, Mr. Polk was transferred to the committee of ways and means, and at that session presented the report of the minority of that committee with regard to certain charges against the United States Bank; this minority report presenting conclusions directly adverse to that institution, which had been the subject of inquiry.

Mr. Polk's course arrayed against him the friends of the bank, but after a severe contest he was re-elected to congress by a majority of over three thousand. In 1833, Gen. Jackson determined upon the removal of the government deposites from the Bank of the United States. At the next session of congress this question elicited much discussion. Mr. Polk, in the house, vindicated the president's measure, and by his coolness, promptitude and skill carried through the resolutions of the committee relating to the bank and the deposites, and sustaining the administration, after which the cause of the bank was abandoned in congress.

In December, 1835, Mr. Polk was elected speaker of the house of representatives, and was again chosen to that station in 1837, at the extra session held in the first year of Van Buren's administration. The duties of speaker, during five sessions, were discharged by him with ability, at a time when party feeling ran high in the house, and in the beginning, unusual difficulties were thrown in his way by the animosities of his political opponents; yet such were his peculiarities in his associations with mankind, that, notwithstanding his firmness upon all questions which arose for decision, that in his actions he carried conviction to the heart of his most bitter political opponents, that if not right Mr. Polk believed he was right. He was highly complimented by resolutions which were unanimously passed in the closing of his labors, which resolutions were introduced by his political opponents.

In 1839, Mr. Polk was elected governor of the state of Tennessee, being the candidate of the democratic party, by a majority of over 2,500.

The state passed into the hands of his political opponents, and Mr. Polk complied with the requirements of the democrats of his own state to become their candidate for governor twice afterwards, and canvassed the state each time, and of course was defeated, although the strongest man the democracy had in that state.

From October, 1841, until his election to the highest office in the union, Mr. Polk remained in private life, not, however, an inert spectator of the wild and troubled drama of politics. He did not conceal his opinions on political subjects, when called upon by his fellow citizens to express them. Those who differed from him had no difficulty in ascertaining the fact of the difference. A proof of this was found in the circumstance which developed his opinions on the subject of the annexation of Texas. The citizens of Cincinnati had, early in 1844, expressed their "settled opposition" to the annexation of that republic to the United States, and invited him to announce his concurrence in their judgment. In his reply, he said:

"Let Texas be annexed, and the authority and laws of the United States be established and maintained within her limits, as also in the Oregon territory, and let the fixed policy of our government be not to permit Great Britain to plant a colony, or hold dominion over any portion of the people or territory of either. These are my opinions: and without deeming it necessary to extend this letter, by assigning the many reasons which influence me in the conclusions to which I come, I regret to be compelled to differ so widely from the views expressed by yourselves, and the meeting of citizens of Cincinnati, whom you represent."

On the 29th of May, 1844, Mr. Polk received the nomination of the democratic National convention, for a candidate for president of the United States. The contest was carried on with much spirit, between the democrats and those who supported Henry Clay, the candidate of the whigs ; but there was a marked difference between that contest and the one of 1840, when General Harrison was put in nomination, in opposition to Martin Van Buren.

	Polk.	*Clay.*
Maine, - - - -	9	
New-Hampshire, - -	6	
Vermont, - - - -		6
Massachusetts, - - -		12
Rhode-Island, - - -		4
Connecticut, - - -		6
New-York, - - - -	36	
New-Jersey, - - -		7
Pennsylvania, - - -	26	
Delaware, - - -		3
Maryland, - - - -		8
Virginia, - - -	17	
North-Carolina, - - -		11
South-Carolina, - - -	9	
Georgia, - - - -	10	
Alabama, - - -	9	
Mississippi, - - - -	6	
Louisiana, - - -	6	
Tennessee, - - - -		13
Kentucky, - - -		12
Ohio, - - - -		23
Indiana, - - - -	12	
Illinois, - - - -	9	
Missouri, - - - -	7	
Arkansas, - - - -	3	
Michigan, - - - -	5	
	170	105

Mr. Polk received 170 electoral votes, and Mr. Clay 105.

On the 4th of March, 1845, we had the pleasure of listening to president Polk's inaugural address delivered in person from the steps of the east front of the capitol of the union, to the largest assemblage of people we ever witnessed in one body.

In person, Mr. Polk was of the middle stature, and a quick penetrating eye. The expression of his countenance was grave, but its serious cast was often relieved by a peculiarly pleasant smile, indicative of the amenity of his disposition.

Mr. Polk in his inaugural address, in referring to the Texas question, said that "the republic of Texas had made known her desire to come into our union, to form a part of our confederacy, and enjoy with us the blessings of liberty, secured and guaranteed by our constitution. Texas was once a part of our country—was unwisely ceded away to a foreign power—is now independent, and possesses an undoubted right to dispose of a part or the whole of her territory, and to merge her sovereignty, as a separate and independent state, in ours. I congratulate my country, that, by an act of the late congress of the United States, the assent of this government has been given to the reunion; and it only remains for the two countries to agree upon the terms, to consumate an object so important to both."

In continuing the subject, Mr. Polk says: "I regard the question of annexation as belonging exclusively to the United States and Texas. They are independent powers, competent to contract; and foreign nations have no right to interfere with them, or to take exceptions to their reunion. Foreign powers do not seem to appreciate the true character of our government. Our union is a confederation of independent states, whose policy is peace with each other and all the world. To enlarge its limits, is to extend the dominions of peace over additional territories and increasing millions. The world has nothing to fear from military ambition in our government. While the chief magistrate and the popular branch of congress are elected for short terms by the suffrages of those millions who must, in their own persons, bear all the burdens and miseries of war, our government can not be otherwise than pacific. Foreign powers should therefore look on the annexation of Texas to the United States, not as the conquest of a nation seeking to extend her dominions by arms and violence, but as the peaceful acquisition of a territory once her own, by adding another member to her confederation, with the consent of that member; thereby diminishing the chances of war, and opening to them new and ever-increasing markets for their products.

"To Texas the re-union is important, because the strong protecting arm of our government would be extended over her, and the vast resources of her fertile soil and genial climate would be speedily developed; while the safety of New-Orleans and of our whole south-western frontier against hostile agression, as well as the interests of the whole union, would be promoted by it."

"In the early stages of our national existence the opinion prevailed with some that our system of confederated States could not operate successfully over an extended territory; and serious objections have, at different times, been made to the enlargement of our boundaries. These objections were earnestly urged when we acquired Louisiana. Experience has shown that they were not well founded. The title of numerous Indian tribes to vast tracts of countries has been extinguished. New territories have been created, and our jurisdiction and laws extended over them. As our population has expanded, the Union has been cemented and strengthened. As our boundaries have been enlarged, and our agricultural population has been spread over a large surface, our federative system has acquired additional strength and security. It may well be doubted whether it would not be in greater danger of overthrow, if our present population were confined to the comparatively narrow limits of the original thirteen states, than it is now that they are sparsely settled over a more extended territory. It is confidently believed that our system may be safely extended to the utmost bounds of our territorial limits; and that as it shall be extended to the utmost bounds of our union, so far from being weakened, will become stronger."

We have given these quotations in order to show the position of Mr. Polk upon the Texas question. He also took ground in his inaugural in favor of maintaining "by all constitutional means, the right of the United States to that portion of country lying beyond the Rocky Mountains." He said "our title to the country of the Oregon is clear and indisputable, and already are our people preparing to perfect that title by occupying it with their wives and children. But eighty years ago, our population was confined on the west by the ridge of the Alleganies. Within that period, our people, increasing to many millions, have filled the eastern valley of the Mississippi; adventurously ascended the Missouri to its head springs; and are already engaged in establishing the blessings of self-government in valleys, of which the rivers flow to the Pacific. The world beholds the peaceful triumphs of the industry of our emigrants. To us belongs the duty of protecting them adequately whenever they may be upon our soil. The jurisdiction of our laws, and the benefits of our republican institutions, should be extended over them in the distant regions which they have selected for their homes."

In his first annual message to congress, under date of the 2d December, 1845, Mr. Polk alluded again to the Texas question, and announced the fact that the terms of annexation which were offered by the United States had been accepted by Texas, and therefore the public faith of both parties was solemnly pledged to the compact of their union.

On the 6th of May, 1844, the Mexican envoy extraordinary and minister plenipotentiary to the United States made a formal protest, in the name of his government, against the joint resolution passed by congress " for the annexation of Texas to the United States, which he chose to regard as a violation of the rights of Mexico, and in consequence of it he demanded his passports. He was officially informed that the government of the United States did not consider the joint resolution referred to as a violation of any of the rights of Mexico, or that it afforded any just cause of offence to his government; that the republic of Texas was an independent power, owing no allegiance to Mexico, and constituting no part of her territory or rightful sovereignty or jurisdiction. He was also assured that it was the sincere desire of this government to maintain with that of Mexico relations of peace and good understanding. That functionary, however, notwithstanding these representations and assurances, abrubtly terminated his mission, and shortly afterward left the country. Our envoy extraordinary and minister plenipotentiary to Mexico was refused all official intercourse with that government, and after remaining several months, by the permission of his own government, he returned to the United States. Thus, by the acts of Mexico, all diplomatic intercourse between the two countries was suspended.

Soon after this, Mexico occupied an attitude of hostility towards the United States; commenced marshalling and organizing armies, issuing proclamations, and avowing the intention to make war on the United States, either by an open declaration, or by invading Texas. Both the congress and convention of the people of Texas earnestly invited this government to send an army into that territory to protect and defend them against the menaced attack. When the terms of annexation submitted by this government to Texas were accepted by the latter, we were bound to protect her territory and people from foreign invasion and agression.

The president, as a precautionary measure, ordered a strong squadron to the coasts of Mexico, and also ordered the concentration of a sufficient military force upon the western frontier of Texas. This latter force was under the immediate command of General Zachary Taylor.

Mr. Polk, in his special message of April 20, 1846, in referring to this force sent to the western frontier of Texas, says, it "was concentrated at Corpus Christi and remained there until I had received such information from Mexico as rendered it probable, if not certain, that the Mexican government would refuse to receive our envoy."

"Meantime, Texas, by the final action of our congress, had become an integral part of our union. The congress of Texas, by its act of December 19, 1836, had declared the Rio del Norte to be the boundary of that republic. Its jurisdiction had been extended and exercised beyond the Nueces.

"The country between that river and the Del Norte had been represented in the congress and in the convention of Texas, had thus taken part in the act of annexation itself, and is now included within one of our congressional districts. Our own congress had, moreover, with great unanimity, by the act of December 31, 1845, recognized the country beyond the Nueces as a part of our territory by including it within our own revenue system; and a revenue officer, to reside within that district, has been appointed by and with the advice and consent of the senate.

"It became, therefore, of urgent necessity to provide for the defence of that portion of our country. Accordingly, on the thirteenth of January last, instructions were issued to the General in command of these troops to occupy the left bank of the Del Norte. This river, which is the south-western boundary of the state of Texas—is an exposed frontier. From this quarter invasion was threatened; upon it and its immediate vicinity, in the judgment of high military experience, are the proper stations for the protecting forces of the government.

"In addition to this important consideration, several others occurred to induce this movement. Among these are the facilities afforded by the ports at Brazos Santiago and the mouth of the Del Norte for the reception of supplies by sea, the stronger and more healthful military positions, the convenience for obtaining a ready and more abundant supply of provisions, water, fuel, and forage, and the advantages which are afforded by the Del Norte in forwarding supplies to such posts as may be established in the interior and upon the Indian frontier.

"The movement of the troops to the Del Norte was made by the commanding General, under positive instructions to abstain from all aggressive acts toward Mexico, or Mexican citizens, and to regard the relation between that republic and the United States as peaceful, unless she should declare war, or commit acts of hostility, indicative of a state of war. He was specially directed to protect private property and respect personal rights.

"The army moved from Corpus Christi on the 11th of March, and on the 28th of that month arrived on the left bank of the Del Norte, opposite to Matamoras, where it encamped on a commanding position, which has since been strengthened by the erection of field-works. A depot has also been established at Point Isabel, near the Brazos Santiago, thirty miles in rear of the encampment. The selection of his position was necessarily confided to the judgment of the General in command."

Mr. Polk, in continuing his war message, of May 11, 1846, said:

"The Mexican forces at Matamoras assumed a belligerent attitude, and on the 12th of April, General Ampudia, then in command, notified General Taylor to break up his camp, within twenty-four hours, and to retire beyond the Nueces river, and in the event of his failures to comply with these demands, announced that arms, and arms alone, must decide the question. But no open act of hostility was committed until the 24th of April. On that day, General Arista, who had succeeded to the command of the Mexican forces, communicated to General Taylor that 'he considered hostilities commenced, and should prosecute them.'' A party of dragoons of sixty-three men and officers were on the same day despatched from the American camp up the Rio del Norte, on its left bank, to ascertain whether the Mexican troops had crossed, or were preparing to cross the river, 'became engaged with a large body of these troops, and after a short affair, in which some sixteen were killed and wounded, appear to have been surrounded and compelled to surrender.'

"The grievous wrongs perpetrated by Mexico upon our citizens throughout a long period of years, remain unredressed; and solemn treaties, pledging her public faith for this redress, have been disregarded. A government either unable or unwilling to enforce the execution of such treaties, fails to perform one of its plainest duties.

"Our commerce with Mexico has been almost annihilated. It was formerly highly beneficial to both nations; bu our merchants have been deterred from prosecuting it by the system of outrage and extortion which the Mexican authorities have pursued against them, while their appeals through their own government for indemnity have been made in vain. Our forbearance has gone to such an extreme as to be mistaken in its character. Had we acted with vigor in repelling the insults and redressing the injuries inflicted by Mexico at the commencement, we should doubtless have escaped all the difficulties in which we are now involved.

"Instead of this, however, we have been exerting our best efforts to propitiate her good will. Upon the pretext that Texas, a nation as independent as herself, thought proper to unite its destinies with our own, she has affected to believe that we have severed her rightful territory, and, in official proclamations and manifestoes, has repeatedly threatened to make war upon us for the purpose of reconquering Texas. In the meantime we have tried every effort at reconciliation. The cup of forbearance had been exhausted, even before the recent information from the frontier of the Del Norte. But now, after reiterated menaces, Mexico has passed the boundary of the United States, has invaded our territory, and shed American blood upon the American soil. She has proclaimed that hostilities have commenced, and that the two nations are now at war.

"As war exists, and, notwithsanding all our efforts to avoid it, exists by the act of Mexico herself, we are called upon, by every consideration of duty and patriotism, to vindicate, with decision, the honor, the rights, and the interests of our country.

"Anticipating the possibility of a crisis like that which has arrived, instructions were given in August last, 'as a precautionary measure,' against invasion, or threatened invasion, authorizing General Taylor, if the emergency required, to accept volunteers, not from Texas only, but from the states of Louisiana, Alabama, Mississippi, Tennessee, and Kentucky, and corresponding letters were addressed to the respective governors of those states.

"These instructions were repeated; and in January last, soon after the incorporation of 'Texas into our union of states,' General Taylor was further 'authorized by the president to make a requisition upon the executive of that state for such of its militia force as may be needed to repel invasion, or to secure the country against apprehended invasion.' On the 2d day of March, he was again reminded, 'in the event of the approach of any considerable Mexican force, promptly and efficiently to use the authority with which he was clothed to call to him such auxiliary force as he might need.'

"War actually existing, and our territory having been

invaded, General Taylor, pursuant to authority vested in him by my direction has called on the governor of Texas for four regiments of state troops, two to be mounted, and two to serve on foot, and on the governor of Louisiana for four regiments of infantry, to be sent to him as soon as practicable.

"In further vindication of our rights and defence of our territory, I invoke the prompt action of congress to recognize the existence of the war, and to place at the disposition of the executive the means of prosecuting the war with vigor, and thus hastening the restoration of peace. To this end I recommend that authority should be given to call into the public service a large body of volunteers, to serve for not less than six or twelve months, unless sooner discharged."

The war was prosecuted with vigor, and the results are familiar to the American people; therefore it is deemed of little importance to treat upon the subject particularly in this connection. Suffice it to say, that the brilliancy of the military achievements acquired by the American army during the various struggles incident to the Mexican war, are not, as yet, duly appreciated. There has not, perhaps, previously been an instance in the known world where an army has been so generally raised by volunteers. No drafting seemed to be necessary, but on the contrary, the greatest trouble on the part of the government seemed to be to keep our men back. They were ready at the call of the government to repair at once to the battle-field to defend their country and their country's honor. The fact that our contest with Mexico was thus carried on by the people of the different states, who voluntarily rushed to the field of battle, has created more surprise and wonderment in foreign countries, than all else which has transpired since the formation of our government. The people of other countries have learned the true cause of the existence of this extraordinary degree of patriotism which prevails in our own. They have learned to attribute it to the cause of education. It is doubtless true that our struggles with Mexico, and the results incident thereto, have had much to do with the struggles for liberty which have transpired in foreign countries within the past eighteen months. There is a spirit of republicanism abroad, which, sooner or later, will cause thrones to totter and empires to be crushed.

In the contest with Mexico General Taylor signalized himself, and his noble and daring exploits will never be forgotten by the American people.

Whatever difference of opinion may have existed in the minds of men relative to the policy of the Mexican war, aside from the duty of protecting our national honor, all must agree that the position acquired by gaining California upon the great pacific ocean, in a commercial point of view, is second in importance to no other enterprise since the formation of our national government. Its importance cannot be known in a day or a year, but time will show that the current of the commerce of the Pacific will be turned, and made tributary to the United States. The minerals of this vast region are attracting the attention of the world, and from the best information we are enabled to gather, the most sanguine anticipations in this regard will be fully realized. Thousands upon thousands of our most enterprising citizens are flocking to the shores of the Pacific—a class of men, or such as those who have heretofore repaired to wilderness homes, and in pursuance of their indomitable perseverance and industry, have caused forests to recede before the woodman's axe, and villages and cities to arise as if by magic.

These are days of progression, and men of enlarged views must see that it is useless to contend against this current, however much they might feel disposed. It is a spirit which the enterprising of all classes, of whatever profession, trade or occupation, are participating in. Old nations, like old garments, are cast off, to make room for the improvements of the age. Many of these improvements are of the most astonishing nature; and not the least of which is the transmission of intelligence from point to point. In olden times, a man would occupy the space of three or four weeks in communicating with his fellow man, a distance of a thousand miles, while at the present day he can converse with his fellow the same distance, as he would with his neighbor by the fire-side. But there are other and important improvements, a recital of which would occupy much space, all going to show the rapid strides of the spirit of progression of the present age.

These remarks are made to show that the results of the Mexican war, the purchase of California particularly, will prove beneficial beyond a doubt to this country, as it will open the door to our men of enterprise to pursue their various occupations, whereas their energies in this older portion of the union did not seem to meet with adequate reward

The course pursued by Mr. Polk upon this whole question, the most important of his administration, all must acknowledge, was dictated by the purest motives. Even in his final negociation for California, he treated it as important only as a commercial position, but lived to learn that the minerals discovered have rendered it equally as important. When time shall have rolled on for a term of years, Mr. Polk's administration will be looked upon as one of unusual brillancy.

Mr. Langdon, the Mayor of the city of Mobile, (Alabama,) and editor of the leading whig paper of that state, in an address to Mr. Polk, on his homeward tour, after concluding his presidential labors at Washington, made these remarks:

"Your acts are on the record. Time will test their wisdom, and the pen of the impartial historian will do you justice. That you have done your duty faithfully and conscientiously with a view to the advancement of your country's best interest, we are free to admit, and for this we honor you. That you have carried out with fidelity, the principles and adhered to the policy which you proposed previous to your election, and to the support of which your life has been devoted, none who know the history of your political life will pretend to deny. For this evidence of your honesty and independence, you have the respect and admiration of those who differ from you in opinion."

During the two last sessions of Mr. Polk's administration, the excitement run high, at Washington and elsewhere, relative to the successor of Mr. Polk. It was thought by many that Mr. Clay would receive the nomination at the hands of the whigs, and that Gen. Cass would be nominated by the democrats.

The Democratic National Convention was holden at Baltimore, on the 23d of May, 1848, and Gen. Cass was nominated. The last ballot, before he was declared unanimously nominated stood as follows: Cass, 179—Woodbury, 38—Buchanan, 33. New-York not voting.

The Whig National Convention assembled at Philadelphia, on the 7th June, 1848, and Gen. Taylor was nominated. The last ballot before he was declared unanimously nominated, stood, Gen. Taylor, 171—Clay, 33—Webster, 14—Scott, 62.

The campaign was conducted with much energy on both sides, but with less bitterness of feeling between the friends of the opposing candidates.

A Convention was called at Buffalo, called a Free Soil Convention, at which Martin Van Buren was nominated for the presidency. This created much feeling in the regular democratic ranks. They had ever looked upon him as the leader and head of their political organization, and who himself owed his political greatness and preferment to the caucus system. Mr. Van Buren having been a democrat, and claiming still, at the time, to belong to that party, and a nomination having been made, his lending himself to defeat that nomination gave rise to much acrimonious feeling.

The result of the vote in the electoral college was as follows:

	Cass.	Taylor.
Maine, - - - -	9	
New-Hampshire, - - -	6	
Vermont, - - -		6
Massachusetts, - - -		12
Rhode-Island, - - - -		4
Connecticut, - - -		6
New-York, - - - -		36
New-Jersey, - - - -		7
Pennsylvania, - - -		26
Delaware, - - - -		3
Maryland. - - - -		8
Virginia, - - - - -	17	
North-Carolina, - - -		11
South-Carolina, - -	9	
Georgia, - - - -		10
Alabama, - - -	9	
Mississippi, - - -	6	
Louuisiana, - - -		6
Tennessee, - - - -		13
Kentucky, - - - -		12
Ohio, - - - -	23	
Indiana, - - - -	12	
Illinois, - - - -	9	
Missouri, - - -	7	
Arkansas, - - - -	3	
Michigan, - - -	5	
Florida, - - - -		3
Texas, - - - -	4	
Wisconsin, - - -	4	
Iowa, - - - -	4	
	127	163

General Zachary Taylor was inaugurated on the 5th day of March, 1849, at 12 o'clock M.

Millard Fillmore, of New-York, was elected vice-president upon the whig ticket over Gen. William O. Butler, of Kentucky, who was supported by the democracy, by the same electoral vote.

The city of Washington was crowded to overflowing, by our people from all quarters of the Union. The ceremony of inauguration was similar to those heretofore described. Gen. Taylor in the afternoon and evening received visitors at the presidential mansion. The house was thronged until a late hour, by people eager to see the hero of the Mexican War, and president of the United States.

The ancestors of General Taylor emigrated from England nearly two centuries ago, and settled in the eastern part of Virginia. His father, Richard Taylor, was born in that state, where he resided until about 1790. Zachary was his second son, and was born in November, 1784, in Orange county, Virginia; he is therefore a native of the same state which gave birth to Washington, Jefferson, Madison, Harrison, and many other illustrious Americans. Besides Zachary, his father had four sons, Hancock, George, William, and Joseph, and three daughters, Elizabeth, Sarah, and Emily.

Richard Taylor seems to have possessed a full share of the restless spirit of active adventure which distinguished the first settlers of America. Accordingly, in a little while after Boon had explored Kentucky, we find him journeying to that wilderness. Here he was not only unappalled by the horrors of a country called by the natives the dark and bloody ground, and by his hair-breadth escapes from the Indians, but he actually formed the design of penetrating to New-Orleans on foot. This he accomplished alone through the forests and wilderness stretching along the Mississippi, and returned by ship to Virginia. When the revolution broke out, the courage and zeal which he had manifested in resisting the encroachments of the mother country, caused him to receive an appointment as colonel in the Continental army, the duties of which office he performed in a manner that fulfilled the high hopes which had been entertained of him. He fought in several of the most important battles of the north, and among others with Washington at Trenton. At the close of the war he retired to his farm in Virginia, where he remained until about the year 1790, when he emigrated with his family to Kentucky. In this journey he was accompanied by Colonels Croghan and Bullitt,both of which names became famous in the annals of their state. They settled upon a spot noted for the long and peculiarly bloody wars of the Indians, and these brave men soon found an ample field in which to display their courage and hardihood. In the burnings and scalpings which happened almost weekly, Colonel Taylor so distinguished himself, that he was soon looked upon as the champion of the white settlers, and the bulwark of their village. After a long time the attacks of the savages became less frequent, and the population had shaken off their fear of the Indian name, and began to assume the appearance of a regular community. Still the usefulness of Col. Taylor did not cease with the causes which had drawn it forth. He became as distinguished a citizen as he had formerly been a soldier, and was entrusted with the duties of several important and responsible stations. He was one of the framers of the constitution of Kentucky; represented Jefferson county and Louisville city for many years in both branches of the state Legislature, and was a member of the electoral colleges which voted for Jefferson, Madison, Monroe, and Clay.

Such are a few points in the history of a man whose name will ever be dear to the American people, as the father of the conqueror of Mexico. All allow him to have been of unflinching perseverance, indomitable courage and zeal and ability to perform the duties of the various offices and stations which he was called to fill.

Under the parentage of such a man, it is nothing singular that young Zachary should early have imbibed a taste for military life. We are told that such was the case; and the common occurrences which daily surrounded him tended to foster this feeling. His nursery tales were stories of Indian butchery which had but recently been perpetrated upon the neighbors of his parents; and as he grew larger, he often heard the shriek of the maiden and innocent, the sharp crack of the rifle that announced their death, and then the fierce conflict between the father and his savage foe. He learned to barricade his own door, and spend the night in watchful intensity, while looking out upon nothing but gloomy forests, and some burning cottage far in the distance.

At the age of six years Zachary was placed at school under the direction of a Mr. Ayers. Even here he was in continual danger of the tomahawk, and many of the larger scholars were obliged to go armed. While here, young Zachary became distinguished among his companions for his activity, decision and bluntness of character, modesty of demeanor, and general intelligence. These are shining qualities in a school-boy, and he soon became the acknowledged and general favorite of a large portion of his comrades. From a child, his mind possessed a keen relish for military narratives, and in youth he began to long for an opportunity to display himself in the field. There still remain of him many anecdotes, all tending to illustrate his fondness for activity and adventure.

The schoolmaster of General Taylor is still living in the town of Preston, near Norwich, Connecticut, where he was born. Though more than seventy years of age, he takes great pleasure in listening to the achievements of his pupil, and in recounting anecdotes of him when a school-boy. He represents him to have been an excellent scholar, possessing an active and inquisitive mind, studious in his habits, though of sanguine temperament, quick of apprehension, and promising fair for a career of usefulness in life. He had mental qualities of thoughtfulness, judgment, shrewdness, and stability, not often found united in youth. But a peculiar trait of his character, and one not often connected with a sanguine temperament, was firmness. This, united with the above named qualities, is an important characteristic in a soldier. Upon many occasions, sudden and warm impulses, when properly directed by judgment and firmness, have produced grand achievements; and though a man may be brave to an eminent degree, yet a phlegmatic temperament is calculated to restrain the exercise of his bravery at a time when it might lead to glorious results.

Upon leaving school, young Taylor continued the exercise of those sports and labors which suited the ardor of his temperament. He often performed feats of strength and difficulty which would excite the wonder and applause of friends, and rivalry of others. His fondness for military life has been mentioned, and it is related that even before he commenced a course of rigid tactical instruction, he might often be seen with his comrades practising the different evolutions of a company drill, with as much gravity and emulation as though under orders before an enemy.

An opportunity was not long wanting for the exercise of the talent thus gradually developing. The difficulties between the United States and England, relative to interruptions of our commerce and the impressment of seamen, now presented so alarming an aspect, that an early rupture was confidently anticipated. This was an excellent opportunity for many of the wild young spirits of the west to wreak their vengeance against an enemy, who, though respected in time of peace, was the object of bitter animosity in war. Volunteer companies were organized in every part of the union, and the "citizen soldiery" became an object of great national importance.

While these events were in progress, the whole country was electrified by the intelligence that a British armed vessel, the Leopard, had fired into the American frigate Chesapeake, killing three of her men, wounding eighteen, and subsequently carrying away four others of her crew. This increased the popular indignation against Great Britain, as well as the spirit of determined resistance to her attacks.

Upon the reception of the news of this affair, young Taylor applied for a commission in the army, and was appointed by President Jefferson a first lieutenant in the 7th regiment of infantry. This step was highly pleasing to his father, who had been instrumental in its accomplishment.

General Taylor, on being sworn into office, as president of the United States, and after he had delivered his inaugural address, appointed his Cabinet as follows: John M. Clayton, Secretary of state; William M. Meredith, of Pa., secretary of the navy; George W. Crawford of Georgia, secretary of war; Thomas Ewing, of Ohio, secretary of the home department; Jacob Collamer of Vermont, post-master-general; and Reverdy Johnson of Maryland, attorney-general.

The first session of the thirty-first congress, which commenced Nov 3, 1849, and closed Sept. 30, 1850, was one of the longest and most exciting ever held. Its ten months' duration was in good part devoted to speech-making—nearly the first month having been consumed by the house in ineffectual ballots for a speaker. The democrats had a small plurality in the house, with a decided majority in the senate; but a number of "free-soil democrats," who could not vote for a speaker so thoroughly adverse as Mr. Cobb to their views of slavery extension, rendered the result doubtful, and would have secured the re-election of Mr. Winthrop, but for the objection of Messrs. A. H. Stephens, Toombs, and Owen, of Ga., Morton of Va., and Cabell of Fla., who refused to vote with their party on speaker without a distinct committal against the Wilmot proviso. This could not be conceded, so Mr. Winthrop was steadily voted against by several pro-slavery whigs, on one side, and anti-slavery men elected by whig votes on the other, while Mr. Cobb lost votes on one side only. Several other candidates were tried on either side with like success, though one (Mr. W. J. Brown of Ia.) came very near an election, having succeeded in uniting both wings of the democracy upon himself, by satisfactory private assurances on the slavery question. The fact that such cross-eyed assurances had been given became pubic barely in time to prevent his election. Finally, the house decided to try a plurality vote, agreeing that the highest candidate at the next ballot should be thereupon elected; and on this vote Howell Cobb of Georgia had 102 votes, Robert C. Winthrop of Massachusetts 100, and there were some fifteen scattering. Howell Cobb was thereupon declared speaker by a resolution moved by Edward Stanley (whig) of North-Carolina. Thomas J. Campbell (whig) of Tennessee was, after a tedious struggle, re-elected clerk, but he soon died, and Richard M. Young of Ill. (once U. S. senator) was chosen in his stead.

Congress being fully organized, a protracted, vehement struggle commenced with regard to the organization of new territories, admission of California, &c. General Taylor at an early day transmitted a special message, recommending in substance that California should be promptly admitted with the constitution her people had framed, and the boundaries they had designated, and that the territories should be left under the military government which had been established upon their conquest, until such time as they should be entitled to and desirous of admission into the Union as states, when they should be received with whatever republican institutions they might present. This plan made no provision for the settlement of the boundary of Texas, which state claimed to include most of the people of New-Mexico and her entire territory east of the Rio Grande, within the former's limits and rightful jurisdiction. To this assumption the people of New-Mexico manifested the most determined and active hostility. Mr. Clay at an early day made a speech to the senate, concurring in Gen.

eral Taylor's preference that each subject should be considered and decided by itself, but insisting that the territories should be promptly organized under regular territorial governments, and the Texas boundary settled. In the progress of the discussion, Mr. Clay waived his own preference of separate action, and assented to the combination of the admission of California, the organization of the territories, and the adjustment of the Texas boundary, all in one bill, which thence obtained the nickname of 'the Omnibus.' A committee of thirteen was raised, with Mr. Clay at its head, from which committee the project known as the Omnibus,' was in due season reported, and thenceforward contested with desperate resolution by all the strength of the senate. When the struggle was the fiercest, General Taylor died, and it was supposed that his decease and the succession of Mr. Fillmore, who was esteemed moderately favorable to 'the omnibus,' would secure its passage, but that expectation was not realized.

General Taylor died on the 9th day of July, 1850, at 10 o'clock P. M. His last words were,—"I am prepared,—I have endeavored to do my duty." The members of the Cabinet and their families were all present at the death-bed and the executive departments were all closed. It has been described as one of the most solemn scenes on record. He was looked upon as a great man for the valiant deeds he had accomplished upon the battle-field; and was then the chosen of the people to administer the affairs of the government. Certain it is, that upon no occasion, within our recollection, has there been regret manifested so generally by all of the people, as upon the death of General Taylor.

Millard Fillmore, the vice-president, was sworn into office as president of the United States, on the day following the death of the president, in pursuance of a provision in the constitution. The cabinet officers appointed by General Taylor, resigned, and after the lapse of a few days, president Fillmore appointed his cabinet, as follows: Daniel

Webster, of Massachusetts, secretary of state; Thomas Corwin of Ohio, secretary of the treasury; Alexander H. H. Stuart of Virginia, secretary of the interior; William A. Graham, of North-Carolina, secretary of war; Charles M. Conrad, of Louisiana, secretary of the navy; Nathan K. Hall, of New-York, post-master-general; and John J. Crittenden of Kentucky, attorney-general.

When business was resumed in congress, and the 'omnibus' being under discussion, after various amendments had been proposed, and mainly rejected, though some of considerable importance were adopted, a motion to strike out all that part relating to the boundary of Texas was carried, and the bill thus crippled, was dismembered limb by limb, until nothing remained but the sections organizing Utah (the "Mormon Deseret") as a separate territory, which was passed and sent to the house.

However, the California admission, the New-Mexico territorial, and the Texas boundary bills, all subsequently passed as independent propositions—the Texas boundary bill giving the same amount ($10,000,000) to Texas for relinquishing her claim to New-Mexico that "the Omnibus" did, while it secured to Texas a larger and more desirable area than she would have had by that bill. The other bills were substantially the same as when included in the omnibus. The Texas boundary bill encountered a formidable resistance in the house—the most determined opponents and the most zealous champions of slavery extension uniting in that resistance—but it was carried through by a small majority, after two failures, by uniting with it the bill to organize New-Mexico as a territory. This union was concurred in by the senate, and all the bills became laws. Two additional bills, reported separately from the senate's compromise committee were likewise passed. One of them abolishes the slave trade in the District of Columbia, while the other (known as the fugitive slave bill) provides more summarily and rigorously for the recapture and return to their masters of all runaways from slavery who shall have taken refuge in the free states. They are the principal results of the session of 1850, and will cause it long to be remembered.

Toward the close of the session, a strenuous effort was made for a revision of the existing tariff, with a view to afford additional protection to the depressed branches of our National industry, especially the production of iron and of cotton and woolen fabrics. The revision was defeated in the house by very close votes. No attempt for it was made in the senate. Cheap postage, mileage reform, and several other desirable changes, were attempted, but failed for want of time and want of favor. But a strenuous attempt to break up the system of executing the printing of Congress by contract, was resisted and defeated in the house, much to the relief of the treasury; and a proviso was fastened to the naval appropriation bill prescribing that flogging in the navy should henceforth be abolished. This proviso is now the law of the land, and likely to remain so. Attempts to engraft the principle of free grants of public lands to actual settlers on our land system were made, but strongly voted down. The session, which had been unusually excited and stormy, closed calmly and quietly.

Mr. Fillmore, the president, has taken a very strong stand as a national statesman. Thus far it seems that no faction can intimidate or influence him from a path he has marked out for his guidance as the chief executive. It is impossible to do justice, we are aware, to an administration in power, as no one, unless he be a member of congress, can possibly have an opportunity of knowing exactly its good or its evil workings.

From Greely's annual almanac we learn that Mr. Fillmore was born at Summer Hill, Cayuga Co., N. Y., January 7th, 1800, and is accordingly now about 50 years old His father was a farmer in very limited circumstances. The family removed to Aurora, Erie county, in 1819, where the father still carries on a farm of moderate dimensions;

the writer hereof has often passed the modest house where reside the family of the President, in a style not more pretending than is common to thriving farmers of that prosperous district. The narrow means of the father did not permit the bestowal on the son of any other than a most limited common-school education. When 15 years old, he was set to learn the trade of a clothier, at which he worked for four years, improving all his spare time in reading books from a little library in the village where he lived. At the age of 19 he made the acquaintance of Judge Wood of Cayuga county, who detected the latent talents of the young man, and induced him to study law, for which he generously furnished the means. Mr. Fillmore remained in Judge Wood's office above two years, studying with that industry and perseverance which have distinguished him through life: during this time he also taught school in the winter months in order himself to provide for his expenses as far as possible. In 1822 he entered a law office at Buffalo and passed a year studying and teaching, when he was admitted to the bar and removed to Aurora to commence the practice of his profession. In 1826 he married Abigail, the daughter of Rev. Lemuel Powers: she now presides at the White House. Several years were now mainly employed by Mr. Fillmore in diligent judicial studies, and in the limited legal practice of a country town. In 1829 he was elected to the Assembly of New-York and for three years (during which time he removed his residence to Buffalo) held a seat in that body. Here he was remarkable for constant devotion to and unwearied industry in his duties. He took a prominent and influential part in the enactment of the law abolishing imprisonment for debt. In 1832 he was elected to the XXIIId Congress and served creditably. In the Fall of 1836 he was again returned to the same office and acted as a member of the Committee of Elections in the famous New Jersey "Broad Seal" case, and in that capacity established his reputation in the House. He was re-elected to the next

Congress, and now assumed the responsible position of Chairman of the Committee of Ways and Means. In the duties of this post at a trying crisis, he manifested the industry, dignity of bearing, efficient practical talent, and ability to secure the confidence of his colleagues, which had before distinguished him. His public reputation perhaps rests more upon the manner in which he filled this post in the XXVIIth Congress than on any other portion of his career.

After this, resisting the importunities of his friends and the Whig Convention of his District, Mr. Fillmore returned at Buffalo, to the practice of his profession. In 1844 he was run by the Whigs of New-York for Governor, and was beaten by Silas Wright. In 1847 he was elected Controller of the State, and removed to Albany to discharge the duties of that office, which he held till February, 1849, when he resigned it, prior to his induction into the Vice-Presidency, to which post he had been elevated by the Presidential election of 1848. On the death of Gen. Taylor in July last, Mr. Fillmore became President. He appointed a new Cabinet with Daniel Webster at its head, and varied so far from the course pursued by Gen. Taylor as to throw the influence of the Administration in favor of the Compromise measures before Congress. At the same time he rebuked with firmness and decision the threats made by Texas against New-Mexico. His course has been governed by an earnest desire to conciliate the warring sections and restore harmony to the Union.

The second session of the 31st Congress, commenced on the second day of December 1850. During this session we are unable to record any measure of particular interest, save the act to reduce and modify the rates of postage in the United States, which will be published in full, when the history of the administrations will be closed.

MODIFICATION OF POSTAGE.

An Act to reduce and modify the rates of postage in the United States, and for other purposes.

Be it enacted by the Senate and House of Representatives of the United States of America in Congress assembled, That, from the thirtieth day of June, eighteen hundred and fifty-one, in lieu of the rates of postage now established by law, there shall be charged the following rates, to wit: For every single letter in manuscript, or paper of any kind upon which information shall be asked for, or communicated in writing, or by marks or signs, conveyed in the mail, for any distance between places within the United States not exceeding three thousand miles, when the postage upon such letter shall have been prepaid, three cents, and five cents when the postage thereon shall not have been prepaid, and for any distance exceeding three thousand miles, double these rates; for every such single letter or paper, when conveyed wholly or in part by sea, and to or from a from a foreign country, for any distance over twenty-five hundred miles, twenty cents, and for any distance under twenty-five hundred miles, ten cents, (excepting, however, all cases where such postage has been or shall be adjusted at different rates by postal treaty or convention, already concluded or hereafter to be made;) and for a double letter, there shall be charged double the rates above specified; and for a treble letter, treble those rates; and for a quadruple letter, quadruple those rates; and every letter or parcel not exceeding half an ounce in weight, shall be deemed a single letter; and every additional weight of half an ounce, or additional weight of less than half an ounce, shall be charged with an additional single postage. And all drop-letters, or letters placed in any post-office, not for transmission, but for delivery only, shall be charged with postage at the rate of one cent each; and all letters *shall* hereafter *be* advertised as remaining over or uncalled for in any post office, shall be charged one cent in addition to the regular postage, both to be accounted for as other postages now are.

Sec. 2. *And be it further enacted*, That all newspapers not exceeding three ounces in weight, sent from the office of publication to actual and *bona fide* subscribers, shall be be charged as follows, to wit: All newspapers published weekly only, shall circulate in the mail free of postage within the county where published, and that the postage on the regular number of a newspaper published weekly, for any distance not exceeding fifty miles out of the county where published, shall be five cents per quarter; for any distance exceeding fifty miles, and not exceeding three hundred miles, ten cents per quarter; for any distance exceeding three hundred miles and not exceeding one thousand miles, fifteen cents per quarter; for any distance exceeding one thousand miles and not exceeding two thousand miles, twenty cents per quarter; and for any distance exceeding two thousand miles and not exceeding four thousand miles, twenty-five cents per quarter; and for any distance exceeding four thousand miles, thirty cents per quarter; and all newspapers published monthly, and sent to actual and *bona fide* subcribers, shall be charged with one-fourth the foregoing rates; and *on* all such newspapers published semi-monthly shall be charged with one-half the foregoing rates; and papers published semi-weekly shall be charged double those rates; tri-weekly, treble those rates; and oftener than tri-weekly, five times those rates. And there shall be charged upon every other newspaper, and each circular not sealed, handbill, engraving, pamphlet, periodical, magazine, book, and every other description of printed matter which shall be unconnected with any manuscript or written matter, and which it may be lawful to transmit through the mail, of no greater weight than one ounce, for any distance not exceeding five hundred miles, one cent; and for each additional ounce, or fraction of an ounce, one cent; for any distance exceeding five hundred miles and not exceeding one thousand five hundred miles, double those rates; for any distance exceeding one thousand five hundred miles and not exceeding two thousand five hundred miles, treble those rates; for any distance exceeding two thousand five hundred miles and not exceeding three thousand five hundred miles, four times those rates; for any distance exceeding three thousand five hundred miles, five times those rates. Subscribers to all periodicals shall be required to pay one quarter's postage in advance; in all such cases the postage shall be one-half the foregoing rates. Bound books, and parcels of printed matter not weighing over thirty-two ounces, shall be deemed mailable matter under the provisions of this section. And the postage on all printed matter other than newspapers and periodicals published at intervals not exceeding three months, and sent from the office of publication to actual and *bona fide* subscribers, to be prepaid; and in ascertaining the weight of newspapers for the purpose of determining the amount of postage chargeable thereon, they shall be weighed when in a dry state. And whenever any printed matter on which the postage is required by this section to be prepaid shall, through the inattention of the postmasters, or otherwise, be sent without prepayment, the same shall be charged with double the amount of postage which would have been chargeable thereon if the postage had been prepaid: but nothing in this act contained shall subject to postage any matter which is exempted from the payment of postage by any existing law. And the Postmaster General, by and with the advice and consent of the President of the United States, shall be and he is hereby authorized to reduce or enlarge, from time to time, the rates of postage upon all letters and other mailable matter conveyed between the United States and any foreign country, for the purpose of making better postal arrangements with other governments, or counteracting any adverse measures affecting our postal intercourse with foreign countries; and postmasters at the office of delivery are hereby authorised, and it shall be their duty, to remove wrappers and envelopes from all printed matter and pamphlets not charged with letter postage, for the purpose of ascertaining whether there is upon or connected with any such printed matter or in such package any matter or thing which would authorize or require the charge of a higher rate of postage thereon. And all publishers of pamphlets, periodicals, magazines, and newspapers which shall not exceed sixteen ounces in weight shall be allowed to interchange their publications reciprocally free of postage: *Provided*, That such interchange shall be confined to a single copy of each publication: *And provided, also*, That said publishers may enclose in their publications the bills for subscriptions thereto without any additional charge for postage: *And provided, further*, That in all cases where newspapers shall not contain over three hundred square inches they may be transmitted through the mails by the publishers to *bona fide* subscribers at one-fourth the rates fixed by this act.

Sec. 3. *And be it further enacted*, That it shall be the duty of the Postmaster General to provide and furnish to all deputy postmasters, and to all other persons applying and paying therefor, suitable postage stamps of the denomination of three cents, and of such other denominations as he may think expedient to facilitate the prepayment of the postages provided for in this act; and any person who shall forge or counterfeit any postage stamp provided or furnished under the provisions of this or any former act, whether the same are impressed or printed on or attached to envelopes or not, or any die, plate or engraving therefor, or shall make or print, or knowingly use or sell, or have in his possession with intent to use or sell, any such false, forged, or counterfeited die, plate, engraving, or postage stamp, or who shall make or print, or authorize or procure to be made or printed, any postage stamps of the kind provided and furnished by the Postmaster General as aforesaid, without the especial authority and direction of the Post Office Department, or who, after such postage stamps have been printed, shall, with the intent to defraud the revenues of the Post Office Department, deliver any postage stamps to any person or persons other than such as shall be authorized to receive the same by an instrument of writing duly executed under the hand of the Postmaster General, and the seal of the Post Office Department, shall, on conviction thereof, be deemed guilty of felony, and be punished by a fine not exceeding five hundred dollars, or by imprisonment not exceeding five years, or by both such fine and imprisonment; and the expenses of procuring and providing all such postage stamps and letter envelopes, as are provided for or authorized by this act, shall be paid, after being adjusted by the auditor of the Post Office Department, or the certificate of the Postmaster General, out of any money in the Treasury arising from the Post Office Department.

Sec. 4. *And be it further enacted*, That it shall be the duty of every postmaster to cause to be defaced, in such manner as the Postmaster General shall direct, all postage stamps attached to letters deposited in his office for delivery, or to be sent by mail; and if any postmaster, sending letters in the mail with postage stamps attached, shall omit to deface the same, it shall be the duty of the postmaster to whose office such letters shall be sent for delivery to deface the stamps and report the delinquent postmaster to the Postmaster General. And if any person shall use, or attempt to use, in prepayment of postage, any postage stamp which shall have been before used for like purposes, such persons shall be subject to a penalty of fifty dollars for every such offence, to be recovered in the name of the United States, in any court of competent jurisdiction.

Sec. 5. *And be it further enacted*, That lists of letters ters remaining uncalled for in any post office in any city, town, or village, where a newspaper shall be printed, shall hereafter be published once only in the newspaper which, being issued weekly or oftener, shall have the largest circulation within the range of delivery of said office, to be decided by the Postmaster General, under such regulations as shall be prescribed by him, at a charge not exceeding *one* [three] at such office, at such time, and under such regulations as the Postmaster General shall prescribe; and at a charge of one cent for each letter advertised. And the postmaster at such office is hereby directed to post in a conspicuous place in his office a copy of such list, on the day or day after the publication thereof; and if the publisher of any such paper shall refuse to publish the list of letters as provided in this section, the postmaster may designate some other paper for such purpose. Such lists of letters shall be published once in six weeks, and as much oftener, not exceeding once a week, as the Postmaster General may specially direct: *Provided*, That the Postmaster General may, in his discretion, direct the publication of German and other foreign letters in any newspaper printed in the German or any other foreign language, which publication shall be in liue of or in addition to the publication of the list of such letters in the manner first in this section provided, as the Postmaster General shall direct.

Sec. 6. *And be it further enacted*, That to any postmaster whose commissions may be reduced before the amount allowed at his office for the year ending the thirtieth day of June, eighteen hundred and fifty-one, and whose labors may be increased, the Postmaster General shall be authorized, in his discretion, to allow such additional commissions as he may deem just and proper: *Provided*, That the whole amount of commissions allowed such postmaster during the fiscal year shall not exceed by more than twenty per cent. the amount of commissions at such office for the year ending the thirtieth day of June, eighteen hnndred and fifty-one.

Sec. 7. *And be it further enacted*, That no post office now in existence shall be discontinued, nor shall the mail service on any mail route in any of the states or territories be discontinued or diminished, in consequence of any diminution of the revenues that may result from this act; and it shall be the duty of the Postmaster General to establish new post offices, and place the mail service on any new mail routes established, or that may hereafter be established, in the same manner as though this act had not passed: *And provided further*, [That the compensation of no postmaster shall be diminished in consequence of the passage of this act.]

SEC. 8. *And be it further enacted*, That there shall be paid to the post office department, in further payment and compensation for the mail service performed for the two houses of Congress and the departments and offices of the government in the transportation of free matter, the sum of five hundred thousand dollars per year, which shall be paid quarterly, out of any money in the treasury not otherwise appropriated; and the moneys appropriated to the post office department by the twelfth section of the act "to establish certain post routes and for other purposes," approved March third, eighteen hundred and forty-seven, and remaining undrawn in the treasury, shall continue subject to the requisition of the Postmaster General, for the service of the post office department, notwithstanding the same may have so remained so undrawn for more than two years after it became subject to such requisition.

SEC. 9. *And be it further enacted*, That there is hereby appropriated, out of any moneys in the treasury not otherwise appropriated, the sum of five hundred thousand dollars to supply any deficiency that may arise in the post office department

SEC. 10. *And be it further enacted*, That it shall be in the power of the Postmaster General at all post offices where the postmasters are appointed by the President of the United States, to establish post routes within the cities or towns, to provide for conveying letters to the post office, by establishing suitable and convenient places of deposit, and by employing carriers to receive and deposit them in the post office; and at all such offices it shall be in his power to cause letters to be delivered by suitable carriers, to be appointed by him for that purpose, for which not exceeding one or two cents shall be charged, to be paid by the person receiving or sending the same; and all sums so received shall be paid into the post office department: *Provided,* The amount of compensation allowed by the Postmaster General to carriers shall in no case exceed the amount paid into the treasury, by each town or city, under the provisions of this section.

SEC. 11. *And be it further enacted,* That from and after the passage of this act it shall be lawful to coin, at the mint of the United States and its branches, a piece of the denomination and legal value of three cents, or three hundredths of a dollar, to be composed of three-fourths silver and one-fourth copper, and to weigh twelve grains and three-eighths of a grain, that the said coin shall bear such devices as shall be conspicuously different from those of the other silver coins and of the gold dollar, but having the inscription United States of America, and its denomination and date; and that it shall be a legal tender in payment of debts for all sums of thirty cents and under; and that no ingot shall be used for the coinage of the three cent pieces herein authorized, of which the quality differs more than five thousandths from the legal standard, and that, in adjusting the weight of the said coin, the following deviations from the standard weight shall not be exceeded, namely—one-half of a grain in the single piece, and one pennyweight in a thousand pieces.

Adproved March 3, 1851.

ABSTRACT.

Of the Laws of the United States in relation to the Naturalization of Aliens.

SECTION 1. Any alien, being a free white person, may be admitted to become a citizen of the United States, or any of them, on the following conditions, and not otherwise:

SEC. 2. *First:* That he shall have declared, on oath or affirmation,before the supreme, superior, district or circuit court of some one of the states, or of the territorial districts of the United States, or a circuit or district court of the United States, or before the clerk of either of such courts, two years at least before his admission, that it was, bona fide, his intention to become a citizen of the United States, and to renounce forever, all allegiance and fidelity to any foreign prince, potentate, state or soverignty, whereof such alien may, at the time, be a or citizen subject.

SEC. 3. From this condition are exempted, any alien, being a free white person, who was residing within the limits and under the jurisdiction of the United States at any time between the eighteenth day of June, 1798, and the fourteenth day of April, 1802, and who has continued to reside within the same.

SEC. 4. An alien, being a free white person and a minor, under the age of twenty-one years, who shall have resided in the United States three years next proceeding his arrival at the age of twenty-one years, and who shall have continued to reside therein to the time he may make application to be admitted a citizen thereof, may, after he arrives at the age of twenty-one years, and after he shall have resided five years within the United States, without having made the declaration, required in the second section, three years previous to his admission: but, such alien shall make the declaration required therin, at the time of his or her admission; and shall further declare, on oath, and prove to the satisfaction of the court, that for three years next preceeding, it has been the bona fide intention of such alien to become a citizen of the United States; and shall, in all other respects, comply with the laws in regard to naturalization.

SEC. 5. When any alien, who shall have complied with the condition specified in section second and who shall have pursued the directions prescribed in the second section of the act of April, 14, 1802, may die, before he is actually naturalized, the widow and the children of such alien shall be considered as citizens of the United States, and shall be entitled to all rights and privileges as such, upon taking the oaths prescribed by law.

SEC. 6. An alien shall at the time of his applications to be admitted, declare, on oath or affirmation, before some one of the courts aforesaid, that he will support the constitution of the United States, and that he doth absolutely and entirely renounce and abjure all allegiance and fidelity to every foreign prince, potentate, state or soverignty whatever, and particularly, by name, the prince, potentate, state or sovereignty, whereof he was before a citizen or subject; which proceedings shall be recorded by the clerk of the court.

SEC. 7. The court admitting such alien shall be satisfied that he has resided within the United States five years, at least, and within the state or territory where such court is at the time held, one year at least; and it shall further appear to their satisfaction that, during that time, he has behaved as a man of good moral character, attached to the principles of the constitution of the United States, and well disposed to the good order and happiness of the same. The oath of the applicant shall, in no case, be allowed to prove his residence.

Sec. 8. In case the alien applying to be admitted to citizenship, shall have borne any hereditary title, or been of any of the orders of nobility in the kingdom or state from which he came, he shall, in addition to the above requisites, make an express renunciation of his title or nobility, in the court to which his application shall be made, which renunciation shall be recorded in the said court; provided, that no alien, who shall be a native citizen, denizen or subject of any country, state or sovereign with whom the United States shall be at war, at the time of his application, shall be then admitted to be a citizen of the United States.

SEC. 9. But persons resident within the United States or the territories thereof, on the eighteenth day of June, in the year one thousand eight hundred and twelve, who had before that day, made a declaration according to law, of their intention to become citizens of the United States; or who, by the existing laws of the United States, were, on that day, entitled to become citizens, without making such declaration, may be admitted to become citizens thereof, notwithstanding they shall be alien enemies, at the times, and in the manner prescribed by the laws heretofore passed on that subject; provided, that herein nothing contained, shall be taken or construed to interfere with, or prevent the apprehension and removal, agreeably to law, of any alien enemy, at any time previous to the actual naturalization of such alien.

SEC. 10. Any alien, being a free white person, who was residing within the limits, and under the jurisdiction of the United States between the fourteenth day of April, one thousand eight hundred and twelve, and the eighteenth day of June, one thousand eight hundred and twelve, and who has continued to reside within the same, may be admitted to become a citizen of the United States, without having made any previous declaration of his intention to become a citizen; provided, that whenever any person, without a certificate of such declaration of intention, shall make application to be admitted a citizen of the United States, it shall be proved to the satisfaction of the court, that the applicant was residing within the limits, and under the jurisdiction of the United States, before the eighteenth day of June, one thousand eight hundred and twelve, and has continued to reside within the same or he shall not be so admitted; and the residence of the applicant within the limits, and under the jurisdiction of the United States, for at least five years immediately preceding the time of such application, shall be proved by the oath or affirmation of citizens of the United States which citizens shall be named in the record as witnesses; and such continued residence within the limits, and under the jurisdiction of the United States, when satisfactorialy proved, and the place or places where the applicant has resided, for at least five years, as aforesaid, shall be stated and set forth, together with the names of such citizens, in the record of the court admitting the applicant; otherwise the same shall not entitle him to be considered and deemed a citizen of the United States.

Sec. 11. Nothing in the foregoing section ten contained shall be construed to exclude from admission to citizenship, any free white person who was residing within the limits and under the jurisdiction of the United States at any time between the eighteenth day of June, one thousand seven hundred and ninety-eight, and the fourteenth day of April, one thousand eight hundred and two, and who, having continued to reside therein without having made any declaration of intention before a court of record as aforesaid, may be entitled to become a citizen of the United States, according to section three. Whenever any person, without a certificate of such declaration of intention, as aforesaid, shall make application to be admitted a citizen of the United States, it shall be proved to the satisfaction of the court, that the applicant was residing within the limits and under the jurisdiction of the United States, before the fourteenth day of April, one thousand eight hundred and two, and has continued to reside within the same, or he shall not be so admitted. And the residence of the applicant within the limits and under the jurisdiction of the United States for at least five years immediately preceding the time of such application, shall be proved by the oath or affirmation of citizens of the United States; which citizens shall be named in the record as witnesses. And such continued residence within the limits and under the jurisdiction of the United States, when satisfactorily proved, and the place or places where the applicant has resided for at least five years as aforesaid, shall be stated and set forth, together with the names of such citizens, in the record of the court admitting the applicant: otherwise the same shall not entitle him to be considered and deemed a citizen of United States.

SEC. 12. The children of persons duly naturalized under any of the laws of the United States, or who, previous to the passing of any law on that subject, by the government of the United States, may have become citizens of any one of the states, under the laws thereof, being under the age of twenty-one years, at the time of their parents' being so naturalized or admitted to the rights of citizenship, shall if dwelling in the United States, be considered as citizens of the United States; and the children of persons who now are, or have been citizens of the United States, shall, though born out of the limits and jurisdiction of the United States; be considered as citizens of the United States. The right of citizenship shall not descend to persons whose fathers have never resided within the United States. And no person hertofore proscribed by any state, or who has been legally convicted of having joined the army of Great Britian during the war of the revolution, shall be admitted a citizen without the consent of the legislature of the state in which such person was proscribed. Children of persons naturalized before the fourteenth of April, 1802, under age at the time of their parents' naturalization, were, if dwelling in the United States on the fourteenth day of April, 1802, to be considered as citizens of the United States.

SEC. 13. Any alien who was residing within the limits, and under the jurisdiction of the United States before the twenty-ninth day of January, one thousand seven hundred and ninety-five may be admitted to become a citizen, on due proof made to some one of the courts aforesaid, that he has resided two years at least, within and under the jurisdiction of the United States, and one year at least immediately preceding his application, within the state or territory where such court is at the time held; and on his declaring on oath or affirmation, that he will support the constitution of the United States, and that he doth absolutely and entirely renounce and abjure all allegiance and fidelity to any foreign prince, potentate, state or soverignty whatever, and particularly, by name, the prince, potentate, state or soverignty whereof he was before a citizen or subject; and moreover, on its appearing to the satisfaction of the court that, during the said term of two years, he has behaved as a man of good moral character, attached to the constitution of the United States, and well disposed to the good order and happiness of the same; and where the alien applying for admission to citizenship, shall have borne any hereditary title, or been of any of the orders of nobility in the kingdom or state from which he came, on his moreover making, in the court, an express renunciation of his title or order of nobility, before he shall be entitled to such admission; all of which proceedings, required in this proviso to be performed in the court, shall be recorded by the clerk thereof.

Sec. 14. Every court of record, in any individual state, having common law jurisdiction, and a seal or clerk or prothonotary, shall be considered as a district court, within the meaning of the naturalization act; and every alien, who may have been naturalized in any such court, shall enjoy the same rights and privileges, as if he had been naturalized in a district or circuit court of the United States.

Sec. 15. No person who shall arrive in the United States, after February the seventeenth, 1815, shall be admitted to become a citizen of the United States, who shall not, for the continued term of five next preceding his admission, have resided within the United States, without being at any time during the said five years, out of the territory of the United States.

ELECTION LAW OF MICHIGAN.

Section 1. In all elections, every white male citizen, every white male inhabitant residing in the State on the twenty-fourth day of June, one thousand eight hundred and thirty-five; every white male inhabitant residing in this state on the first day of January, one thousand eight hundred and fifty, who has declared his intention to become a citizen of the United States, pursuant to the laws thereof, six months preceding an election, or who has resided in this state two years and six months, and declared his intention as aforesaid, and every civilized male inhabitant of Indian descent, a native of the United States, and not a member of any tribe, shall be an elector and entitled to vote; but no citizen or inhabitant shall be an elector or entitled to vote, unless he shall be above the age of twenty-one years, and has resided in this state three months, and in the township or ward in which he offers to vote, ten days next preceding such election.

Sec. 2. All votes shall be given by ballot, except for such township officers as may be authorized by law to be otherwise chosen.

Sec. 3. Every elector, in all cases except treason, felony or breach of the peace, shall be privileged from arrest during his attendance at election, and in going to and returning from the same.

Sec. 4. No elector shall be obliged to do militia duty on the day of election, except in time of war or public danger, or attend court as a suitor or witness.

Sec. 5. No elector shall be deemed to have gained or lost a residence by reason of his being employed in the service of the United States or of this state; nor while engaged in the navigation of the waters of this state or of the United States, or of the high seas; nor while a stduent of any seminary of learning; nor while kept at any almshouse or other asylum at public expense; nor while confined in any public prison.

SEC. 6. Laws may be passed to preserve the purity of elections, and guard against abuses of the elective franchise.

SEC. 7. No soldier, seaman, nor marine in the army or navy of the United States, shall be deemed a resident of this state in consequence of being stationed in any military or naval place within the same.

SEC. 8. Any inhabitant who may hereafter be engaged in a duel, either as principal or accessory before the fact, shall be disqualified from holding any office under the constitution and laws of this state, and shall not be permitted to vote at any election.

UNITED STATES GOVERNMENT.

SALARIES.

President of the United States,	$25,000
Secretary of State,	6,000
" of the Treasury,	6,000
" " " Interior,	6,000
" " War,	6,000
" of the Navy,	6,000
Postmaster-General,	6,000
Attorney-general,	4,000

STATE GOVERNMENTS.—1851.

States.	*Governor.*	*Term expires.*	*Salary.*
MAINE,	John Hubbard,	Jan. 1852	$1,500
N. HAMPSHIRE,	Samuel Dinsmoor,	June, '51	1,000
VERMONT,	*Chas K. Williams,*	Oct. '51	750
MASSACHUSETTS,	George S. Boutwell,	Jan. '52	2,500
RHODE-ISLAND,	Phillip Allen,	May '52	400
CONNECTICUT,	Thos. H. Seymour,	May '52	1,100
NEW-YORK,	*Washington Hunt,*	Jan. '53	4,000
NEW-JERSEY,	George F. Fort,	Jan. '55	1,600
PENNSYLVANIA,	*Wm. F. Johnston,*	Jan. '52	3,000
DELAWARE,	William H. Ross,	Jan. '55	$1,333\frac{1}{3}$
MARYLAND,	Enoch L. Lowe,	Jan. '54	3,600
VIRGINIA,	John B. Floyd,	Jan. '52	$3,333\frac{1}{3}$
NORTH-CAROLINA,	David S. Reid,	Jan. '53	2,000
SOUTH-CAROLINA,	John H. Means,	Jan. '52	3,500
GEORGIA,	Geo. W. Towns,	Nov. '51	3,000
FLORIDA,	*Thomas S. Brown,*	Oct. '53	1,500
ALABAMA,	Henry W. Collier,	Dec. '51	2,500
MISSISSIPPI,	John A. Quitman,	Jan. '52	3,000
LOUISIANA,	Joseph Walker,	Jan. '54	6,000
OHIO,	Reuben Wood,	Dec. '52	1,200
INDIANA,	Joseph A. Wright,	Dec. '52	1,300
ILLINOIS,	Augustus C. French	Jan. '53	1,500
MICHIGAN,	John S. Barry,	Jan. '52	1,000
WISCONSIN,	Nelson Dewey,	Dec. '51	1,250
IOWA,	Steph. Hempstead,	Dec. '54	1,000
KENTUCKY,	*J. L. Helm,* (acti'g)	Aug. '51	2,500
TENNESSEE,	William Trousdale,	Oct. '51	2,000
ARKANSAS,	John S. Roane,	Nov. '52	1,800
TEXAS,	Peter H. Bell,	Dec. '51	2,000
MISSOURI,	Austin A. King,	Dec. '52	2,000
CALIFORNIA,	Peter H. Burnett,	Dec. '51	10,000

The names of Governors in *italics* are whigs.

ELECTORAL VOTES FOR PRESIDENTS AND VICE PRESIDENTS FROM 1789 TO 1849.

		Maine,	N.Hampshire	Vermont,	Massachusets	Rhode-Island	Connecticut,	New-York,	New-Jersey,	Pennsylvania	Delaware,	Maryland,	Virginia,	N. Carolina,	S. Carolina,	Georgia,	Alabama,	Mississippi,	Louisiana,	Tennessee,	Kentucky,	Ohio,	Indiana,	Illinois,	Missouri,	Arkansas,	Michigan,	Florida,	Texas,	Wisconsin,	Iowa,	Total,
1789	George Washington, Va.		5		10		7		6	10	3	6	10		7	5																69
	John Adams, Mass.		5		10		5		1	8			5																			34
	Scattering,						2		5	2	3	6	5		7	5																35
1793	George Washington, Va.		6	4	16	4	9	12	7	15	3	8	21	12	7	4					4											132
	John Adams, Mass.		6	4	16	4	9		7	14	3	8			6																	77
	George Clinton, N. Y.							12		1			21	12	sc	4					sc											50
1797	John Adams, Mass.		6	4	16	4	9	12	7	1	3	7	1	1																		71
	Thomas Jefferson, Va.									14		4	20	11	8	4				3	4											69
	Thomas Pinckney, S. C.			4	13		4	12	7	2	3	4	1	1	8																	59
	Aaron Burr, N. Y.									13		3	1	6						3	4											30
	Scattering.		6		3	4	5					2	19	5		4																48
1801	Thomas Jefferson, Va.							12		8		5	21	8	8	4				3	4											73
	John Adams, Mass.		6	4	16	4	9		7	7	3	5		4																		65
	Aaron Burr, N. Y.					sc		12		8		5	21	8	8	4				3	4											73
	Chas. C. Pinckney, S. C.		6	4	16	3	9		7	7	3	5		4																		64
1805 Pres	Thomas Jefferson, Va.		7	6	19	4		19	8	20		9	24	14	10	6				5	8	3										162
	Cha's C. Pinckney, S. C.						9				3	2																				14
V.P	George Clinton, N. Y.		7	6	19	4		19	8	20		9	24	14	10	6				5	8	3										162
	Rufus King, N. Y.						9				3	2																				14
1809 Pres	James Madison, Va.			6				13	8	20		9	24	11	10	6				5	7	3										122
	Cha's C. Pinckney, S. C.		7		19	4	9	sc			3	2		3																		47
V.P	George Clinton, N. Y.							13	8	20		9	24	11	10	6				5	7	sc										113
	Rufus King, N. Y.		7	sc	19	4	9	sc			3	2		3																		47
1813 Pres	James Madison, Va.			8						25		6	25	15	11	8			3	8	12	7										128
	De Witt Clinton, N. Y.		8		22	4	9	29	8		4	5																				89
V.P	Elbridge Gerry, Mass.		1	8	2					25		6	25	15	11	8			3	8	12	7										131
	Jared Ingersoll, Pa.		7		20	4	9	29	8		4	5																				86

1817	James Monroe, Va.		8	8		4		29	8	25		8	25	15	11	8			3	8	12	8	3									183
Pres	Rufus King, N. Y.				22		9				3																					34
V. P.	D. D. Thompkins, N. Y.		8	8	sc	4	sc	29	8	25	sc	8	25	15	11	8			3	8	12	8	3									183
1821	Pres. James Monroe, Va.	9	7s	8	15	4	9	29	8	25	4	11	25	15	11	8	3	3	3	8	12	8	3	3								231
V. P.	D. D. Thompkins, N. Y.	9	7s	8	7s	4	9	29	8	25	sc	10	25	15	11	8	3	3	3	8	12	8	3	3								218
1825	Andrew Jackson, Tenn.							1	8	28		7		15	11		5	3	3	11			5	2								99
Pres	John Quincy Adams, Ms	9	8	7	15	4	8	26			1	3							2					1								84
	Wm. H. Crawford, Ga.							5			2	1	24			9																41
	Henry Clay, Ky.							4													14	16			3							37
V. P	John C. Calhoun, S. C.	9	7	7	15	3		29	8	28	1	10		15	11		5	3	5	11	7		5	3								182
	Nathan Sanford, N. Y.		sc				sc	7			sc	sc	sc			sc					7	16			sc							30
Vote in the House of Representatives.	Adams,	7	6	5	12	2	6	18	1	1		5	1	1			3		2		8	10		1	1							13
	Jackson,							2	5	25		3	1	2	9			1	1	9	4	2	3									7
	Crawford,				1			14			1	1	12	10		7						2										4.
1829	Andrew Jackson, Tenn.	1						20		28		5	24	15	11	9	5	3	5	11	14	16	5	3	3							178
Pres	John Q. Adams, Mass.	8	8	7	15	4	8	16	8		3	6																				83
	John C. Calhoun, S. C.	1						20		28		5	24	15	11	2	5	3	5	11	14	16	5	3	3							171
V. P	Richard Rush, Pa.	8	8	7	15	4	8	16	8		3	6																				83
	William Smith, S. C.															7																7
1833	Andrew Jackson, Tenn.	10	7					42	8	30		3	23	15	sc	11	7	4	5	15		21	9	5	4							219
Pres	Henry Clay, Ky.			sc	14	4	8				3	5									15											49
V. P	Martin Van Buren, N. Y.	10	7					42	8			3	23	15		11	7	4	5	15		21	9	5	4							189
	John Sergeant, Pa.			sc	14	4	8			sc	3	5			sc						15											49
1837	Martin Van Buren, N.Y.	10	7			4	8	42		30			23	15	sc	sc	7	4	5	sc				5	4	3	3					170
Pres	William H. Harrison, O.			7	sc				8		3	10									15	21	9									73
V. P	R. M. Johnson, Ky.	10	7			4	8	42		30				15			7	4	5					5	4	3	3					147
	Francis Granger, N. Y.			7	14				8		3	sc	sc		sc	sc				sc	15	21	9									77
1841	Wm. H. Harrison, Ohio.	10		7	14	4	8	42	8	30	3	10		15		11		4	5	15	15	21	9				3					234
Pres	Martin Van Buren, N. Y.		7										23		11		7							5	4	3						60
V. P	John Tyler, Va.	10		7	14	4	8	42	8	30	3	10		15		11		4	5	17	15	21	9				3					234
	R. M. Johnson, Ky.		7										22		sc		7							5	4	3						48
1845	James K. Polk, Tenn.	9	6					36		26			17		9	10	9	6	6				12	9	7	3	5					170
Pres	Henry Clay, Ky.			6	12	4	6		7		3	8		11						13	12	23										105
V. P	George.M. Dallas, Pa.	9	6					36		26			17		9	10	9	6	6				12	9	7	3	5					170
	Theo Frelinghuysen, NY			6	12	4	6		7		3	8		11						13	12	23										105
1849	Lewis Cass, Michigan.	9	6										17		9		9	6				23	12	9	7	3	5		4	4	4	127
Pres	Zachary Taylor, La.			6	12	4	6	36	7	26	3	8		11		10			6	13	12							3				163
V. P	William O. Butler, Ky.	9	6										17		9		9	6				23	12	9	7	3	5		4	4	4	127
	Millard Fillmore, N. Y.			6	12	4	6	36	7	26	3	8		11		10			6	13	12							3				163

RECAPITULATION.

1st Term, 1789. Electors 69, and 69 votes for George Washington' John Adams had 34. John Jay had New-Jersey, 5, Delaware, 3, Virginia 1--9 in all. R. H. Harrison had Maryland, 6. J. Rutledge had South Carolina, 6. John Hancock had Pennsylvania, 2, Virginia, 1, South Carolina, 1--4 in all. G. Clinton had Virginia, 3. S. Huntington had Connecticut, 2. J. Milton had Georgia, 2. J. Armstrong had Georgia, 1, Edw. Telfair had Georgia, 1. B. Lincoln had Georgia, 1--Total 69. Rhode-Island, New-York, and North-Carolina did not assent to the constitution in season to vote for President in 1789.

2nd Term, 1793. Electors, 135, 132 votes for George Washington, and 3 vacancies, (Maryland, 2, and South-Carolina, 1). John Adams received 77 votes; George Clinton, 50. Thomas Jefferson had Kentucky, 4 votes. Aaron Burr had South-Carolina, 1 vote--Total 132.

3d Term, 1797. Electors, 138. John Adams received 71 votes. Thomas Jefferson had 68 votes. Thomas Pinckney had 59 votes. Aaron Burr had 30 votes. S. Adams had Virginia, 15 votes. O. L. Elsworth had New-Hampshire, 6, Massachusetts, 1, Rhode-Island 4--11 in all. George Clinton had Virginia, 3, Georgia 4--7 in all. John Jay had Connecticut, 5. James Iredell had North-Carolina, 3. George Washington had Virginia, 1, North-Carolina, 1--2 in all. J. Henry had Maryland, 2. C. C. Pinckney had North-Carolina, 1. S. Johnson had 2 from Massachusetts.

4th Term, 1801. Electors, 138. Thos. Jefferson received 73 votes; Aaron Burr received 73 votes; J. Adams had 65 votes; Chas. C. Pinckney had 64 votes. John Jay had Rhode-Island, 1. The election was carried to the House of Representatives, and Mr. Jefferson was, on the 36th ballot, chosen President by the votes of New-York, New-Jersey, Pennsylvania, Maryland, Virginia, North-Carolina, Georgia, Tennessee and Kentucky. Mr. Burr was also chosen Vice-President. After this the Constitution was altered so as to require the President and Vice-President to be voted for separately.

5th Term, 1805. See table.

6th Term, 1809. For President, J. Madison, 122 votes; Chas. C. Pinckney, 47; G. Clinton, 6 votes from the State of New-York. Vacancy in Kentucky. Total, 176. For Vice-President, G. Clinton, 113; Rufus King, 47; J. Langdon, 9, (6 from Vermont and 3 from Ohio); J. Madison, 3, (from N. Y.); J. Monroe, 3, (from N. Y.); 1 vacancy in Kentucky. Total, 176.

7th Term, 1813. See table. One vacancy in Ohio.

8th Term, 1817. For President, J. Monroe, 183 votes; Rufus King, 34. Four vacancies, (Del. 1, Md. 3). Total, 221. For Vice-President, Dan'l D. Tompkins, 183 votes; John E. Howard, 22 votes from Mass.; James Ross, 5, from Conn.; J. Marshall, 5, from Conn.; R. G. Harper, 3 from Delaware. Four vacancies as before. Total 221.

9th Term. 1821. For President, J. Monroe, 231; J. Q. Adams, 1, from

Mass. Total, 232. For Vice President, D. D. Tompkins, 218; R. Stockton, 8, from Mass.; D. Rodney, 4, from Delaware; R. Rush, 1, from N. H.; R. G. Harper, 1, from Maryland. Total, 232.

10th Term, 1825: For President, Andrew Jackson, 99 votes; J. Q. Adams, 84; Wm. H. Crawford, 41; Henry Clay, 37. Total, 261. Mr. Adams was chosen by the House of Representatives. See table. For Vice President, J. C. Calhoun, 182; N. Sandford, 30; N. Macon, 24, from Va.; A. Jackson, 13, (1 from N. H., 8 from Conn., 1 from Md., and 3 from Mo.;) M. Van Buren, 9, from Georgia; Henry Clay, 2, from Del. One vacancy in Rhode Island. Total, 261.

11th Term, 1829. See Table.

12th Term 1833. For President, Andrew Jackson, 219 votes; Henry Clay, 49; J. Floyd, 11, from S. C.; Wm. Wirt, 7, from Vt. Two vacancies from Maryland. Total, 286. For Vice President, M. Van Buren, 189; John Sergeant, 49; Wm. Wilkins, 30, from Pa.; Henry Lee, 11, from S. C.; Amos Ellmaker, 7, from Vt. Total, 286.

13th Term, 1837. For President, Martin Van Buren, 170; Wm. H Harrison, 73; Hugh L White, 26; Daniel Webster, 14; W. P. Mangum, 11. Total, 294. For Vice President, Richard M. Johnson, 144; Francis M. Granger, 77; John Tyler, 47, Wm. Smith, 23. Total, 294.

14th Term, 1841. For President Wm. H. Harrison, 234 votes; M. Van Buren, 60. Total 294. For Vice President, John Tyler, 234; R. M. Johnson, 48; L. W. Tazewell, 11; J. K. Polk, 1. Total, 294.

15th Term, 1845. (See Table.)

16th Term, 1849. (See Table.)

SINGULAR COINCIDENCE.

The presidents left the chair of state at periods of life as follows:

George Washington, -	in the 66th	year of his age,
John Adams, - - -	" 66th	"
Thomas Jefferson, - -	" 66th	"
James Madison, - -	" 66th	"
James Monroe, - -	" 66th	"
John Quincy Adams, - -	" 62d	"
Andrew Jackson, - -	" 70th	"
Martin Van Buren, - -	" 59th	"
William H. Harrison, -	" 68th	"
James K. Polk, - -	" 54th	"
Zachary Taylor, -	" 66th	"

Had the younger Adams been elected a second term, he would have retired in his 66th year.

FIRST CENSUS OF THE U. S. FOR 1790.

Whites, and all others not slaves,	3,231,930
Slaves,	697,897
Total population,	3,929,827

Apportionment.—The apportionment, under the first census, in 1790 of Representatives among the several States, agreeable to the act of April 14, 1792, was 1 Representative to every 33,000 souls, after March, 3, 1793.

SECOND CENSUS OF THE U. S. FOR 1800.

Whites, &c.,	4,412,900
Slaves,	893,041
Total,	5,305,941

Apportionment of Representatives, according to act of Jan. 14, 1802, was 1 Representative to every 33,000 souls, after March 3, 1803.

THIRD CENSUS OF THE U. S., FOR 1810.

Whites, &c.,	6,048,450
Slaves,	1,191,364
Total,	7,239,814

Apportionment of Representatives, according to act of Dec. 21, 1811, was 1 Representative to every 35,000 souls, after March 3, 1813.

FOURTH CENSUS OF THE U. S., FOR 1820.

Whites, &c.,	8,100,163
Slaves,	1,538,028
Total,	9,638,191

Apportionment of Representatives, according to act of March 7, 1822, was 1 Representative to every 40,000 souls, after March 3, 1823.

FIFTH CENSUS OF THE U. S., FOR 1830.

Whites, &c.,	10,856,977
Slaves,	2,009,043
Total,	12,866,020

Apportionment of Representatives, according to act of May 22, 1832, was 1 Representative to every 47,700 souls, after March 3, 1833.

SIXTH CENSUS OF THE U. S., FOR 1840.

Whites, &c.,	14,582,098
Slaves,	2,487,355
Total,	17,069,453

Apportionment of Representatives, according to act of June 25, 1842, was 1 Representative to every 70,680 souls, after March 3, 1843.

Under each apportionment, two-fifths of the slave population was deducted.

SIXTH CENSUS OF THE U. S., FOR 1840.

	White population, and all others not slaves.	Slaves.	Total.
Maine,	501,793		501,793
New Hampshire,	284,574		284,574
Massachusetts,	737,699		737,699
Rhode Island,	108,825	5	108,830
Connecticut,	309,061	17	309,978
Vermont,	291,948		291,948
New York,	2,428,917	4	2,428,921
New Jersey,	372.659	647	373,306
Pennsylvania,	1,723,969	64	1,724,033
Delaware,	75,480	2,605	78,805
Maryland,	380,282	89,737	470,019
Virginia,	790,810	448,987	1,239,797
North Carolina,	507,602	245,817	753,419
South Carolina,	267,360	327,038	594,398
Georgia,	410,450	280,942	691,392
Alabama,	337,224	253,532	590,756
Mississippi,	162,440	195,211	375,651
Louisiana,	183,957	168,454	352.411
Tennessee,	646,151	183,059	829,210
Kentucky,	587,570	192,258	779,828
Ohio,	1,519,464	3	1,519,467
Indiana,	685,863	3	685,866
Illinois,	475,852	331	476,183
Missouri,	335,462	58,240	383,702
Michigan,	212,267		212,267
Arkansas,	77,637	19,937	97,574
Florida,	28,760	25,717	54,477
Wisconsin,	30,934	11	30,945
Iowa,	43,096	16	43,112
District of Columbia,	39,018	4,694	43,712
			17,063,353

Total number of persons on board vessels of war in the U. S. service, June 1, 1840,.................................. 6,100

Total of the United States,................................ 17,065,439

SIXTH CENSUS OF THE U. S. FOR 1850.

The Superintendent of the Census furnished the Washington Republic, at Washington, in May last, the following statement of the census or 1850, which is the only list now before the public. It is supposed to be nearly correct, although there may be some slight inaccuracies. It also gives the ratio of representation and number of Representatives to each state, which that amount of population will give, the fractions being given in a separate column, as left to each state.

States.	Free Population.	Slaves.	Representative population.	No. of Representatives and fractions.
Maine,	583,232			6 21,020
New-Hampshire,	317,831			3 36,725
Massachusetts,	994,721			10 57,251
Vermont,	313,466			3 32,360
Rhode Island,	147,555			1 53,853
Connecticut,	370,604			3 89,498
New-York,	3,090,022			32 91,558
New-Jersey,	488,552	119		5 20,113
Pennsylvania,	2,311,681			24 62,533
Ohio,	1,977,031			21 9,289
Indiana,	988,734			10 51,714
Wisconsin,	304,226			3 23,113
Michigan,	395,703			4 20,120
Illinois,	858,298			9 20,980
Iowa,	192,122			2 4,718
California,	200,000			2 12,956
Maryland,	492,706	89 800	546,586	5 78,086
Virginia,	948,055	473,026	1,231,870	13 13,744
North-Carolina,	583,544	288,412	753,505	8 3,889
South-Carolina,	289,000	384,925	514,499	5 45,989
Georgia,	515,669	515,669	733,448	7 77,534
Florida,	48,046	39,341	71,750	1
Alabama,	428,765	342,894	634,501	6 72,289
Mississippi,	292,434	300,419	472,685	6 20,895
Louisiana,	269,955	230,817	408,440	4 33,632
Texas,	134,057	53,346	166,064	1 72,362
Arkansas,	162,658	46,983	190,848	2 3,444
Missouri,	594,843	89,289	648,416	6 86,204
Tennessee,	733,599	249,519	923,310	9 89,992
Kentucky,	779,728	221,768	912,788	9 75,470
Delaware,	89,239	2,289	90,612	1

ENTIRE POPULATION.

	Free.	Slaves.
Free States, - - - - - -	13,533,328	
Slave States, - - - - - -	6,393,938	3,067,234
District and Territories, - - -	160,824	3,500
	20,087,909	3,710,724

The entire representative population is about 21,832,625. The ratio of representation will be about 93,702.

As the law of 22d May, 1850, determines the number of representatives, at 233, and as but 220 of these are provided for in the foregoing table without taking them from fractions, it will be necessary to select from the thirteen states having the largest fractions, to each of which are to be assigned a representative, to make up the entire number.

The states entitled to representatives for such fractions will most probably be Alabama, Georgia, Indiana, Illinois, Kentucky, Massachusetts, Maryland, Missouri, New York, Pennsylvania, Rhode Island, Tennessee, Texas.

The states which gain, irrespective of the fraction, will be Pennsylvania 1, Illinois 2, Mississippi 1, Michigan 1, Missouri 1—6.

The states which gain, in all, are as follows, viz: Arkansas 1, Indiana 1, Illinois 2, Massachusetts 1, Mississippi 2, Michigan 1, Missouri 2, Pennsylvania 1--10.

The following states lose, viz: Maine 1, New-Hampshire 1, New-York 1, North-Carolina 2, South-Carolina 2, Vermont 1, Virginia 2--11.

The free states gain six members and lose four; the slave states gain four and lose six.

INDEBTEDNESS OF THE SEVERAL STATES.

United States,	$64,228,238	Mississippi,	7,271,707
Maine.	979,000	Louisiana,	16,238,131
Massachusetts,	8,091,017	Texas,	11,050,201
New-York,	23,937,249	Arkansas,	3,862,172
New-Jersey,	62,596	Tennessee,	3,337,806
Pennsylvania,	40,424,737	Kentucky,	4,531,913
Maryland,	15,900,000	Ohio,	19,173,223
Virginia,	14,400,507	Michigan,	2,849,939
North-Carolina,	977,000	Indiana,	6,556,437
South-Carolina,	3,622,039	Illinois,	16,612,795
Georgia,	1,903,472	Missouri,	956,261
Alabama,	10,385,938	Iowa,	55,000

Total in 1850, - - - - - -	$275,480,676
Total in 1843, - - - - - - -	198,818,735
Increase in seven years, - - - -	$76,671,940

INDEBTEDNESS OF BANKS, RAILROADS, CITIES & COUNTIES

Bonded debts of cities and counties, 1851,	$75,000,000,00
Bonded debts of railroad and canal companies, 1851,	80,000,000,00
Loans and discounts of banks in the United States, 1851,	450,000,000,00
Total, - - - - - -	$605,000,000,00

CENSUS OF MICHIGAN BY TOWNS.

ALLEGAN COUNTY.

TOWNSHIPS.	1840	1845	1850	TOWNSHIPS.	1840	1845	1850
Allegan,	634	843	752	Monterey,			238
Dorr,			124	Newark,	121	241	246
Fillmore,			527	Otsego,	480	507	819
Ganges,			246	Pine Plains,			34
Gunplain,		476	587	Plainfield,	397		
Leighton,			112	Trowbridge,		217	313
Manlius,	35	84	82	Watson,		205	313
Martin,	116	235	329	Wayland,		133	406
					1,783	2,041	5,127

BARRY COUNTY.

TOWNSHIPS.	1840	1845	1850	TOWNSHIPS.	1840	1845	1850
Assyria,		312	336	Johnstown,	227	285	451
Barry,	343	216	478	Maple Grove,			153
Baltimore,			90	Orangeville,			364
Castleton,		200	324	Prairieville,		437	555
Carlton,		218	272	Rutland,			177
Hope,			99	Thornapple,	99	177	336
Hastings,	279	236	554	Woodland,		205	377
Irving,		139	214	Yankee Springs,	130	177	292
					1,078	2,602	5,072

BERRIEN COUNTY.

TOWNSHIPS.	1840	1845	1850	TOWNSHIPS.	1840	1845	1850
Bainbridge,	251	613		Niles,	1,420	1,884	
Bertrand,	1,298	1,395		Oronoko,	335	664	
Benton,		237		Pipestone,		274	
Berrien,	593	566		Royalton,	146	283	
Buchanan,	264	630		St. Joseph,	489	622	
Galien,		141		Weesaw,	142	155	
New Buffalo,	123	401					
					5,011	7,865	11,412

BRANCH COUNTY.

TOWNSHIPS.	1840	1845	1850	TOWNSHIPS.	1840	1845	1850
Algansee,	424	776	609	Gilead,	214	420	503
Batavia,	400	636	724	Kinderhook,		282	356
Bethel,	335	449	679	Mattison,	170	333	475
Bronson,	622	561	713	Noble,		434	451
Butler,	234	469	611	Ovid,	369	393	710
California,			473	Quincy,	498	841	1,111
Cold Water,	1,123	1,467	2,166	Sherwood,	367	613	686
Girard,	452	675	934	Union,	507	715	1,271
					5,715	9,064	12,474

CASS COUNTY.

TOWNSHIPS.	1840	1845	1850	TOWNSHIPS.	1840	1845	1850
Calvin,	209	359	624	Ontwa,	543	626	781
Howard,	370	622	766	Penn,	415	536	698
Jefferson,	471	684	887	Porter,	556	948	1,259
La Grange,	769	1,030	1,327	Pokagon,	516	618	994
Mason,	318	398	570	Silver Creek,	183	335	491
Marcellus,		187	222	Volinia,	411	531	607
Milton,	439	478	610	Wayne,	335	474	682
Newburgh,	175	252	388				
					5,710	8,078	10,906

CALHOUN COUNTY.

TOWNSHIPS.	1840	1845	1850	TOWNSHIPS.	1840	1845	1850
Albion,	932	1,358	1,666	Homer,	824	830	929
Athens,	134	375	532	Lee,	59	208	381
Battle Creek,	993	1,652	1,897	Leroy,	326	582	878
Bedford,	220	455	740	Marshall,	1,763	2,250	2,823
Burlington,	411	659	811	Marengo,	872	1,080	1,013
Clarence,		326	485	Newton,	235	387	569
Clarendon,	506	692	669	Pennfield,	377	517	598
Convis,	292	539	621	Pinckney,	201		
Eckford,	555	711	715	Sheridan,	584	791	978
Emmet,	647	1,122	1,582	Tekonsha,	375	530	651
Fredonia,	343	536	623				
					10,599	15,594	19,169

CHIPPEWA COUNTY.

Sault Ste Marie 534 | 1,017 | 898

CLINTON COUNTY.

TOWNSHIPS.	1840	1845	1850	TOWNSHIPS.	1840	1845	1850
Bath,		151	222	Greenbush,		105	318
Bengal,		49	143	Lebanon,		114	192
Bingham,		72	185	Olive,		159	228
Dallas,		108	185	Ovid.		102	172
De Witt,		418	706	Riley,		134	191
Duplain,		213	419	Victor,		229	277
Eagle,		364	521	Watertown,		198	315
Essex,		193	410	Westphalia,		401	618
					1,614	3,010	5,102

EATON COUNTY.

TOWNSHIPS.	1840	1845	1850	TOWNSHIPS.	1840	1845	1850
Bellevue,	529	653	769	Kalamo,	139	256	429
Benton,		186	344	Oeinda,	265	280	492
Brookfield,		147	255	Roxand,		166	358
Carmel,	85	288	567	Sunfield,		112	122
Chester,	195	201	380	Tyler,		680	
Delta,		110	242	Vermontville,	182	272	324
Eaton,	868	397	539	Walton,	116	286	464
Eaton Rapids,		457	1,525	Windsor,		122	253
					2,379	4,813	7,058

GENESEE COUNTY.

TOWNSHIPS.	1840	1845	1850	TOWNSHIPS.	1840	1845	1850
Argentine,	177	384	436	Genesee,	425	843	
Atlas,		780	1,207	Grand Blanc,	782	1 029	1,165
Clayton,			418	Hearsley,	115		
Cavison,		203	367	Montrose,			52
East Genesee,			844	Mundy,	440	632	786
Fenton,	660	953	873	Richfield,		427	482
Forest,		126	179	Thetford,		172	303
Flint,	984	2,008	3,304	Vienna,	212	342	389
Flushing,	473	1,211	708	West Genesee,			232
Gaines,		156	286				
					4,268	9,266	12,031

HILLSDALE COUNTY.

TOWNSHIPS.	1840.	1845.	1850.	TOWNSHIPS.	1840.	1850.	1850.
Adams,	554	794	1,129	Litchfield,	691	929	1,362
Allen.	466	704	1,033	Moscow,	758	883	942
Amboy,			252	Pittsford,	641	833	1,223
Camden,	174	345	594	Ransom,			549
Cambria,		421	716	Reading,	331	620	956
Canaan,	164			Rowland,	83	324	
Fayette,	807	1 720	895	Scipio,	634	644	864
Florida,	297	499		Somerset,	716	776	913
Hillsdale,			1,067	Wheatland,	718	1,125	1,358
Jefferson,			763	Woodbridge,	226	217	404
Jonesville village.			565	Wright,		277	574
					7,240	11,111	16,159

HOUGHTON COUNTY.

Eagle Harbor			126	L'Anse,			126
Houghton,			546				
							798

HURON COUNTY.

Total,							207

INGHAM COUNTY.

Alaidon,	221	296	377	Locke,		212	321
Aurelius,	148	318	501	Meridan,		169	367
Brutus,	97			Onondaga,	276	559	819
Bunker Hill,	93	226	374	Phelpstown,	121	191	393
Delhi,		243	402	Stockbridge,	385	552	657
Ingham,	273	534	754	Vevay,	223	604	783
Lansing,		88	1,229	Wheatfield,		180	231
LeRoy,	110	164	254	White Oak,	270	422	508
Leslie,	281	509	673		2,498	5,267	8,597

IONIA COUNTY.

Berlin,		348	391	North Plains,		264	292
Boston,	85	241	424	Odessa,			81
Campbell,			40	Orange,		348	378
Cass,	202			Orleans,			491
Danby,		150	362	Otisco,	212	607	1,018
Easton,		278	397	Portland,	441	654	763
Ionia,	486	654	774	Ronald,		201	452
Keene,		390	737	Sebewa,		100	247
Lyons,	497	705	850				
Montcalm,		161			1,923	5,101	7,597

JACKSON COUNTY.

Columbia,	952	1,089	1,142	Parma,	525	769	1,081
Concord,	814	901	984	Pulaski,	394	653	760
East Portage,	532	922		Rives,	400	550	518
Grass Lake,	1,127	1,342	1,281	Sandstone,	654	789	823
Hanover,	714	931	931	Spring Arbor,	775	935	1,075
Henrietta,	277	422	830	Springport,	294	476	759
Jackson	2,773	3,427	4,147	Tompkins,	209	341	623
Leoni,	1,037	1,331	1,290	Waterloo,			1,098
Liberty,	525	692	891				
Napoleon,	1,098	1,255	1,208		13,130	16,825	19,433

KALMAZOO COUNTY.

TOWNSHIPS.	1840.	1845.	1850.	TOWNSHIPS.	1840,	1846.	1850.
Alamo,	194	305	420	Pavillion,	283	407	495
Brady,	1,175	581	578	Portage,	446	547	726.
Cooper,	376	482	733	Prairie Ronde,	623	720	690
Comstock,	624	945	1,202	Richland,	518	638	795
Climax,	310	581	504	Ross,	386	419	680
Charleston,	605	890	846	Schoolcraft,		1,089	1,101
Kal. vil.			2,507	Texas,	249	352	410
Kal. town,	1,290	1,924	777	Wakeshma,			128
Oshtemo,	310	400	587				
					7,380	10,163	13,179

KENT COUNTY.

Ada,		497	593	Grattan,			648
Algoma,			233	Lowell,			234
Alpine,			618	Muskegon,		104	
Bowne,			220	Oakfield,			404
Byron,		493	309	Paris,		484	521
Cannon,			696	Plainfield,		565	659
Cascade,			358	Sparta,			309
Courtland,		400	406	Vergennes,		850	876
Caledonia,		127	99	Walker,		1,122	823
Gaines,			319	Wyoming,			543
Grand Rapids, city,			2646				
Grand Rapids, town,		1,510	503		2,587	6,153	12,017

LAPEER COUNTY.

Almont,		409	1,452	Metamora,	350	266	821
Attica,		900	462	Mayfield,			
Dryden,	805	219	1,131	Oregon,			204
Elba,	101	607	255	Atlas,	660	1,258	
Hadley,	365		846	Bristol,	884		
Imlay,		858	183	Davison,	69		
Lapeer,	746	230	1,467	Richfield,	193		
Marathon,	92	567	205				
					4,265	5,314	7,02

LENAWEE COUNTY.

Adrian,	2,496	2,821	3,008	Palmyra,	828	1,118	1,098
Blissfield,	778	860	924	Raisin,	1,117	1,216	1,267
Cambridge,	644	817	974	Ridgeway,		561	634
Dover,	841	1,116	1,223	Riga,		139	208
Fairfield,	837	1,163	1,327	Rollin,	581	952	1,080
Franklin,	1,023	1,204	1,231	Rome,	1,128	1,460	1,528
Hudson,	599	956	1,544	Seneca,	581	849	1,092
Madison,	1,067	1,780	2,320	Tecumseh,	2,503	2,624	2,678
Medina,	760	1,176	1,685	Woodstock,	674	766	949
Macon,	1,146	925	1,030				
Ogden,	286	420	579		17,889	22,923	26,380

LIVINGSTON COUNTY.

Brighton,	786	922	1,015	Iosco.	395	552	645
Conway,		269	460	Jena,	141		
Deerfield,	440	697	882	Marion,	345	601	873
Genoa,	504	610	753	Osceola,	523	706	960

TOWNSHIPS	1840.	1845.	1850.	TOWNSHIPS.	1840.	1845.	1850.
Green Oak,	764	884	941	Putnam,	597	887	797
Hartland,	570	831	996	Tuscola,	247	418	454
Howell,	321	708	1,155	Tyrone,	394	676	867
Hamburg,	602	780	895	Unadilla,	643	945	1,027
Handy,	158	301	484				
					7,430	10,787	13,475

MACOMB COUNTY.

TOWNSHIPS	1840.	1845.	1850.	TOWNSHIPS.	1840.	1845.	1850.
Armada,	652	1,069	1,146	Richmond,	602	415	1,000
Bruce,	1,128	1,375	1,555	Ray,	805	1,166	1,232
Chesterfield,		845	1,002	Shelby,	1,262	1,290	1,482
Clinton,	1,115	1,754	2,130	Sterling,	677	831	876
Erin,		721	974	Washington,	1,314	1,518	1,541
Harrison,	395	528	483	Warren,	337	421	7C0
Lenox,	284	513	654	Orange,	193		
Macomb,	952	646	757				
					9,716	13,491	15,532

MACKINAC COUNTY.

TOWNSHIPS	1840.	1845.	1850.	TOWNSHIPS.	1840.	1845.	1850.
Holmes,		1,151		St. Ignace,		234	3,5978
Moran,		281					
					923	1,166	

MARQUETTE COUNTY.

Total, 136

MASON COUNTY.

Total, 93

MIDLAND COUNTY.

Total, 65

MONTCALM COUNTY.

TOWNSHIPS	1840.	1845.	1850.	TOWNSHIPS.	1840.	1845.	1850.
Eureka,			461	Bushnell,			66
Montcalm,			135				
Fairplain,			229				891

MONROE COUNTY.

TOWNSHIPS	1840.	1845.	1850.	TOWNSHIPS.	1840.	1845.	1850.
Ash,	949	1,382	1,229	London,	425	594	626
Bedford,	499	849	889	Milan,	363	433	642
Dundee,	773	1,004	1,239	Monroe, (town)	693	856	837
Erie,	852	1,016	I,1 4	Monroe, (city,)	1,703	2,455	2,809
Exeter,	233	376	458	Raisinville,	683	860	967
Frenchtown,	833	979	1,242	Summerfoid,	395	474	472
Ida,	251	422	345	Whitford,	363	564	696
Lasalle,	905	1,003	1,100				
					9,922	13,287	14,695

NEWAYGO COUNTY.

Total, 510

OAKLAND COUNTY.

TOWNSHIPS.	1840.	1845.	1850.	TOWNSHIPS.	1840.	1845.	1850,
Addison,	537	728	924	Oakland,	918	974	978
Avon,	1,630	1,831	1,456	Orion,	769	1,036	1,119
Bloomfield,	1,508	1,735	1,603	Oxford,	574	874	1,019
Brandon,	442	691	893	Pontiac,	1,904	2,861	19
Commerce,	939	1,465	1,428	Rose,	415	750	886
Farmington,	1,684	1,755	1,844	Royal Oak,	860	957	1,092
Groveland,	655	910	988	Southfield,	1,061	1,240	1,658
Highland,	566	994	851	Springfield,	573	873	956
Holly,	429	657	941	Troy,	1,482	1,583	1,426
Independence,	830	1,281	1,279	Waterford,	946	1,017	1,085
Lyon,	1,206	1,195	1,134	WhiteLake,	549	726	905
Milford,	880	1,362	1,470	West Bloomfi'ld,	938	1,217	1,085
Novi,	1,351	1,529	1,428				
					23,646	30,241	31,267

OCEANA COUNTY.

Total,	300

ONTONAGON COUNTY.

Total,	389

OTTAWA COUNTY.

TOWNSHIPS.	1840.	1845.	1850.	TOWNSHIPS.	1840.	1845.	1850.
Allendale,			168	Ottawa,	398	321	430
Chester,			216	Oceana,	31	45	
Crockery,			247	Polkton,		98	268
Georgetown,	38	133	196	Ravenna,			77
Holland			1,829	Spring Lake,			545
Jamestown,			72	Tallmadge,	139	351	534
Muskegon,		119	484	Wright,			521
Norton,	98	350					
					704	1,417	5,587

SAGINAW COUNTY.

TOWNSHIPS.	1840.	1845.	1850.	TOWNSHIPS.	1840.	1845.	1850.
Bridgeport,			374	Taymouth,		21	58
Buena Vista,			251	Tittabawassee,		254	341
Hampton,		194	546	Tuscola,	55	104	
Northampton		47	122				
Saginaw,	837	598	917		892	1,218	2,609

SANILAC COUNTY.

TOWNSHIPS.	1840.	1845.	1850.	TOWNSHIPS.	1840.	1845.	1850.
Lexington,			1,176	Worth,			600
Sanilac,			339				
							2,115

SCHOOLCRAFT COUNTY.

TOWNSHIPS.	1840.	1845.	1850.
Grand Island,			16

SHIAWASSEE COUNTY.

TOWNSHIPS.	1840.	1845.	1850.	TOWNSHIPS.	1840.	1845.	1850.
Antrim,	117	167	282	Perry,		197	313
Bennington,	403	559	601	Sciota,		182	191
Burns,	257	488	717	Shiawassee,	326	649	810
Caledonia,	114	331	500	Venice,		97	186
Hazleton,			26	Vernon,	373	506	674
Midlebury,	32	59	132	Woodhull,	147	171	259
New Hav'n & Rush		103	150				
Owosso,	234	413	392		2,103	3,921	5,233

ST. CLAIR COUNTY.

TOWNSHIPS.	1840.	1845.	1850.	TOWNSHIPS.	1840.	1845.	1850.
Berlin,		396	533	Lexington,		695	
Brockway,			252	do in Sanilac,		173	
Burchville,		353	472	Lyn,			55
Casco,			134	Port Huron, vil.		1,184	1,584
China	610	870	1,037	do town,			717
Clay,	387	569	821	Polk, in Huron,		72	
Columbus,	155	315	377	Riley,		219	311
Cottrelville,	602	726	913	St. Clair,	413	1,004	1,728
Clyde,		482	691	Wales,		113	189
Ira,	204	391	597				
					2,371	7,562	10,411

Sanilac has been cut off from St. Clair since the census of 1845.

ST. JOSEPH COUNTY

Bucks,	787			Lockport,		873	1,143
Burr Oak	286	421	658	Mendon,		603	860
Colon,	420	683	847	Mottville,	465	581	610
Constantine,	751	1,042	1,494	Nottawa,	1,226	964	1,165
Fawn River,	220	461	473	Park,	331	567	823
Fabius,		370	504	Sherman,	683	252	354
Florence,	528	739	732	Sturgis,		657	839
Flowerfield,	281	429	563	White Pigeon,	680	787	794
Leonidas,	410	668	858				
					7,068	10,097	12,717

TUSCOLA COUNTY.

Total, 291

VAN BUREN COUNTY.

Almena,		350	420	Keeler.	126	280	486
Antwerp,	316	546	614	Lawrence,	243	317	510
Arlington,		123	240	La Fayette.	327	752	1,145
Bloomingdale,		122	160	Pine Grove,			62
Columbia,		104	265	Porter,		314	444
Clinch,	250			South Haven,	99	142	220
Decatur,	328	115	386	Waverly,		95	
Hamilton,	145	279	370				
Hartford,	76	204	296		1,910	3,743	5,618

WASHTENAW COUNTY.

Ann Arbor,		4,143	4,870	Saline,	1,390	1,636	1,631
Augusta,	646	695	808	Salem,	1,364	1,242	1,343
Bridgewater,		1,073	1,148	Scio,		1,737	1,195
Dext'r, t'n & vil.		775	1,435	Sharon,		800	869
Freedom,	956	1,222	1,214	Superior,	1,398	1,269	1,127
Lyndon,		763	901	*Sylvan,		865	924
Lodi,	1,077	1,154	1,234	Webster,		950	924
Lima		966	912	York,	1,146	1,312	1,360
Manchester,		1,279	1,274	Ypsilanti,	2,419	2,651	3,052
Northfield,		1,070	1,116	Residue of co.	12,024		
Pittsfield,	1,151	1,197	1,232		......	......	......
					23,571	26,979	28,561

WAYNE COUNTY.

TOWNSHIPS.	1840.	1845.	1850.	TOWNSHIPS.	1840.	1845.	1850.
Brownstown,	793	811	1,047	Nankin,	1,109	1,420	1,617
Canton,	1,081	1,225	1,333	Plymouth,	2,163	2,602	2,431
Detroit City,	9,102	12,642	21,028	Rensselaer,	464		
Dearborn,	1,248	1,300	1,385	Redford,	1,108	1,467	1,645
Ecorse,	738	835	653	Springweils,	916	1,548	1,263
Greenfield,	738	1,203	1,674	Sumpter,	193	815	}
Grosse Point,			1,392	Taylor,			}
Huron,	307	377	482	Romulus,			}2828
Hamtramck,	1,797	2,219	1,628	Van Buren,	940	1,262	}
Livonia,	1,169	1,353	1,375	Wayne,		605	
Monguagon,	307	555	984		......	......	......
					24,173	31,737	42,765

RECAPITULATION.

Comparative Table showing the population of the State of Michigan by Counties, for the years 1840, 1845 *and* 1850.

COUNTIES.	1840.	1485.	1580.
Allegan,	1,783	2,941	5,127
Barry	1,078	2,602	5,072
Berrien,	5,011	7,865	11,417
Branch,	5,715	9,064	12,472
Calhoun,	10,599	15,594	19,169
Cass,	5,710	8,078	10.906
Chippewa,	534	1.017	898
Clinton,	1,614	3,010	5,102
Eaton,	2,379	4,613	7,058
Genesee,	4,268	9,266	12,031
Hillsdale,	7, 40	11,1I1	16,159
Houghton,			708
Huron,			207
Ingham,	2,498	5,267	8,597
Ionia,	1,923	5,101	7,597
Jackson,	13,130	16,825	19,433
Kalamazoo,	7,380	10,163	13,179
Kent,	2,587	6,153	12,017
Lapeer,	4,265	5,314	7,026
Lenawee,	17,889	22,923	26,380
Livingston,	7,430	10,787	13,475
Macomb,	9,716	13,491	15,532
Mackinac,	923	1,166	3'597
Marquette,			136
Mason,			93
Midland,			65
Montcalm,			891
Monroe,	9,912	13,287	14,695
Newaygo,			510
Oakland,	23,646	30,241	31,267
Oceana,			300
Ontonagon,			389
Ottawa,	740	1,417	5,587
Saginaw,	892	1.218	2,609
Sanilac,			2,115
Schoolcraft,			16
Shiawasse,	2,103	3,921	5'233
St. Clair,	2,371	7,562	10,411
St. Joseph,	7,068	10,097	12,717
Tuscola,			291
Van Buren,	1,910	3,743	5,681
Washtenaw	23,571	26,979	28,569
Wayne,	24,173	31,747	42,765
	210,032	302,553	397,536

UNITED STATES SENATE.—62 MEMBERS.

OF THE CONGRESS COMMENCING IN DECEMBER, 1851.

Whigs in *Italics*; Democrats in Roman; Free Soilers in SMALL CAPS. The figures before each Senator's name denote the year when his term closes.

ALABAMA.
1853 Jeremiah Clemens,
1855 William Rufus King.

ARKANSAS.
1853 William K. Sebastian,
1855 Solon Borland.

CALIFORNIA.
1851 No election,
1855 William M. Gwin.

CONNECTICUT.
1851 No election,
1855 *Truman Smith.*

DELAWARE.
1857 James A. Bayard,
1853 *Presley Spruance.*

FLORIDA.
1851 No election,
1855 *Jackson Morton.*

GEORGIA.
1853 *John Macpherson Berrien,*
1855 *William C. Dawson.*

INDIANA.
1857 Jesse D. Bright,
1855 James Whitcomb.

ILLINOIS
1853 Stephen A. Douglass,
1855 James Shields.

IOWA.
1853 Geo. W. Jones,
1855 Augustus C. Dodge.

KENTUCKY.
1853 *Joseph R. Underwood,*
1855 *Henry Clay.*

LOUISIANA.
1853 Solomon U. Downs,
1855 Pierre Soulé.

MAINE.
1857 Hannibal Hamlin,
1853. James W. Bradbury.

MASSACHUSETTS.
1857 CHARLES SUMNER,
1853 *John Davis.*

MARYLAND.
1857 *Thomas G. Pratt,*
1855 *James A. Pearce.*

MICHIGAN,
1857 Lewis Cass,
1853 Alpheus Felch.

MISSISSIPPI.
1857 Jefferson Davis,
1853 Henry Stuart Foote,

MISSOURI.
1857 *Henry S. Geyer,*
1855 David R. Atchison.

NEW HAMPSHIRE.
1853 JOHN P. HALE,
1855 Moses Norris, Jr.

NEW YORK.
1857 *Hamilton Fish,*
1855 *William Henry Seward.*

NEW JERSEY.
1857 Robert F. Stockton,
1853 *Jacob W. Miller.*

NORTH CAROLINA.
1853 *Willie P. Mangum,*
1855 *George E. Badger.*

OHIO.
1857 BENJAMIN F. WADE,
1855 SALMON P. CHASE.

PENNSYLVANIA.
1857 Richard Brodhead,
1855 *James Cooper.*

RHODE ISLAND.
1857 Charles T. James,
1853 *John H. Clarke.*

SOUTH CAROLINA.
1853 R. Barnwell Rhett,
1855 Andrew P. Butler.

TENNESSEE.
1851 No election,
1853 *John Bell.*

TEXAS.
1857 Thomas J. Rusk,
1853 Samuel Houston.

VERMONT.
1857 *Solomon Foot.*
1855 *William Upham.*

VIRGINIA.
1857 James M. Mason,
1853 Robert M. T Hunter.

WISCONSIN.
1857 Henry Dodge,
1855 Isaac P. Walker.

INDEX.

A

B

U

V

W

www.ingramcontent.com/pod-product-compliance
Lightning Source LLC
LaVergne TN
LVHW010210110826
845151LV00004B/1048

* 9 7 8 1 4 2 5 5 2 8 2 0 1 *